AF856066

Principles and Techniques of Mental Health Consultation

Current Topics in Mental Health

Series Editors: Paul I. Ahmed
Southeastern University

and

Stanley C. Plog
Plog Research, Inc.

STATE MENTAL HOSPITALS: What Happens When They Close
Edited by Paul I. Ahmed and Stanley C. Plog

COPING WITH PHYSICAL ILLNESS
Edited by Rudolf H. Moos

PRINCIPLES AND TECHNIQUES OF MENTAL HEALTH CONSULTATION
Edited by Stanley C. Plog and Paul I. Ahmed

Principles and Techniques of Mental Health Consultation

Edited by

Stanley C. Plog

Plog Research, Inc.
Reseda (Los Angeles), California

and

Paul I. Ahmed

Southeastern University
Washington, D.C.

Plenum Medical Book Company · New York and London

Library of Congress Cataloging in Publication Data
Main entry under title:

Principles and techniques of mental health consultation.

(Current topics in mental health)
Includes bibliographical references and index.
1. Psychiatric consultation. I. Plog, Stanley C. II. Ahmed, Paul I. [DNLM: 1. Mental health services. 2. School health. WM30 P957]
RC455.2.C65P74 362.2'04'25 76-42189
ISBN-13: 978-1-4684-2288-7 e-ISBN-13: 978-1-4684-2286-3
DOI: 10.1007/978-1-4684-2286-3

Softcover reprint of the hardcover 1st edition 1977
227 West 17th Street, New York, N.Y. 10011

Plenum Medical Book Company is an imprint of Plenum Publishing Corporation

To

GORDON W. ALLPORT

Mentor, Master Psychologist, True Christian

Contributors

PAUL I. AHMED, M.A., L.L.B., Professor, Southeastern University, Washington, D.C.

IRVING H. BERKOVITZ, M.D., Senior Psychiatric Consultant for Schools, Los Angeles County Department of Mental Health Services.

IRVING N. BERLIN, M.D., Head, Child Psychiatry, Division of Mental Health, Sacramento Medical Center.

STANLEY L. BRODSKY, Ph.D., Professor of Psychology, Associate Director, Center for Correctional Psychiatry, University of Alabama.

GERALD CAPLAN, M.D., Director, Laboratory of Community Psychiatry, Harvard University.

RAQUEL E. COHEN, M.D., Associate Professor, Department of Psychiatry, Harvard School of Medicine.

RALPH G. HIRSCHOWITZ, M.D., Assistant Professor of Psychiatry, Harvard Medical School.

KENNETH R. MITCHELL, Ph.D., Director, Division of Religion and Psychiatry, The Menninger Foundation.

STANLEY C. PLOG, Ph.D., President, Plog Research, Inc., Reseda, California.

ALEXANDER S. ROGAWSKI, M.D., Professor and Director, Division of Social and Community Psychiatry, University of Southern California.

FRANK M. TIMS, M.A., National Institute of Drug Abuse, Rockville, Maryland.

Preface

The raison d'être of the mental health profession is supposed to be concerned with helping. Our involvement is with people's problems—the psychological problems that incapacitate and prevent otherwise capable individuals from leading fulfilling and "self-actualized" lives. Perhaps more than most of the specialties and subdisciplines within the broad field, mental health consultation is even more concerned with helping people. Because the focus in consultation is on reaching larger numbers of people, the discipline has an even greater dedication to doing something about troubled lives. The emphasis of most consultations is on improving the quality of life for various groups of people, on making impossible living situations more bearable, and broadly on assisting people to face the daily challenges in their lives.

Mental health consultation is an effective tool for achieving these goals (see Chapter 4). And it is an art—a difficult art that requires not only special skills and special training but special kinds of personalities that can relate well to people of different walks of life, different ethnic backgrounds, different religious or political beliefs, and different status or economic position. But, unfortunately, far too many individuals who are engaged in consultation have neither the requisite background nor the special skills to become the kind of artist that is required. They have stumbled into consulting relationships with school districts, industrial organizations, or welfare agencies because of a felt need by these organizations for a continuing relationship with someone who understands human behavior and who can help them overcome some difficult problem situations.

The mental health professional (psychiatrist, psychologist, or social worker) often responds to this challenge—out of interest in doing something new or challenging or because his professional reflexes automatically react when someone calls for help. But this ideal situation—a client who wants help and a helper who is available to provide that help—far too often ends in frustration and discouragement for both parties. The agency expected too much and the consultant provided too little. The situation may have been impossible because of internal resistances within the organization, or community pressures may have prevented the consultant from working directly with the groups that needed the greatest amount of help. But, more often than not, the failure has been with the consultant, for he knew little or nothing about the techniques and practices of consultation and he attempted to apply his previously learned clinical skills—usually based on techniques applicable to clinical private practice—to the consulting relationship. This innocent but strategic error now has destroyed a potentially productive relationship that both the fledgling consultant and the "new" client desired.

In such situations, it is typical for the consultant to blame his client for its inbred conservatism and unwillingness to enter the 20th century with its concerns about people problems. Not as frequently is he willing to question his own practices and procedures and whether or not he contributed to any of the problems he encountered by the way he approached the organization or pursued his consultation efforts. If he chooses the latter course, he may seek to learn more about consultation—what it is and how to do it—and ultimately become a topflight consultant through extensive reading and specialized training. Whatever the problems of the organization receiving consultation, the expert consultant recognizes that he often must begin under less than ideal conditions and gradually, through his own efforts, educate his client organization to the point that more important mental health goals can now be accomplished because the client implicitly trusts everything he may want to do.

Unfortunately those who desire more training in consultation can receive it at only a handful of centers, located primarily on both coasts of the United States. To receive this training, a scholarship or other support funds are usually necessary, and extended time away from an important and very demanding job may be required.

A more viable course of action for many individuals is to read about consultation in available articles and books. But what should be read?

What is current? What is enduring? And where do you find it? There are theoretic and pragmatic expositions by individual authors, but it is difficult to find a compendium that places mental health consultation in perspective and offers examples of specialists in action in a variety of settings, thereby providing relevance to the current activities of both existing and would-be consultants. Because of this apparent need for more information on consultation techniques and practices, the present volume was assembled. It is meant to be pragmatic in focus—to offer insight into how to operate as a consultant in varied but demanding settings, such as schools, local churches, and correctional institutions. The emphasis is on providing information to the consultant practitioner and the advanced novice on what is current, pragmatic, and useful. It is a volume for "doers": for activists who want to function more effectively in self-chosen roles as mental health consultants and for professionals who want to learn about consultation practices in related fields.

The book is divided into two primary sections: theoretic overview (Part I) and practical applications (Part II). In the theoretic section, the two major theorists of mental health consultation (Gerald Caplan and Irving N. Berlin) summarize their current beliefs as based, for each individual, on more than 25 years of direct experience in the field. In the applied section, successful consultation in action is described in various settings requiring very diverse kinds of skills and value systems by the consultant. The hope is that the reader, by being exposed to both the theoretic material and pragmatic application, will receive a perspective that is not possible through any other method.

Like most books, this one has been long "aborning," but the labor has been one of love and affection. The editors are firm believers in the utility of mental health consultation, and we are pleased with the distinguished and creative group of consultants who agreed to participate in this effort. Our debt to them is great—for their patience and understanding throughout the extended period of correspondence and editing. And we owe a special thanks to Mrs. Jean Eggen, who assumed full responsibility for the typing and final production of all papers.

STANLEY C. PLOG
Granada Hills, California
PAUL I. AHMED
Silver Spring, Maryland

Contents

I

The Principles of Effective Mental Health Consultation

1

The Common Basis of Consultation

STANLEY C. PLOG AND PAUL I. AHMED

Although all authors in this volume are unique in their approach to consultation and they are working in almost incomparable settings, there are some common messages that grow out of their writings. These form a backdrop for understanding the special demands that are placed on consultants, especially in contrast to the role of private-practice therapists. This distinction is important since the most typical route for becoming a consultant is by enlarging the scope of one's clinical therapeutic practice to include consulting roles or assignments with agencies that have contacted local practitioners in order to receive help with specific problems of adults or children. When they enter the new consulting relationship, far too frequently they naïvely or arrogantly attempt to work with consultees as though they are "patients" who are simply being seen in a new or different setting. Inevitably, the relationship is quickly terminated and mental health receives another black eye. Wiser individuals, entering into unfamiliar situations, recognize their own professional inexperience and seek information and guidance before they become too deeply enmeshed.

The messages derived from the authors in this volume divide into several conclusions, which can best be summarized as *mental health consultation grows out of and builds on skills developed for clinical psychiatry*

STANLEY C. PLOG · President and Founder, Plog Research, Inc., Reseda (Los Angeles), Ca.
PAUL I. AHMED · Southeastern University, Washington, D.C.

and psychology, but it is not synonymous with these skills. Clinical skills are useful, and perhaps necessary, to becoming a successful consultant, but they are very different from the requirements for success in the consultation profession. Specifically, some of the common conclusions from these chapters are the following.

1. Mental health consultation requires the professional providing the services to have a broader armamentarium of skills and capabilities than is true of an individual in private practice. The mental health consultant may be called upon to diagnosis the meaning of the behaviors of an individual (client), delicately handle the emotional problems of a consultee, defuse a potentially explosive political situation threatening to destroy a community organization, work constructively in a small-group setting, help plan the mental health programs and services for his consultee agency, and work effectively with a broad spectrum of ages, income groups, and ethnic backgrounds—all within a single day. An individual engaged in private practice, on the other hand, may frequently limit himself to the specific types of behavioral or emotional problem cases with which he feels most comfortable and which are drawn from a narrow income and age range (and within a restricted geographic area within his own city). Even when his practice is more broadly defined, he is not likely to be faced with the dizzying array of problems and demands that confront most mental health consultants. The restrictiveness of private practice and the more narrow view of life it provides are frequently two of the primary reasons why private practitioners seek out consulting relationships. They simply are tired of four walls and neurotic housewives or acting-out teen-agers.

2. The typical consultant must be much more flexible and professionally adaptable than an average individual engaged in psychotherapy. The number and diversity of the situations the consultant is likely to encounter demand greater adaptiveness. In contrast, most psychotherapists, however flexible they might feel they are, demand that their patients learn to adapt to and work within their usual framework for conducting psychotherapy.

3. A mental health consultant must be prepared for the shock of having his services evaluated. Whatever the agency, it is typical for its program director to review what have been the accomplishments, or lack of them, by the consultant on at least a once-a-year basis. This review may occur at the annual budget meeting, in which the decision is made about whether or not to renew the contract for the consultant's services; or it may be more formally structured in the form of a research design that attempts to evaluate the impact of the services on the staff or children; or it may be on the basis of a more informal discussion with the program director "over

a cup of coffee.'' Whatever the occasion, the consultant is likely to receive fairly direct feedback on how well he is doing and, typically, on how his consultees would like to see him change.

On the other hand, the average psychotherapist, operating behind closed doors, is far better insulated from the world of professional or lay evaluation of the quality of his work. No colleagues are available to indicate a degree of satisfaction or dissatisfaction with any aspect of his activities. His only clientele, his patients, are far too dependent upon him for emotional support to be critical, and more important, they lack a basis on which to compare his work with the services of any other practitioner or any other method of treatment. As a result, private-practice therapists often tend to become insulated and unresponsive to pressures or demands for change, whatever the source.

4. The typical consultant has to be responsive to the sociological setting in which he is operating in addition to the personal psychology of the individuals with whom he is consulting. A frequent criticism of the private-practice therapist is that many of the recommendations he offers to his patients do not take into account the social milieu in which they operate. Thus, the decision may be for the patient to return to work because it would be therapeutic for him. But neither his family nor his work confederates were involved in that decision, and very often they are not prepared to accept him in his new role as a breadwinner or co-worker.

The mental health consultant, however, must constantly be aware of the variety of social forces impacting on his client and, rather than condemning their negative influence, must learn to work with these realities to achieve acceptable final outcomes for the many individuals participating in the same social network. Very often it is his greater sensitivity to the true sociology of the situation and his more accurate assessment of the variety of possible courses of action that contribute to his overall usefullness. He can assist the school superintendent to walk the delicate line in working with conflicting parent groups, the welfare agency to deal more effectively with its own stifling bureaucracy, or the local church minister to understand and distinguish between problems of human relations and problems of theology.

5. Because of their awareness of the social milieu in which they work, the vast majority of mental health consultants have a deeper respect for the ''establishment.'' Through working with administrators, executives, and others in positions of responsibility, the consultant develops a greater understanding of the problems faced by these individuals and the risks that these executives must face in all courses of action they take. And

the consultant is often more willing to side with them and support their efforts to achieve certain goals because he understands the implications of alternative courses of action. Blanket criticism of established rules and regulations is a luxury not available to a good consultant.

6. An operating assumption of all approaches to the consulting relationship described in this volume is that the consultant and his client have coequal professional status. Each respects the other for a specialized area of knowledge and draws from the other in this area. The consultant is recognized as an expert in human relations but not in education, or criminology, or business, or engineering, etc. The typical psychotherapeutic encounter, on the other hand, tends to place the patient in a subordinate relationship (even the word *patient* implies a subordinate relationship) and he tends to seek guidance from the therapist in broad areas of life. This point is likely to be denied by those therapists who say that they leave those decisions up to their patients and that they stick only to the care of the emotional problems or difficulties their patients are facing. Actually the influence of therapists on their patients is unusually pervasive and extends very often to areas greater than they would be willing to admit.

7. Finally, there is a tacit assumption in most of the articles, which is defined in some way by a few authors, that the average mental health consultant has to be a much more emotionally stable and far better "put together" individual than a typical therapist in private practice. The consultant is bombarded by a crossfire of political, psychological, and sociological forces, and if he is to be successful, he has to be able to handle attacks against his own ego and against the agency with which he is working. The consultant will be tested frequently in his interpersonal relationships and, if he is found to be overly rigid or insensitive to others, will be rejected by his consultees. Deviancy or strange behavior is likely to be recognized quickly and can become the source of private jokes and stories or a concerted effort to remove him from the agency. For the private practitioner, in contrast, iconoclastic behavior may be the source of some discussion by patients with their relatives or friends, but it is often presumed to be the source of his brilliance and therefore his usefulness as a therapist.

These are some of the commonalities of consultation. But there is diversity too—more so than commonality—for consultation must be adapted to the unique personalities of the consultants offering their services. This is what makes consultation an art—through holding on to what is common across all consultants, while emphasizing uniqueness in goals, the forms in which the services are offered, or the pragmatic application of specific techniques. Art involves both creativity and discipline. The effective consultant recognizes the requirement to be innovative and creative, so as to adapt to the unique demands of each consulting relationship; but he also possesses the necessary professional skills and personal discipline to deliver the services required in each situation so that he is not inappropriately challenged by his consultees to demonstrate competency.

Mental health consultation is an exciting and professionally rewarding enterprise. It is an area begging for new recruits. It demands more commitment from professionals than has generally been the case to date, but its rewards are enormous. Our hope is that some of our enthusiasm for consultation will be transmitted to those who wander across these pages.

2

Mental Health Consultation: Retrospect and Prospect

GERALD CAPLAN

During my quarter of a century of consultation work, a number of issues have become apparent that have helped clarify what is useful or effective in consultation and what is not. Although it is difficult to evaluate scientifically the effectiveness of various techniques or approaches to mental health consultation, personal contact with thousands of consultants over the years in the United States and other countries has produced a perspective at the Laboratory of Community Psychiatry about those techniques in consultation that have stood the test of time and those that have not. It is useful to review some of these ideas in order to bring them up to date.

This chapter represents a continuation of material published previously in *The Theory and Practice of Mental Health Consultation*[1] and in *Helping the Helpers to Help*,[2] in which I wrote two chapters that present some of these ideas in a preliminary way. The latter book is about the development of a consultation program in the Episcopal church, first in the Diocese of Massachusetts and then as it spread through the rest of the country. It provides a relatively short digest of the theory and techniques of my approach to consultation, and it also offers detailed examples of group consultation sessions (based on analysis of tape-recorded consultation sessions) that are not available elsewhere.

GERALD CAPLAN Director, Laboratory of Community Psychiatry, Harvard University.

The Enduring Principles of Consultation

From the vantage point of today, what are some of my ideas that appear to have stood the test of time?

First, education and emotional support are good, but they are not enough. A consultant can and must offer more than just an addition to his consultee's knowledge about mental health problems, and he must do more than increase the feelings of emotional security of the consultee. He can make a precise contribution to improving his professional capacity and that of his institution in dealing with the problems of today and the future, on their own, through the vehicle of the type of cases for which they are currently enlisting his help. This assistance is invaluable for it leads to considerable personal growth and a capacity for competent and independent professional action on the part of the consultee.

Second, the coordinate relationship (the nonhierarchical relationship of equality between consultant and consultee) provides the quickest and the most lasting results. Whatever disagreement there is about some of the specialized techniques described in *The Theory and Practice of Mental Health Consultation,*[1] almost no experienced consultant today would argue about the importance of the coordinate relationship. This principle states that the consultant should not have any power or administrative leverage over his consultee, that is, that he should not be able to force his consultee to do what he says.

Allied with this concept is the principle that the consultant should not be personally responsible for the outcome of the consultee's work, freeing the consultant from feeling an obligation to force the consultee to accept what he has to say. That, paradoxically, in our culture, provides the best opportunity for consultees to take those ideas of the consultant that they find meaningful within their own setting. And what they select is theirs, not the consultant's. In certain cases, the actual status discrepancy between consultant and consultee can be large, as, for example, where a consultant clearly has high status in the community and his consultee is low-status. As a professor at the Harvard School of Public Health, I often found it difficult to provide consultation to junior public-health nurses. Under those circumstances, the perceived status differential was such that it was impossible by any kind of technical maneuvering to maintain a coordinate relationship—to arrange that the junior nurse should feel on equal terms with the consultant. Nevertheless, when the consultant makes a sincere attempt to maintain a coordinate status, even though he may never really succeed, the consultee appreciates his efforts and this has an effect in maintaining a feeling of autonomy within the consultee. The implied statement to the client is, for example, "I am a psychiatrist and not a public health nurse. You are a specialist in public health nursing. Even though it is true that you need me as a specialist consultant, I need you because a consultant actually needs consultees. So each of us needs the other, and there is no question that you know more about the realities of your work situation than I will ever know. Although I am an expert in mental health, you are an expert in public health nursing."

Many may argue that in the final analysis it is not possible to convince that young nurse of the coordinate-status relationship. She will never believe that she need not pay a great deal of attention to what the consultant has to say: if he believes something is green, she had better not decide it is blue, even though the consultant may be the one who is color blind. Nevertheless, any attempt to produce that coordinate relationship does have an important result: it conveys the message of great personal respect by the consultant for the consultee. It is impossible to pretend to respect someone of a different age, sex, profession, or cultural group. It is a help that, by and large, a consultant who works with members of another profession for a period of time and keeps his eyes and ears open gradually develops respect for the other profession. Developing respect for public health nurses may seem to be difficult for some, but after one works with them for a while, it will become apparent that they do a job that is beyond the capabilities of the consultant because (1) he does not have training in public health nursing and (2) most consultants would not dream of living with the number of difficulties that are part of their daily lives. Most of us require our lives to be more comfortable than what is acceptable to these women.

The Laboratory of Community Psychiatry has developed a film of a consultation session between a psychiatrist and a public health nurse relating to one of her patients who is dying of cancer. As part of that film, what this nurse is doing in her everyday work becomes clear. Psychiatrists watching that film who have not had much experience with public health nurses soon realize that these young women are often working in intimate contact with dying patients, handling all kinds of messy dressings until the moment of death. Meanwhile, doctors in hospitals send patients home and do not have to deal with them when they die in a few weeks or a few months. These young women must take care of patients on a daily basis and in intimate contact, encountering a broad panorama of cognitive and emotional burdens. Working with someone in another profession leads to respect for what they are doing—a natural outgrowth of the process of working together.

The third principle that has stood the test of time quite well is the principle of the separation of professional role and private life. In work with a consultee, it is necessary to safeguard the separation of his private life from his professional role. This was a point on which there were many debates 15 or 20 years ago. There may still be debate today in some places, but it has not surfaced publicly for almost 15 years. If the boundary is broken and personal-life conflicts become part of the consultation relationship, the consultant must deal with a technical problem of the highest order.

The fourth principle is the value of using the displacement object of the case in consultation. This technique is described in detail in *The Theory and Practice of Mental Health Consultation.*[1] Despite a general respect for the separation of private problems from professional roles among mental health professionals, there is no question that in real life there is often an intrusion of private material into the consultation session. Instead of behaving as an objective professional, the consultee becomes subjectively involved in the case and that subjective involvement distorts his professional functioning and perspectives. That is one of the commonest reasons why he may have some cognitive deficit, because some aspect of the situation he is describing is triggering him emotionally.

It has become obvious over the years that when a consultee's personal life invades his work setting, his personal difficulties interfere with his work functioning. These personal problems may now be displaced onto a case he is discussing with his consultant, which can provide considerable benefit for him. The consultee vicariously works out his personal problem, not inside himself but, as it were, "out there" on the case. He defends himself by displacement, and from the point of his own mental economy, he benefits in the form of current relief of tension. There is considerable value in accepting the consultee's defensive displacement and working "out there" with the case. The consultation discussion focuses entirely on the case, without making the link explicit between this case and what is going on inside the consultee. *The consultant does not confront,* even in an age when confrontation techniques have become so popular. It seems to be popular currently to use confrontation techniques as the royal road to success, much in the manner that it once was popular to believe that the royal road to success was "to make the unconscious conscious." Both techniques have their place. However, in many areas of life and in many aspects of professional functioning, making the unconscious conscious, producing insight, and forcing confrontation, although highly satisfying from the point of view of the abreactive fireworks that may take place (and the outpouring of tears, sweat and feeling), do not necessarily improve the functioning of the person and very often leave a considerable amount of personal wreckage. If the situation provides an opportunity to deal with that wreckage, the person may benefit. But, most often this is not possible and a competent professional person ends up very dissatisfied with the entire consultation process and still unable to deal with the problems presented by a particular client.

The use of the displacement object means that the consultant acts in congruence with the consultee, and the two of them operate on the basis of an unspoken contract to talk as though the work problem "out there" with the client is the only problem, even though the consultant is aware that that particular problem has some very special meaning for the consultee. Nevertheless, he does not interpret that special meaning, does not deal with it explicitly, and continues to focus only on the "out there." Many consultants have never read about theme interference reduction, but they have discovered on their own the importance of this principle.

The fifth principle that has survived well over time is the importance of an orderly and unhurried reflection process that increases the consultee's range of options. This tends to counteract emotionally toned, premature closure of important issues. Effective consultation provides a consultee with a rare opportunity in a supportive setting for an unhurried reflection on what he has been doing in this job and how he has been acting toward a particular case. That in itself is extremely valuable, since personal and professional growth can be considerable.

The sixth principle, enunciated in the *Theory and Practice* book,[1] has become more obvious than at the time the book was released. Broadly defined, consultation is important, but it is only one of many community mental health interventions that are available. Heavy reliance on mental health consultation techniques by a consultant may make him into a professional "gimmicker," that is, someone who has a gimmick to solve all problems in all situations. Consultation is appropriate in certain settings and it is not appropriate in others. A well-trained professional should realize that consultation is only one of the techniques available, and it should be used only where it is appropriate.

Altered Perspectives about Consultation

During the past 25 years, my views have also changed on some important topics. For instance, since the *Theory and Practice*[1] book was written, the full value of the group approach in consultee-centered consultation has become apparent. Many professionals attacked me because the group approach was downgraded in this book, especially in consultee-centered case consultation. In the book by Ruth Caplan,[2] however, there is clear documentation of the advantages of the group approach. That book centers on an analysis of consultee-centered group-case consultation between mental health specialists and groups of Episcopal clergymen.

In the *Theory and Practice* book, concern was expressed that the presence of the other group members would upset the consultant's delicate assessment of the problem and his interventions in theme-interference reduction. A competent consultant who is intent on using the displacement in the case to deal with emotionally significant issues in his consultee without ever making this explicit relies on maintaining the consultee's unconscious displacement. This, in turn depends upon the consultee's not discovering that he is personally involved in this particular aspect of the case and that he must not develop insight into *its* personal meaning to him. A consultant working alone in a room with a consultee can control the interview and the closeness to or distance from the emotionally toned material of personal significance to the client. The main technique of consultee-centered consultation depends upon being able to feel the consultee's emotional pulse as the interview progresses and never permitting the topics to become too emotionally charged. As the consultee begins to become more and more upset while discussing emotionally toned material, it may be necessary to lead the discussion away to an emotionally neutral issue. Later it is possible to come around gradually to the "hot" issue from another point of view, never forcing the consultee into a situation in which his own personal involvement erupts into his consciousness. This procedure is exactly the opposite to the techniques of uncovering pscyhotherapy, in which the purpose is to probe for preconscious material that is emotionally burdensome and to bring it out. It is desirable for the patient to verbalize these feelings unless he has a very weak ego. If it is felt he cannot bear the insight, the method of displacement is used in a manner similar to the process employed in consultation.

When this approach is used with a single consultee, it is possible to have control of the situation. The consultee may try to guide the direction of the discussion, but it is up to the consultant to come up with the techniques to prevent this from happening. In a group situation (and especially in a sophisticated group), however, it always seemed possible that some intelligent group member would see the tears welling up in the eyes of the consultee and say, "Look here, the way you are talking about this case, I just wonder whether it hasn't got some personal significance for you? Did you have similar kinds of conflicts with your own mother?" The fear was that it might happen so quickly that it would be impossible to control and a catastrophe would occur for the consultant—the tears would well over the edge of those eyes, and the consultee would lose face and be revealed as someone whose personal life was interfering with his work. Although greatly concerned about this possibility, the staff at the Laboratory of Community Psychiatry discovered in experiments with this approach to consultation that fears that the other group members would interpret the consultee's personal references were exaggerated, provided certain rules were followed. The primary ground rule was explained to the group in the manner of "This is a consultation group in which discussion is restricted to the work situation only. It is not a therapy group. We will, therefore, not discuss the private life of any member of this group." That rule must be understood and repeated over and over again because, however closed the group is initially, there are usually some people who join in after three or four sessions and have not been exposed to this requirement. It is the new group members who are apt to infringe the ground rules, especially since more and more people have been exposed to sensitivity group training and other new forms of group communication. They believe in confrontation, touching, and "authentic" communication. In the early stages of the group they may struggle with the consultant because they believe that each person should openly and honestly say what he feels about another person and that he must deal the same way with you. These may feel that it is useful to break down each other's personal defenses. It is up to the consultant to make it clear that this particular method is linked with a very different mental health approach. He may be forced to say, "If you want to have that kind of group, you may have it. But you won't have me. What we will do here is discuss work situations only, and we will not, under any circumstances, discuss the private life or personality of anyone in this room."

If this ground rule is well understood and its merits appreciated, the members of the consultation group not only do not infringe it, but occasionally, if the consultant makes a mistake in that area, they bring him into line. In *Helping the Helpers to Help,*[2] there are examples in which an inexperienced consultant violated this rule and an experienced consultee in the group tactfully steered him back onto course. What very often happens is that there is a kind of polite refocusing of attention: someone talks about a private personal issue and reveals some normally hidden aspect of his life, and the discussion immediately veers away. It is as though the group members did not hear it. They turn their eyes aside from observing its implications. That was very interesting to discover, and it means that the danger, in practice, is not very important.

A second point made in the *Theory and Practice* book[1] that now appears not to be valid was the belief that the group would interfere with the assessment of the consultee's problem because when one member of the group raises a case issue, everyone in the group is likely to have a different sensitivity to the issue or a different interest in it. Instead of the consultant's being able to move systematically in assessing the consultee's problem, the fear was that the group would move the discussion over a variety of unrelated topics. What was discovered, instead, was that the group learns how to help the consultant assess the consultee's problem by asking the correct questions of the consultee's material.

Third, at one time it appeared to be a wasteful procedure to do consultation in a group setting because while one member of the group discussed a problem and the consultant was working with him on it, the rest of the group would be mere spectators waiting to bring up their own case material. With 10 members in the group, 1 person would be presenting and there would be 9 observers. The assumption was that 9 might be able to learn intellectually from hearing discussion about their colleague's problem, but it would be similar to the kind of work of some group therapists who do individual therapy in a group setting versus those who try to do analytic group therapy, in which they are conducting therapy on the group as a unit. It seemed that it would be very rare to get a situation in which a theme would develop that was common to all members of the group. Thus the fear was that an individual might have to wait for 9 weeks for an opportunity to discuss material that was meaningful to him—a great waste of professional time. In point of fact, however, group consultation provides a more potent opportunity for other group members not only to benefit intellectually from a consultation discussion but also to identify emotionally with the discussant. While a single consultee is presenting his own material, it reverberates with some aspect of their own experiences. Much more important, however, is that they alternate between the roles of "vicarious consultee" and "vicarious consultant."

Through this interactive-process consultation, the group members gradually learn several important principles that tend to guide many facets of their daily professional lives. They are not restricted to identifying with the consultee when they are not presenting. The consultant can arrange events so that members of the group act as co-consultants in helping one of their colleagues who is currently the consultee. This produces a very potent situation in which everyone in the group alternates in his role from consultant to consultee. One week he is the consultee and he is cognitively confused or emotionally involved in a case and is asking for the help from the consultant. In that session, he experiences the meaning of receiving help and assistance. He discovers that it is possible to get out of an emotional or intellectual trap, even though he primarily felt there were only two ways out and both of them were undesirable in outcome. Through the consultation process, he gradually begins to discover new factors that lead to new options. And he has the opportunity to work with the consultant to help a colleague. This alternating of roles is a tremendously powerful learning experience, probably one of the most powerful learning experiences in consultation practice.

Thus, for all concerned, every case discussion, whether.one is participating as a consultee or as an "assistant consultant," provides a vicarious experience of problem solving. Several principles seem to be communicated in this process.

1. The consultees learn to avoid stereotyping or at least to be alert to their own stereotyping and to recognize it as a normal, natural, human response. And they learn that if they go about it the right way, they can break through their own stereotyping. This implies a reduction in their dehumanization of their clients, and they are better able to penetrate their complicated idiosyncrasies as human beings.

2. Related to this, they discover how to remedy their own stereotyping, the overly simplified view of another person, usually emotionally toned, by discovering how to enlarge their original views of actors and outcomes. The stereotyping includes not only perceptions of the situation in a work setting but also the expected outcomes and how to go about changing these.

3. They also come to realize that if one gets enough information and investigates enough connections, both intrasystemic and intersystemic, the most inexplicable human behavior can be understood. And they learn that if the situation under discussion is difficult to understand, a thorough search for additional information gradually makes what was not understandable become understandable. Several years ago in a consultation seminar in Seattle, Washington, organized by a community organization specialist, Dan Prossor, he said, "You know, it strikes me that the object of consultation could be stated very simply—it is to complicate the thinking of the consultee." What was simple, and therefore impossible, is made complicated and begins to be understandable. Most people think that when things get more complicated, they are more burdensome, but they also provide an increased opportunity to understand and to act.

4. Consultees also learn increased tolerance for feelings in their clients and in themselves. And they learn how feelings can constrict and

distort a cognitive view and how such distortions can be reduced by personal effort and support from others, *but not necessarily through discussion that focuses on feelings*. Similar results can be obtained through a focus on the feelings involved, but it is more efficient to maintain a cognitive focus on the complications of the case.

5. The members of the group similarly come to realize the value of a calm, methodical analysis of confusing situations and to avoid premature closure of judgment and action. What consultee groups learn, and what the co-consultant learns through helping the consultee, is how to maintain poise despite confusion and frustration. Many psychoanalysts state that this is a basic aspect of ego strength. It is also possible to discover how to extend oneself through personal effort in difficult situations and through the guidance and support of peers and authority figures. Consultees learn how to pull themselves up by their own bootstraps. The goal of consultation is not just to help the consultee with a particular case. *The real focus of consultation is help plus education.* The consultant helps the consultee in such a way that this corrective emotional and cognitive experience can be used to understand future cases of a similar type. Through this process he becomes more independent of the consultant and better able to deal with a variety of problem situations on his own.

6. Finally, the widening range of intervention possibilities that become apparent during consultation increases the feeling of personal mastery for most consultees. This fact deals with a very significant problem in most professions. The great majority of us come to recognize how nonideal our actual work situation is, how limited our power is to effect useful change, and how easy it is to fail on a day-to-day basis. We may begin to think less of ourselves and our accomplishments and begin to doubt our mission in life even while vigorously defending our profession to others. As a result, speakers at professional meetings often make speeches addressed to colleagues about how marvelous they all are. They develop mythical histories of their profession, carefully written to show all the heroes of the past, and they preach to each other about their own merits. *Psychiatry and the Community in Nineteenth Century America*[3] details the fact that when American psychiatry was at its lowest ebb and the nonprofessional world was most dissatisfied, guild psychiatrists were very busy giving testimonials to each other and recounting how wonderful psychiatrists are. Usually there was a direct correlation between the external *invalidation* of this self-view and the internal guild attempts at self-validation.

One fundamental value of consultation for a consultee, especially when the consultant is from another profession, is the validation of the intrinsic worth of the consultee's mission. One of the most professionally satisfying statements ever given to me came from Bishop Stokes of Massachusetts at the end of 2 years of consultation.

The bishop had to explain to his Jewish consultant what his Episcopal church was all about, what being a bishop was, and so on. The discussion covered, in detail, the quandaries, perplexities, and difficulties of the life of a bishop in Massachusetts during turbulent years when his church was under attack because of turmoil within and without.

Bishop Stokes said one day, "I want you to know that from talking to you, I have understood the significance and importance of my role as a bishop." He had been a bishop 25 years and had begun to think that although as a bishop he had high status, it was questionable whether he had actually accomplished anything important. He was aware of his own failures, he was tired, and he was coming to the end of his professional life questioning, "What have I done anyway?" Having the chance to talk to a stranger—a sympathetic stranger—and having to explain the complexities of his church and its problems gave him the chance to reflect. Eventually he decided, "Well, you add it all up, and maybe I have been doing an important job after all."

What consultation does, apart from complicating the thinking of the consultee, is to give the consultee a chance for subsequent reflection about broad aspects of his work. Disciplined reflection is also important for consultants. Anyone wanting to develop as a consultant needs regular opportunities to reflect on what has been happening in his own professional life.

Beyond Consultation

On the basis of 25 years of consultation practice, it is readily apparent to me that the method has real value. And the road ahead appears to be leading in two directions, both promising real gains.

The first road was envisioned in the last chapter of *Theory and Practice of Consultation*.[1] Consultation, especially consultee-centered case consultation, was developed in long-term, stable institutions. It depends upon effective personnel-selection policies, in-service training, supervision, and the availability of a variety of forms of technical consultation.

Within these settings, most personnel are professionals and they are trained for their roles. Consultation adds to their full complement of professional skills. However, many of the programs utilizing mental health specialists today in this and other countries do not include stable institutions. Therefore, it is necessary to develop other defined techniques in addition to consultation. Examples of some of these are intercession, mediation, adult education, administrative action, and program development. A consultant, operating in an antipoverty agency, for example, must be prepared to involve himself in direct action and must be prepared to take on operational responsibilities. In a situation in which there are inadequate personnel-selection procedures and no regular training programs, he must be prepared to do many jobs for which he has not been specifically trained. He must be constantly aware that he is filling a gap. Therefore, he should do the job, develop the role, and then model the role and make sure that there is someone to take it over at an appropriate time. Thus, he will tend to move from one area to another actively searching for new roles he must fill and model for others. The consultant must move on and continue to move on. This is the work of a good consultant, but it is not traditional consultation.

The second road leads in a somewhat different direction. It involves utilizing mental health workers to stimulate the development of supportive structures inside institutions or in the open community that capitalize on some of the principles developed in consultation, except that they are not being accomplished in the consultation mold at all. The ends are similar but are achieved by different techniques. Many of the functions of a specialist consultant can be handed over from the start for development by key people in the institution or program. Instead of doing the job and modeling it for someone else, the consultant assists the institution in choosing its own people to assume these positions. The consultant occupies the role of trainer and supervisor in helping them develop effective intervention procedures within their system. The interventions and roles that develop are not copies of what the consultant would have done if he were doing it himself. Rather they are unique to the institution and fit their own reality. It must be recognized that the contributions of mental health workers are also paralleled by other types of professionals who also have considerable competence in the field of human nature. They can do many things that mental health specialists can do and some things they cannot do, catalyzing the development of human relations operations by other people within their own system or institutions. In *Support Systems and Community Mental Health,*[4] these ideas have been developed in greater depth. This field of work is still in its early stages, but it has promise of being a most effective mission for mental health specialists because its results will not be limited to the face-to-face interactions of a consultant, even when working in a group setting. The support systems approach for the first time holds out a reasonable hope of community coverage and significant improvement in the mental health of an entire population. It must discover how to reach all members of a population it serves, especially all who are vulnerable, by strategic interventions that have a potency in strengthening people when they need help the most.

References

1. Caplan, G. *The theory and practice of mental health consultation.* New York: Basic Books, 1970.
2. Caplan, R. B. *Helping the helpers to help.* New York: Seabury Press, 1972.
3. Caplan, R. B. *Psychiatry and the community in nineteenth century America.* New York: Basic Books, 1969.
4. Caplan, G. *Support systems and community health:* Lectures in concept development. New York: Behavioral Publications, 1974.

3

Some Lessons Learned in 25 Years of Mental Health Consultation to Schools

IRVING N. BERLIN

In a period of 25 years of work in the schools, one learns much about the process of consultation, including the factors that make for success and failure. Sometimes the end of a quarter of a century is a good time to look back and review one's efforts and decide what has been found that is useful or effective and what some of the typical problems are that inexperienced consultants tend to encounter.

In this chapter, we will review the mental health consultation process in three settings: with teachers, with school administrators, and, finally, with the focus on community problems. Consultants who operate within the schools are likely to be called upon to provide each of these very vital forms of consultation and need to be informed of the similarities and differences in skill and approach required in each setting.

The Mental Health Consultation Process

Mental health consultation can be described as a process in which a consultant tries to help a consultee from another profession with a work-

---

IRVING N. BERLIN · Head, Child Psychiatry, Division of Mental Health, Sacramento Medical Center; President, American Academy of Child Psychiatry.

related problem. The method involves several steps and processes, including:

1. A diagnostic appraisal of the conflicts in and between consultee and client that cause the work problem.
2. The development of a dynamic understanding of the consultee's underlying anxieties and of the form in which they are presented to the consultant.
3. An assessment of the integrative capacities of the consultee.
4. The use of various approaches to reduce anxieties by the consultant's comments (which indicate his understanding).
5. Acceptance of the feelings and conflicts engendered in the consultee by the behavior of his clients.
6. Discussion of how similar problems have been or may be handled by others so that the consultee is able to get some sense of how he might deal with the problem he presents.

The Handicap of Traditional Practice

The mental health professional—social worker, psychologist, or psychiatrist—who begins to learn consultation methods often must unlearn some of his traditional ways of working with people.

In this process, the consultee is a collaborator, not a patient, a client, or a counselee. His personal psychopathology is not the focus of discussion, which means that the mental health professional requires considerable reorientation. Since the process is an indirect one, it is also often a slow process. The results may not be evident for a considerable period of time and perhaps are recognized only in the reduced need for consultation. Thus, the satisfactions and rewards of individual psychotherapeutic efforts are often not present in the same way they are in the individual practice of psychotherapy. Even more than in individual work, when the process is effective the consultee may matter-of-factly accept the improvement in his work, sometimes not being aware of how he has been helped. When he is aware, he may not acknowledge it to the consultant. Since the usual ways of gauging one's effectiveness and usefulness are missing, at critical moments it is often difficult for the consultant to refrain from using the tried and true methods of individual psychotherapy. The result is usually an increase of problems in consultation.

Over the years, it has become clear that trainees who have had previous experience and practice in psychotherapeutic work with children and their parents learn consultation practice readily. They have long ago learned to hear—in the complaints of the parent about the other parent or the child—disguised statements about the immediate patient. Therefore, in consultation they can hear in the consultee's statements about his concern with a client what he is saying about himself.

Normal Anxiety in Consultation

Each mental health profession has its traditional roles and attitudes for reducing the practitioner's anxieties in dealing with the patient. The role of the person asking for help is also fairly clearly delineated. Thus, the self-expectations and the expectations of the other person are quite clear. In consultation, however, there is no traditional role, and no clear expectation of consultee and consultant.

In fact, in any consultation session one may be faced with unpredictable crises and demands for their solution; unsolvable problems may be presented in which the etiological factors are unknowable for the time being, and understanding of the consultee's troubles and their meaning at that moment may be impossible to achieve.

As one colleague stated, anxiety is to be taken for granted as a part of the consultant's expected experience in most consultation sessions.

On one occasion our consultation team arrived in a ghetto high school directly after a riot. The principal turned to me glaringly and demanded, "OK, Berlin, no shit this time. You tell me why we had this riot and how we stop them. I'm tired of your dodging these direct questions and asking us what we think. Now you tell us!" I replied that without information about the events that led up to the riots, my guesses would be worthless. He screamed at me, "Well, guess then, damn it! We've had enough of these riots!"

My two co-consultants to the administrative team of principal, vice-principal, and deans of men and women and head counselor whispered to me, "Say something." I stood fast, reminding them that I had no magic but that we could start with some questions, like: Had there been any warnings about the riots?

Again the principal flared up, though not so violently: "Always questions. How about a few answers?" The dean of men then interceded and said, "Yes, there had been rumblings of a fight between black and Chicano groups two days ago." The principal said, "Yeh, and these guys [the Deans] wanted me to have a conference with the gang leaders and I said 'Nuts!' I increased the patrols of the halls and grounds."

From this beginning, we began to piece together the demands student groups had made of the administration, the administrators' fear of confrontations, and the divided opinion about what to do.

Our discussion led to a rehearsal of how such demands could be listened to and dealt with. The principal, in his anger, acted the part of a confrontive student and I, as his target, acted as administrator. As I listened to outrageous demands and acknowledged some of the issues raised as problems and tried to involve him as a student in how they could be solved, he seemed to be watching and listening carefully as I dealt with his anger and outrage by trying to elicit a collaboration in solving problems of concern to students. That this demonstration was helpful was borne out the next month: a riot was avoided when the administrative team did get student leaders together in a listening–problem-solving session.

As so often occurs in consultation, the principal never acknowledged that my stand and demonstration had been helpful to him. I heard indirectly from the dean of men.

The Communication of Mental Health Principles to Teachers

The mental health consultant in a school system often has a unique opportunity to communicate and sometimes to demonstrate mental health principles to teachers.

Perhaps the most important principle he can communicate to school people is the fact that all human feelings can be talked about without shame, blame, or passing judgment on the teacher as a "bad" person. The consultant, by his attitude of concern, attentiveness, and respect for his professional colleague, demonstrates his relationship to the teacher as a colleague whose problems, with their attendant mixed feelings, are of mutual concern. The consultant's encouragement of verbal expression of all the teacher's feelings about his work is greatly enhanced as the consultant progressively clarifies that he is not there to analyze the teacher's personal problems. He demonstrates in many ways that his job as an expert in interpersonal relations is to help the teacher understand himself in terms of the job he is doing and, in particular, to help him be consciously aware of his feelings about the particular child who is a problem for him. The purpose is always to enable the teacher to do his work more effectively.

Through this process, the consultant communicates that every person has limitations, both professionally and personally. Unreal self-expectations and their aftermaths of tension and exhaustion from increasing conflict may seriously interfere with teaching. Thus, the understanding, acceptance, and assessment of one's own limitations are important for good mental health.

Case Examples of Communicating Mental Health Principles

Two experiences illustrate the consultant's role in demonstrating the mental health principle that all feelings aroused by a pupil can be talked about.

A third-grade teacher and her principal asked to talk with me about a nonlearning black youngster whose size and aggression made him a terror in and out of the classroom. The principal described the boy's behavior in the classroom and schoolyard and the difficulties of the teacher and the administrator in handling the boy. While the principal talked, the teacher sat very quietly by and appeared frozen. When asked to add her comments to the principal's, she remarked in a barely audible voice that it had all been said and sat stiffly in her chair. As I began to comment that this must be a handful for the teacher to contend with all day and that we psychiatrists were pretty lucky because at the worst we had to deal with such a child for only an hour once or twice a week, the teacher grinned tightly. I then talked about a learning experience of my own of which this child had reminded me. This was a severely hostile, aggressive 10-year-old boy who presented a constant dilemma in the early weeks of treatment. If I tried to stop him from attacking me and breaking up the playroom *before* he got started, he accused me of jumping him before he had done anything, and I felt guilty and uncomfortable about being unfair to such a disturbed child. If I waited until things did get started, it required all my efforts to contain him, and I found myself full of mounting rage and revengeful feelings as I struggled to prevent him from hurting me or destroying equipment. After seven or eight sessions, in 1 hour I found myself full of murderous fury, having been hurt by him and finally finding myself on the floor with a scissor lock around his legs and arm locks holding this 10-year-old down. I was working very hard only to restrain him and not to hurt him.

Beside myself with impotent rage, I told this boy how terribly angry I felt and of my own fear that the anger he provoked in me might cause me to hurt him. If that happened I would feel very guilty and sorry. I told him further that to avoid this possibility I had just decided to restrain him the moment he even looked as if he were about to be violent and that I was quite prepared to be unfair to him at times. I was determined to continue this until he had shown me that he could begin to control himself. After 3 more hours of testing and protesting as I restrained him at every sign of incipient trouble, he began to settle down and express his feelings through the materials in the playroom.

As I was talking, I could see this teacher's face relax; there were little nods as I described my own feelings in the playroom with respect to the child, and when I finished, she sighed mightily and began to talk rapidly of her own fears, the anger, hatred, and helpless feelings occasioned by this boy's behavior. She accepted my suggestion that she try to anticipate this boy's beginning unrest and stay with him, helping him do schoolwork. Her personal attention at such moment rather than a half hope from a distance that the ominous signs might not bring their inevitable result might slowly begin to help this child. Also, she might in time aid this boy to begin to communicate in words his feelings and to find a way out of his tension through beginning successes in schoolwork. On my next trip to this school about 6 weeks later, the administrator commented that a great change had taken place in the teacher. Since the consultation in which the administrator had participated, the teacher seemed more able to talk with the administrator about her problems. The boy, although still a school and classroom problem, was gradually settling down.

On another level, a male high-school teacher, after several conversations around other problems, recounted his difficulties with several, huge, explosive boys who seemed to dare him to stop them. Although no weakling himself, he found himself indecisive. He feared a fight and a riot if he interfered and tried to stop the hostile, provocative behavior, and he felt ineffectual and at the boys' mercy if he did not take some action. Involved in this also was his feeling that he could not ask the administrator's help with this recurring problem lest he be thought a poor teacher. As the teacher recounted his experiences, the dean of boys who sat by became more and more uncomfortable.

My comment that this was a hell of a fix to find oneself in brought a "You ain't kidding" from the teacher and a nod from the dean. I then recalled a particularly difficult situation in the army with a psychotic soldier who had been a wrestler as well as a much-decorated paratrooper. He terrorized the psychotic ward and was reigning as king when I took over the service. During the first ward rounds, he made his stand clear as he towered over me flexing his muscles, saying, "I am running things, see." Since my fear was evident to all in my trembling hands and legs, there seemed no point in denying it. I told this psychotic patient that I was scared of him and what he might be able to do physically to me, but that I could not let him run the ward; I was prepared personally and with all the MPs in the hospital, if necessary, to run it as it must be run. The man glared at me for an interminably long minute. I did my best to meet his gaze. Finally, he shrugged his shoulders and disdainfully said, "OK, Doc, have it your way," and returned to his bedside. I had felt that being painfully honest about my fear as well as clearly demonstrating my determination to carry out my job by whatever means were necessary had been the effective elements of this interchange.

Both teacher and dean then began to discuss how they could work together to help these youngsters settle down in the classroom. It was clear to me from the dean's avid following of my account and from his relieved look when our discussion began that he had felt as stymied as the teacher by these boys and, therefore, unable to be of much help. The humorous aftermath of this consultation came when the dean, weeks later, commented that this teacher now had a reputation among the tough youngsters for great fearlessness because he could admit being scared.

Problems in Initiating Consultation

The contract in consultation that is to be an ongoing process may present problems because it may be honored in different ways. In all varieties of individual psychotherapy, the understanding at the beginning of the work forms the framework for treatment. At least the person seeking help agrees to certain appointment times and fees and also commits himself to try to talk about his troubles.

In consultation where there is no crisis, the initial agreement may be ignored; the time, place, and conditions of consultation may seem never to have been talked about. The consultant is then faced with redefining the conditions of consultation by his own attitudes and behavior with the consultee. His efforts to help the consultee with the obstacles to his keeping the contract may be a necessary demonstration of the consultation process and vital to the development of the consultation relationship. The consultant may find himself initially giving lectures to staff, doing much direct service, etc., as part of developing the relationship.

In one instance, a principal asked the consultant to do a different kind of task each time (e.g., interview a child or a parent, visit a classroom, make a referral, or give a speech to the PTA), until he finally became convinced that the consultant really was concerned with understanding and helping the administrator and was not another prima donna from the superintendent's office concerned only with his special little project and his own professionally narcissistic satisfactions.

The Introductory Phase of Consultation

The honeymoon is an aspect of the get-acquainted period of most relationships. In the consultation process the honeymoon period is especially trying and deceptive because often everything is overtly going well, and covertly the consultee is complaining to superiors and colleagues that consultation is a waste of time and a humbug. Often the more anxious and insecure the consultee, the greater the discrepancy between the overt and covert communications.

Thus, the trainee consultant may be completely surprised and devastated when he hears the complaints. He also finds it difficult, then to deal with the consultee about the complaints in such a way as to clarify and strengthen the consultation relationship. Furthermore, effective consultation may sometimes evoke anxiety and complaining that reflects the particular reality situation that neither the consultant nor anyone else can change. Only continued consultation might reduce the consultee's turmoil. As in the matter of the problems around the contract, the consultant's efforts to explore the dissatisfactions, his ability to be nondefensive and to admit mistakes, and his honest and earnest desire to be of help may solidify the consultation relationship as a result of such "honeymoon" problems; this might otherwise take many, many more months of consultation to achieve.

While the foregoing comments apply to ongoing or continuous consultation in general—as contrasted with crisis consultation—they have a particular bearing on mental health consultation with agency administrators. This is the most difficult and trying aspect of consultation to learn and, therefore, to teach.

Learning about Transference and Countertransference

The community mental health person must learn to become aware of countertransference attitudes and feelings as well as their subsequent manifestation in his behavior, otherwise his actions may be inappropriate or destructive to the situation. The psychotherapist learns to be aware of his countertransference attitudes so that he will not act on them to the disservice of his patients. He also learns to use these feelings as important data in treatment. Countertransference attitudes are derived from our relations to parents and other important persons in the past that are unconsciously evoked in us by behaviors of persons in the present.

The development and refinement of the understanding and use of transference and countertransference manifestations takes a long time and results primarily from two kinds of psychiatric experiences: personal analysis and training in psychotherapy. Perhaps the most common way to gain such awareness is through supervised learning of individual psychotherapy over a sufficiently long period of time with a sufficient number of patients so that the nuances of these attitudes come into awareness and can be used. The second method through which one gains such awareness is through a personal psychoanalytic or psychotherapeutic experience of sufficient intensity and duration to permit exploration of one's own childhood experiences and their effect on one's perception and misperceptions of others.

Transference and Countertransference in the Consultation Setting

The community mental health specialist and the consultant should be trained to understand that behavior of people toward them in a variety of settings is determined not only by the immediate circumstances but also by how individuals view the consultant resulting from his professional role, his position in the community, and stereotypes that have developed about mental health professionals. Thus, attitudes that develop from previous experiences (such as with parents, siblings, teachers, classmates, friends, and other relationships of dominance, equality, and subordination that are operative in most interpersonal interactions) may be understood and used by the community psychiatrist for advancing the work of the group of which he is a part. These transference attitudes, if not understood, may lead to certain unconscious expectations of the consultant and may result in a sense of bewilderment, anger, disappointment, unrealistic self-expectations, and most of all, ineffectual collaboration. In the consultation setting, invitations to form alliances, to join rebellions, or to support the status quo may occur without any overt stimulation by the consultant and may reflect both current power struggles and eddies of group process on the one hand and, on the other, old parent–child and sibling relationships that need to be understood.

Variety of Transference Problems in Consultation in the Schools

Perhaps the most difficult problem confronting the mental health consultant is that of dealing with the omnipotence and omniscience that are ascribed to him by agency executives and groups as they look to him to apply his knowledge of individual psychopathology and psychotherapy to a wide variety of community phenomena. There is nothing more ego-deflating than to have educators turn to the consultant for solutions to the problems of school dropouts or underachievement. They are usually acutely disappointed when they discover that the mental health specialist's ideas are not very new or that they require careful collaborative assessment of a variety of factors, including the role of the educator. The educator's manifest disenchantment with the magic of the mental health specialist may be a difficult thing with which to deal, especially when expressed in a group situation. Similarly, when the board of a probation agency, the judge, or the chief probation officer turns to the consultant to solve the community's juvenile delinquency problems, with equal disappointment, it becomes difficult to feel that one can ever be of use to these overworked, harassed, and important people in the community.

It is vital, therefore, for the consultant to be prepared for this univeral phenomenon—that is, that the mental health specialist may be looked to as the expert who can make things right in much the same way that parents are looked to to solve the world's problems out of their wisdom and parental powers without requiring work from those who solicit help.

Another very difficult recurrent phenomenon to understand and work through presents an apparent paradox. When the consultant talks with individual agency executives, workers, or board members, there seem to be excellent communication and mutual understanding. As individuals, they appear to comprehend his limitations, his mode of operation, and how he might be helpful to them. In the group meeting, this awareness often disappears and actually seems never to have existed, only to reappear at the next individual meeting. Some background experience in group process, especially group therapy, as well as an understanding of such phenomena from individual psychotherapy may be vital to the consultant's own mental health.

It is essential for the consultant to recognize that he may be regarded as an intruder into a group. They know little of his methods of operation. Frequently, group members fear that the mental health specialist will analyze and dissect them both as individuals and as a group and find some hidden troubles. This aspect of the transference situation must be understood. Sometimes he is expected to understand situations without the data's having been made explicit, as if he were an all-wise and all-knowing parent. He will be expected to prove magically that he is a benign, nonhostile, accepting, and understanding person who does not assign blame or assess fault. He must demonstrate that he is indeed a collaborator and that his understanding of human beings as individuals and in groups is used only in the service of the common work. In this context, the consultant needs to be alert to the undue weight often given to his comments and to the fact that some of his innocent and defensive remarks will be misconstrued, taken out of context, and repeated back to him at moments of impasse in a way he never intended them to be used.

An awareness of the transference phenomena may enable him to understand how and why individual members of the group react to him as they do and why their comments are used by others in defensive or aggressive ways. He slowly comes to understand the individual needs and pressures, the hierarchical problems in the group, the status needs of various members, the power struggles, the sibling rivalries in which he is a participant, and the behind-the-scene manipulations. He also becomes aware of how his presence and comments may be used to fulfill both individual and group needs.

Failure

Despite their best efforts, teachers will sometimes fail to help a disturbed child, and they need to be able to accept such failure. The consultant's readiness to illustrate from his own experience that he, too, has on occasions failed to be helpful demonstrates his understanding of their problem. It seems to be helpful to the teacher when the consultant comments that one can fail with a clear conscience after one has literally done everything one can within his own present scope of knowledge and professional development. As many of us have experienced, the readiness to give up and to admit failure often frees both people in a working relationship to try again. I have often witnessed that the consultant's understanding and acceptance of the administrator's and the teacher's desire to exclude a child from school because they are at the end of their rope with the child resulted in the teacher's relief. Thus, the contemplated action about which the teacher or the administrator feels some guilt is accepted as reasonable in the light of the situation that has been discussed. Often later in the same discussion, after close examination of the problems and their possible causes, the teacher has reconsidered the exclusion and has been willing to try to work with the child again.

The Experimental Model of Mental Health Consultation

In recent years some of us have attempted to restructure our methods of consultee-centered consultation to resemble more closely a scientific experimental model that would lend itself to better theory testing and measurement of results.

The experimental approach is perhaps best exemplified by a vignette of Alan, with the steps of the process to be described later.

The Case of Alan

A fourth-grade teacher referred Alan because of his disruptive behavior, aggressiveness toward other students, constant restlessness, distractibility, and inability to learn—he was reading at the first-grade level. The administrator indicated that this teacher seemed to have special problems in teaching children like Alan.

At the initial meeting, the worker noted an edge of hostility as the teacher described Alan's behavior and refusal to learn. As the consultant sympathized with these problems, the teacher questioned whether there might not be something wrong with her since these problems bothered her so much. In the face of the teacher's searching, half-beseeching look, the consultant commented that such children were very difficult for anyone to handle and that this persistent nonlearning was certainly going to defeat any teacher worth her salt. The consultant suggested that data on Alan's previous school experiences and home situation be obtained. The teacher commented that she had met with his parents several times to discuss Alan's school problems. The mother had been very hostile and accused the schools of failing to interest Alan, who was a well-behaved, alert, and delightful child at home. The consultant acknowledged that he had had experience with parents who vented anger on anyone who criticized their child, and he thereby implied some parental responsibility for the child's problems. He promised to meet with the teacher the following week, after interviewing the family, so that they could together consider how Alan's emotional problems could best be worked with in the classroom.

An interview with both parents and a review of Alan's cumulative record revealed considerable information. The mother was very hostile in talking about Alan early in the interview, and his father seemed withdrawn and removed from the discussion. After the mother's hositility abated, she described Alan as a hyperactive, colicky, and demanding infant. He was her first child and she had become pregnant again barely 1 year after his birth. She felt overwhelmed at being pregnant again and was frequently sick with nausea and vomiting. During the first year, Alan's father, who was a heavy-equipment mechanic, had been away much of the time on out-of-state construction jobs, and the mother had been left to cope with this difficult infant alone. As she recounted these events, she glared balefully at her husband, who rather sheepishly said he had to go wherever his company sent him.

The birth of the second child, a girl, delighted the mother. Lucy was a serene, lovely child who slept all the time and gave little trouble. As Alan began to walk, he was into everything. The mother was alternately punitive about his destructive explorations and then let him do as he wanted in the hope that he would amuse himself and leave her alone. Alan frequently hit and bit Lucy, but the father once spanked him hard for attacking her. After this, Alan became more subtle in his attacks.

Both the cumulative record and the mother's report indicated that Alan was a terror in nursery school and in kindergarten and that he was shunned by other children and barely tolerated by his teachers. Both parents felt helpless in their efforts to get him to read or do arithmetic, both of which he stubbornly refused to do. Each effort ended in a battle, with Alan the victor. As his aggression was focused more in school, he was less hostile at home but more willful, obstinate, and contentious.

The consultant met with the teacher and made clear that this behavior and negativism had a long history. The teacher began to relax and become less defensive in describing her problems with Alan. The consultant suggested that the teacher keep a log so that they could look at the specifics of his behavior related to various areas of learning and at different times of the day.

The following week the teacher documented her problems with Alan. As he entered the classroom, he seemed restless and it was difficult to settle him down. During any formal learning exercise, he left his seat and wandered around the room harassing the other children. The teacher moved his seat next to her desk, but frequent reminders that he had a particular assignment to do kept him seated only briefly. The teacher stated that she had never before worked with such an exasperating child. The consultant nodded and then related the story of a similar problem he had had with a very hyperactive little girl who drove him to distraction. The teacher smiled, her face softened, and she remarked, "Yes, these are very difficult children to help. What did you do?" The consultant recalled that in discussions with his supervisor, he had begun to understand the child's behavior as possibly saying that as a responsible adult he ought to prevent her distractible and provocative actions. The consultant decided, after recurrent discussion, to remain close to the child and restrain her physically until she settled down and finally realized that he was determined to follow through. It had not been easy.

The teacher sniffed and said, "That's well and good for one mental health worker and one child, but how does it apply to a classroom with thirty kids?" The consultant replied, "It's not easy, but there must be a way to help Alan feel someone cares enough about him to help him settle down and learn. Let's see what we can think of. What has worked with other youngsters?'' The teacher reflected for a moment and hesitantly said, ''Well, maybe if first thing in the morning I go him started on arithmetic. He likes that, although he even messes up the papers he has done correctly. If I got him started and kept an eye on his progress, it might help.''

Slight progress was reported the next week. Alan was sitting a little longer and doing slightly better in arithmetic, although he returned to old form after completing his assignments. The consultant commented that it seemed like a good start and wondered how this could be extended to other areas. Forcefully, the teacher replied, ''Well, I can't devote all my time to him. There are twenty-nine other children who need to learn.'' The consultant responded, ''How true. What a monumental job to settle Alan down and help the rest of the class learn. I'll bet he takes up lots of your time during the day that other kids need.'' She speculated that perhaps giving Alan the extra time he required might, however, save both time and wear and tear. They agreed that the teacher would try to give him some extra individual attention.

For the next 5 weeks, it appeared that this technique was helping. In addition, the teacher had Alan stay after school once to do some special reading aloud, since he seemed inhibited, acted silly, and disrupted the group each time he was called on. This also seemed to be useful. However, in the sixth week the teacher appeared depressed and harassed, relating that Alan was worse than ever before. The consultant guessed it might have to do with his mother's hospitalization for a tumor biopsy. The father had called him that morning to say that Alan was withdrawn and noncommunicative. He related that the parents had not prepared the children for this hospitalization previous to the day their mother was admitted. The consultant said he felt the teacher had a good relationship with Alan and wondered if she might keep him after school to express her concern about his mother and her hope that he would talk to her about any worries he had or the fears children have when a parent is in the hospital, such as the possibility of the parent's dying.

At the next meeting, the teacher glowingly reported that the talk had really done the trick. Alan had cried and she had comforted him; now his mother was home again and all right, and Alan was really shaping up in class. The four to five succeeding meetings were spent in discussing and pinpointing new areas in which Alan needed help in learning. The teacher and the consultant discussed which subject areas he needed to be brought up to grade in and how he might be helped to socialize with the other children who now more readily accepted him. He especially needed help in working on cooperative projects with classmates.

The teacher appeared at the subsequent meeting looking somber and tired. She reported that Alan was now latching onto her and too frequently wanted her undivided attention. He was reluctant to leave each afternoon, and she felt drained and uneasy about turning this needy child away. She said, ''I'm not sure which is worse. At least before I didn't feel guilty when I got mad at him. Now those big, brown eyes look so beseeching I feel sick.'' The consultant mused aloud that he really should have anticipated this with such an emotionally deprived child. He pointed out the necessity of the teacher's helping the youngster experience the limits of her patience and endurance, and they discussed how this might be done by clearly specifying to Alan how much time could be spent with him and where and when and by conveying to him that the setting of limits is not the same as rejection or not caring. Hopefully, repeated efforts would reduce the extra concessions that he was able to obtain through arousing the teacher's guilt.

This phase took several weeks of discussion, examination of details of interaction, and speculation by both teacher and worker about how these interchanges could be handled differently before the teacher was able to be firm and clear about limits. Then Alan settled down and remained that way.

The consultant made sure that the teacher knew how to contact him should there be any future need and expressed pleasure that the teacher had been able to help such an emotionally disturbed child change so markedly. The teacher responded that she would not have been able to do it alone. No further regular consultation meetings were held.

The Experimental Model Defined

In this model, several stages are apparent. The first relates to the initial effort of developing a colleague relationship, which was facilitated by the consultant's statements that to understand any problem and to begin to think about solutions certain information or data had to be collected. The basic initial hypothesis was that a child's early life experience provided a basis for later behavior and may be predictive of later behavior. The involvement of the consultee in data collection takes time and reinforcement from the consultant. Obtaining information from cumulative records, from parents, and, when necessary, from other sources like pediatricians and preschools is difficult and time-consuming, but such data are essential to a mutual understanding of the factors that contribute to problems. The consultant's offer to obtain some information from health facilities, etc., through the principal's office or direct phone calls enhances the collaboration. The data-collection process is usually resisted and requires the consultant's conviction that it is vital and that only the teacher can get the necessary information for them both to put together and review.

After much of the data from the past are collected, then the student's behavior can be assessed in terms of the past information and certain patterns tentatively outlined, with reduction of the consultee's sense of blame for current problems.

The second phase also enhances the collaboration and indicates the consultant's view of the problem as one that can be better understood in the light of a log of the consultee's observations of the student in both a time frame (what happens when in the day) and a social frame (what happens in interaction with others). A behavioral data base is thus established for finding out the situations that appear to be related to behavior problems and the duration of these problems under varying circumstances.

During this phase, the consultee is helped to see himself as a participant in making observations, being helped to refine his observational skills. Most consultees, as they are helped, encouraged, and praised for their increasing precision of observation, in fact become more effective and objective observers in general. Sometimes they will even try to include their own behavior with the student as elements of the process to be understood.

The third phase is one of hypothesis generation. Both consultant and consultee comb through the data to evolve the most meaningful hypothesis about why the child (like Alan) behaves as he does. From these hypotheses, several ways of testing their relevance evolve; that is, interventions are planned to test out a hypothesis that reasonably could account for most of the behavior. One of several possible interventions is chosen and the effect of the application of the intervention on the student is examined. In subsequent meetings the data from the interventions are used to test the hypothesis and to revise the hypothesis and the interventions based on the new data.

In this process, the client is helped and the consultee consciously learns as he is helped to evolve a method of understanding student behavior. He learns through repetition and collaboration the importance of data collection and of close and precise observation, which leads to hypothesis construction and testing.

The method also helps to clarify for other consultees in group consultation what is expected of them, and it enhances their involvement in a nonjudgmental consultative process. As often happens in group consultation, a number of consultees with problem students similar to the one being presented begin to apply the same methods.

Consultation with School Administrators

Most of the techniques and methods of approach described earlier for working with teachers are applicable for working with school administrators, but there are some special problems that deserve attention.

The administrator's position makes him especially sensitive and vulnerable in the area of authority, status, and possible failure in dealing with difficulties related to teaching staff or parents. As a result, many administrators feel they must never acknowledge any problems to superiors. They must also not admit to a mental health professional that he might have knowledge or techniques that might be of use to them.

One consultant found that while a school administrator made relevant referrals and seemed to appreciate help in understanding and working with parents, she also felt that the scheduling of regular meetings would be an acknowledgement that she was not a self-sufficient and completely competent administrator. It was only when this administrator was enlisted as a collaborator (in preventive mental health evaluations of children and in helping her teachers to be more effective in understanding, evaluating, and using educative methods to help some of these very young, potentially disturbed children) and she could accept regular work with the consultant and eventually discuss a few of her problems as an administrator.

One of the most difficult problems in consultation, especially with school administrators—although this is true also of some other agency heads—stems from the combination of realistic pressures that keep them constantly busy and unavailable and their relative autonomy in the school. This makes it possible for a few administrators to shift their responsibilities to subordinates. They may provide little leadership in the school and yet prevent subordinates from operating effectively with other administrative personnel by fragmenting their authority.

The pressures incumbent in the job make it possible for the anxious administrator to be always too busy to sit down with the consultant for very long. Parents, staff, visitors, and various meetings come first. These pressures also permit ostensibly legitimate demands to be made in terms of urgent referrals, direct service, etc., and may make it impossible for the consultant and the administrator to meet to discuss other problems.

A frequent problem in working with public agency administrators stems from their conviction that they must undertake every assignment given to them, that they must carry out every suggestion made by superiors, and that they must never say no to any demands from the community. These administrators are literally overwhelmed and often frightened by the enormity of their jobs and the fact that they can see no relief in sight.

Even more difficult is the situation presented by an administrator who responds to the consultant's attitude of expertness by handing all his problems over to the consultant for solution. He often demands constant reassurance from the consultant as well. Such administrators, and they are relatively few, react to the consultant's confidence and aura of competence and especially to his ready and helpful suggestions with regressive helplessness, as if they could not possibly exist unless the consultant remained constantly at their sides to advise and help them.

Another very difficult aspect of consultation with administrators comes from the fact that sometimes one's most effective consultative work is most threatening to them. This is especially so in the kind of continuous consultation I teach, in which the administrator is present at consultation with his subordinates.[2] He can thus sanction any action that comes from consultation but, most important, as he is exposed to the consultation process, he can slowly learn by identification with the consultant how he may help his own subordinates more effectively with their problems.

If the consultant is not clearly aware of the administrator's anxieties and competitive feelings with the consultant, he may attend only to the subordinate's problems and, through his accurate and precise understanding of those problems, help him with such apparent ease that the administrator may feel impotent and worthless because he had failed to help his subordinate. Thus, the consultative relationship may be jeopardized. It is necessary (although difficult) for the mental health consultant to learn to think on many levels at once, not only about the dynamics of the individual in front of him but also about the dynamics of the entire agency and its varied personnel.

Program Consultation to School Systems

Program consultation to school systems relies on the methods described in the previous sections. A case example will demonstrate the principles.

A small suburban school system requested consultation because of increased nonlearning and behavior problems of 3rd-grade to 12th-grade students. In the last 5 years, the area had changed in composition after a low-cost housing unit was built at one end of the district. Middle- and upper-middle-class families were beginning to remove their children from the schools as the character of the schools changed.

The superintendent was urged by one of his staff to obtain consultative help with these problems because of the resistance of the school administrators to new ideas about changing some teaching procedures.

The superintendent and the cabinet at their first meeting outlined the problems primarily as decreased learning in school with a major increase of complaints by middle-class parents that their children found the school less interesting and classes more disrupted. The primary complaint was that the nonlearners were altering the general level of teaching and that the new, individualized, programmed, self-learning curriculum was not working because little individual or group help was available. This circumstance was most glaring in math, English, and the sciences. Efforts to involve principals in the review of present methods were not effective.

When the administrators turned to the consultant for possible solutions, he raised the issue of needing to obtain specific data about how class composition had changed, how the change had affected teachers and their efforts to deal with these issues, how individual programmed learning had been introduced and how teachers felt about this, and how teachers and principals felt about their current efforts. It was suggested that some of the data could be gathered by the consultant in individual meetings at the school with teachers, special education and pupil services personnel, principals, and assistant superintendents for instruction. This last idea was resisted because the principals felt that they had enough to do and because they were resistant to any new efforts. The hypothesis to be tested by the information gathering was that a change in district population and in school population made the usual methods of engaging students in learning difficult for teachers and that the curriculum change had not really altered the problems. When this hypothesis was spelled out to a meeting chaired by an assistant superintendent, it became evident that there were two major groups of principals: those very concerned with the problems and wanting to alter programs (mostly younger administrators) and those who believed that only a get-tough, kick-them-out-of-school position would be helpful. Rather than trying to deal with the entire group, the consultant asked some principals to volunteer to get the data together from their schools.

In the meeting with the younger principals, it became clear that most of them were uneasy about the unrest and the lack of learning in their schools. They were also disturbed about the teachers' anxiety and lack of leadership in the school district. Several areas were delineated for fact finding: First, how do these new children differ from the usual students? Second, what does it take to teach them? Third, what seems to interfere with teaching and learning? Fourth, what help do teachers need to do a competent job? The administrators undertook to ask their assistants and counselors to meet with teachers and to make classroom observations. They were asked to note especially any good, effective teaching and learning that occurred to provide models for other teachers.

By the next meeting, 2 weeks later, all of the younger principals had done their jobs. When they presented their findings, it became clear that most of the children from the housing projects were not ready to learn. In the early grades, they were ignored or given preprimer activities with little support in catching up with the middle-class students. By third grade, these youngsters were labeled as nonlearners and stupid. Individual teachers' efforts to reach them usually failed, and the teachers became discouraged and angry when their efforts were ignored or obviously responded to with misbehavior. With few exceptions, these children stood out. They were poorly dressed, handled themselves awkwardly socially, and were friendly only with each other, and their acting out also often occurred in groups.

The individualized-progress curriculum through which each child could start at any level in a programmed-learning sequence and proceed in steps deteriorated because individual assessments of achievement were not made. Those students who began to learn on their own found out that no one cared about them or encouraged them. The better middle-class students began to perform poorly also because this individualized method required some involvement of the teacher in assessing progress and encouraging further work. The classroom discipline problems made such encouragement rarely possible. Students often repeated their errors or worked far below their levels of capability.

As a result of the mass of data gathered, a number of ideas about effecting change were brought forth. Most of them were to test the hypothesis that the early experiences of not being ready to learn required extra attention and help in learning-readiness skills with personalized efforts to help new students become interested in learning, especially through rewarding them for their efforts. Another hypothesis was that learning readiness depended on parental interest in education and that parents would need to be involved. A third hypothesis was that these students needed opportunities to learn in noncollegebound tracks with more emphasis on manual skills and business skills.

With the agreement of the administrative staff, several kinds of interventions were tried. In the first and second grades, volunteer tutors began to work with all new students singly and in small groups to enhance their learning. Volunteers also brought mothers to school to explain the new efforts and to get the mothers' cooperation in finding a quiet place for study without TV for a short while each evening. Volunteers demonstrated how mothers could help their children practice reading. In the fifth through seventh grades, more sewing, woodshop, and typing classes were made available with ever-increasing enrollment until two teachers decided to keep their shop and sewing rooms open two evenings a week for students and their families. In a short time, these evenings were so busy that a third and fourth evening were added to accommodate the demand.

It became clear in these schools that the students were responding and that more learning in a better classroom atmosphere was occurring.

In 2 months, a report was presented to all administrative staff. The superintendent and his staff were pleased that the problems had been delineated and that some efforts were being made to reduce them. The older principals were skeptical of the findings, saying that they did not apply to their schools. Their volunteer tutors were not reliable, and these children did not appreciate the help offered. Efforts by two principals to point out their need to admit that they did not understand the special needs of the housing project students drew violent objections from most principals. As one put it, his teachers did their best and that was all right with him.

At this point, the superintendent and his staff became concerned and met with the consultant about how these very conservative administrators and teachers could be helped to change. The consultant recognized that this was a difficult situation, since the administrators and teachers could undermine any plan for change. Discussions then focused on how the present crisis could be made more vivid to these resistant principals and teachers. Most cabinet members agreed that a strong volunteer program of regular help and efforts to work closely with kids, to involve them early, and to provide relevant family activities might work.

The superintendent and the assistant superintendent for instruction and curriculum undertook to describe this program to the principals. Almost en masse they rejected this proposal as an invasion of their schools. The superintendent did not feel strongly enough to force the issue.

A backdrop to most of these efforts was a concern by the superintendent about community reaction to school taxes, which were to be voted upon in the near future. At the next meeting, the consultant predicted a serious defeat of the school levy and proposed that he work with the school administrators in those schools where old and conservative teachers were feeling strain because of the new program.

The consultant returned to a staff meeting, on request, 1 week after the levy was badly defeated. After some discussion of bad public-relations efforts, a review was made of the precincts that had turned down the levy. With one exception, they occurred in elementary-school areas where no special efforts were made to work with students. At this point, the superintendent became firm with his reluctant administrators, and group sessions with all administrators were worked out to discuss problems of helping reluctant staff to change.

The next levy passed. The changes in the elementary schools were very evident. The secondary schools were still in bad shape, and further data gathering and hypothesis generation were requested.

The Consultant in the Community

Mental health consultants in the schools are usually not concerned with community needs and priorities. Most remediation of students' problems ignores the community's priorities and its frustrations with a nonresponsive school district. Relevant interventions that involve the community, the students, the parents, and the educators as collaborators are rare.

Professional training and background also influence the responsiveness of the mental health consultant to community needs. The psychiatrist and psychologist trained in individual psychotherapy, research techniques, and testing know how to interact with middle-class patients who are like themselves and who respond to the methods they have learned. Social workers, who have been historically concerned with community needs, especially with poor and economically powerless persons, have become the emulators in practice of the well-paid, high-status psychiatrists. Only recently have some become increasingly concerned with the needs of their clients and begun to espouse the clients' positions in their welfare councils.

Professional Training versus Community Involvement

Why are mental health professionals reluctant to involve themselves with relevant groups from the community? It is clear from some of our studies that lack of prior experience in working with community members and students is a central problem. Since their only experience is with patients who ask for help or with school consultees whose troubled existence makes any offer of help quite welcome, they are not forced to venture out. Thus community residents—students and adults—may want help, but for *their* goals and on *their* terms. Mental health consultants need to learn to hear behind the anger and the rhetoric the issues that require their expertise. Traditional mental health professionals employed by the schools are in competition with each other and seek power by serving the educational establishment. They have difficulty in thinking in terms of community needs.[11]

Psychologists' sophistication about learning theory and the use of behavior modification as a tool to help teachers to work with students who have learning or behavior problems are rarely used to effect a meaningful collaboration between student and teacher to realize the *student's* particular goals. Child psychiatrists, as consultants, are often well trained in normal and abnormal physical and emotional development as well as in the stages of cognitive and affective development. However, it is striking how often the need to be omnipotent and omniscient interferes with a problem-solving, scientific approach to a child's dysfunctional behavior that might involve the educator, the administrator, the child, and the parents in a collaborative effort. Since most social workers have had little training either in child development or in learning theory and behavior modification, their most frequent tool is to try to understand the student's problems in light of his past behavior and the intrafamilial conflicts. Often, working in this way, they are helpful to student and parents but, as consultants, they have not been trained to help educators do a more effective job. Therefore, they are seen as persons to whom administrators can give the problem for solution rather than as enhancing the capacities of educators to do a more effective job with students and their families. None of these "mental health" professionals is, by training, concerned with prevention in their work.

Redefinition of the Consultant's Role

Mental health professionals and educators often find themselves alienated from a community that they do not know or understand, or that they may fear. Community priorities in education, jobs, or health care are difficult for middle-class professionals to respond to and facilitate, since these professionals usually conceptualize problem solving from their own middle-class framework. They have no way of understanding the community feelings of impotence with regard to altering any part of the system and the mistrust they evoke as representatives of the system when they seek to be helpful. Students and other adolescents in the community are often seen by professionals as strident and difficult patients, rather than as participants in a process of mutual learning. Especially difficult for mental health professionals is to reconsider their role as one of using their expertise on behalf of the community, placing their skills at the disposal of the community to accomplish those tasks most vital to them.

The usual professional role, the one most comforting, is to use one's knowledge in a traditional way; that is, the professional knows what is best for his patients or the community and provides those services as he sees fit. For example, in public health care, there can be little question that wiping out disease in every contagious form is a professional's job. However, when it comes to ridding the same population of dangerously contaminated drinking water, pollution that comes from the effluent of a nearby industry, unsanitary housing conditions, or serious overcrowding injurious to health, mental health, and children development, then the public health physician must have the vigorous, informed, sustained backing of the population he serves. Without it, his knowledge and authority are not sufficient to offset the wealth, propaganda, promises, and rhetoric of a well-financed company or nonresponsive city, state, or national government. Thus, in the instance of environmental pollution, health professionals put themselves in the position of lending their expertise as informed educators to the community and its leaders so that they may use it for the community's benefit. The real leadership in the fight against environmental pollution and environmental hazards must come from the concerned and articulate citizens who utilize the data provided by the health professionals. Citizens are learning to do this effectively on the local and national political scenes.[9,10]

Consultation to Change Traditional Roles

The educator and the mental health consultant need to collaborate to overcome the many obstacles within any institution so as to introduce new methods of teaching and learning. The mental health consultant knows from other experiences that system changes are upsetting to many within the hierarchy. The role of the consultant clearly becomes one of helping concerned community participants and pioneering school personnel to anticipate resistance to innovative school changes and to mobilize to minimize it. Mental health consultants need to be in constant touch with key people in the schools and the community, who will be subject to the greatest pressure, the most anxiety, and in some instances threats, so that they can be supported through this onslaught and be helped to maintain their positions despite pressures to revert to the status quo.[10,12]

Conclusion

Mental health consultation has evolved as a useful tool to help educators cope with nonlearning and disturbing behavior of students. Throughout the years, many of us have turned to group consultation as a more effective tool to help more teachers deal with problems in their classrooms.

In some instances, we have also begun to help other mental health personnel in the school to learn consultation techniques so that they, as school counselors, social workers, psychologists, or nurses, can be more helpful to an ever-growing body of disenchanted teachers faced with overwhelming problems.

Most recently, many of us have turned to the problems of the school system as appropriate areas of our concern and have sought to consult with top-level personnel to evaluate and find new ways for a school system to deal with new and troubling problems.

A few of us have also turned to working with the community, the consumers, to help them learn to make better use of the schools and often to help parents take a more active part in the early education of their children and to be more personally involved in the impact of the schools on their children.

Innovative efforts, of which the teaching and learning of problem-solving methods as the basic contribution of the school are an example, have been one way of helping discouraged educators and their students to seek new solutions in a rapidly changing world.

Finally, mental health consultation needs to be responsive to the changing times and needs of the schools. The consultants must acquire new skills never taught to them in their generic training. However, the constant new learning required in consultation is one of its most invigorating assets for the consultant who seeks to grow and learn and who recognizes that there are no final answers in this process.

References

1. Berlin, I. N. Some learning experiences as psychiatric consultant in the schools. *Mental Hygiene*, 1956, *40*, 215–236.
2. Berlin, I. N. Psychiatric consultation on the antidelinquency project. *California Journal of Secondary Education*, 1960, *35*, 198–202.
3. Berlin, I. N. Mental health consultation in schools as a means of communicating mental

health principles. *Journal of the American Academy of Child Psychiatry*. 1962, *1*, 671–679.

4. Berlin, I. N. Learning mental health consultation, history, and problems. *Mental Hygiene*, 1964, *48*, 257–267.
5. Berlin, I. N. Preventive aspects of mental health consultation to schools. *Mental Hygiene*, 1967, *51*, 34–40.
6. Berlin, I. N. Mental health consultation for school social workers: A conceptual model. *Community Mental Health Journal*, 1969, *5*(4), 280–288.
7. Berlin, I. N. Professionals' participation in community activities: Is it part of the job? *American Journal of Orthopsychiatry*, 1971, *41*(3), 494–500.
8. Berlin, I. N. An effort to update mental health consultation methods. In *Mental Health Consultation to the Schools: Directions for the Future*. Los Angeles, California: Behavior Science Corporation, 1973, Pp. 23–44. (BASICO No. 645-02; Proceedings of a Conference at San Diego, California, March 15–16, 1973. NIMH Contract.)
9. Geiger, H. J. Hidden professional roles: The physician as reactionary, reformer, revolutionary. *Social Policy*, 1971, *1*(6), 24–33.
10. Leininger, M. Some anthropological issues related to community mental health programs in the United States. *Community Mental Health Journal*, 1971, *7*(1), 24–28.
11. Sarason, S. B., Levine, M., Goldenberg, I. I., Cherlin, D. L., and Bennett, E. M. *Psychology in community settings*. New York: John Wiley and Sons, 1966.
12. Sheldon, A. On consulting to new, changing, or innovative organizations. *Community Mental Health Journal*, 1971 *7*(1), 62–71.

4
Effectiveness, Leadership, and Consultation

STANLEY C. PLOG

Introduction

This chapter reports on the results of a study conducted for the National Institute of Mental Health (NIMH) evaluating the impact or effectiveness of mental health consultation services to school districts. The investigation produced many insights into what are the differences between effective and ineffective mental health consultants and the prerequisites for developing a quality consultation program.

Successful consultants alone do not make successful consultation programs. From this study it is obvious that executive leadership often is lacking, leading to the early demise of many attempts to offer services to school districts. When strong and effective leadership is present, it often will be expressed in pragmatic form, that is, in attempting to develop a consistent and focused program of consultation services, rather than allowing each consultant to offer his or her services in an idiosyncratic and uncoordinated manner. Thus, successful programs more often are directed by good administrators who tend to:

1. Select and recruit consultants whose views are consonant with their own broad perspectives on consultation.

STANLEY C. PLOG · President and Founder, Plog Research, Inc., Reseda (Los Angeles), Ca.

2. Rely primarily on consultants with appropriate mental health and consultation backgrounds and provide opportunities for continued in-service training for all consultant staff.
3. Approach school districts on a flexible basis by describing the variety of services that can be offered and by inviting school administrators to become part of the planning process for developing the consultation programs.
4. Offer services that are perceived as relevant to the immediate needs of school districts before suggesting new and more pragmatic directions for future services.
5. Maintain continuous communication with school administrators during the time that consultants are working with teachers.

The study produced positive results that point to the benefits of consultation; but it also leads to some disturbing conclusions requiring considerable thought about the direction of mental health consultation programs and the characteristics of the people who serve in the programs. Stated briefly, the primary findings from the research are:

1. Mental health consultation is an effective tool in the programs of community mental health centers primarily when conducted by highly trained mental health specialists.
2. However, it tends to be infrequently employed by community mental health centers (CMHCs) because of:
   a. Inertia or resistance to change by mental health professionals who are accustomed to providing *treatment* services rather than *preventive* services (consultation and education).
   b. A lack of understanding by mental health administrators at community mental health centers of the requirements and the responsibilities of their executive and administrative positions.

These conclusions will be elaborated in the material that follows.

The focus on school settings for consultation efforts is the most obvious and natural location for the development of prevention-based services. It is the only place where a captive population of almost all available children can be found. As a recent NIMH report by Quinn and Wegner[7] states:

> Schools are the main institutions with a sustained influence over children during their vital formative years. The schools day by day deal with many times more emotional and behavioral disturbances in children than do community mental health centers. They are. because of their daily influence upon

> the children, strategic agencies for primary prevention in mental health It is estimated that mental health clinics are seeing 1 out of 14 disturbed children, while school systems are dealing with almost 14 out of 14.

Thus, effective consultation programs have the potential for reaching nearly every child in a given school district—and the corresponding potential for significant positive mental health impact.

Research Methods

In the study, a total of 20 community mental health centers were visited that had ongoing programs of mental health consultation services to school districts. The sample requirements for selecting CMHCs were based on a general random draw of all centers receiving funds from the NIMH that met the criteria of having an ongoing program in school consultation services, whether large or small, and having provided continuous service to at least one school district for 2 years or more. In addition, special requirements of the sample were that:

1. A broad geographic distribution of centers across the United States would be represented.
2. Various ethnic populations, subcultures, and income groups would be represented in the populations served by these centers.

It is obvious from these sampling characteristics that both exemplary and nonexemplary programs were included in the final selection, since nominations or recommendations were not asked of persons familiar with community mental health centers as to which were the best programs. The inclusion of both types of programs ultimately provided the opportunity to make meaningful comparisons between above-average and below-average school consultation programs.

The focus of the research effort was on evaluating the impact of mental health consultation on school systems. In this case, the question of impact (effectiveness) was measured primarily by determination of the degree of acceptance by the users of the service: Did the users of the services (consultees) find benefits from consultation, as applied to classroom problem situations, or did they really wish to terminate the services, if given the opportunity? It was impossible, within the scope of this study, to evaluate the impact on the children's lives (most of whom never saw the consultant). However, acceptance by consultees (primarily classroom teachers) could be used as a measure of determining whether or not the consultants were influencing the teachers in such a way that they accepted consultant recommendations and implemented these recommendations in the classroom setting.

The primary method of data collection was through in-depth personal interviews at these centers. More than 400 personal interviews were completed with consultants, consultees, community mental health center directors and directors of the school consultation programs, school administrative staff, and business or administrative personnel of both CMHCs and school districts. The interviews were all completed by Ph.D.-level psychologists, who visited each center (two psychologists were assigned to each center) using an extensive questionnaire that included both structured and semistructured questions. In addition, self-administered questionnaires were completed by consultees (primarily teachers) in which they were asked to rate the specific degree of help they had received from their consultant in a variety of areas typically related to student mental health problems.

Programs were divided into exemplary, average, and nonexemplary on the basis of research team evaluations after the site visit had been completed. These exemplary–nonexemplary ratings were based on separate and broad judgments by each team member visiting each center and its school districts in the areas of:

1. The length of time the center had been successful in maintaining a continuous program of services to a school district in relation to the number of years the center had offered a program. Thus, a relatively new program of services was not penalized for its newness. (Conversely, the number of times a center's program had been terminated by various school districts was a measure of an unsuccessful program.)
2. The willingness of the school district to assume some of the costs of supporting the program when the supporting funds were to be removed (determined from a question in the school administrator's questionnaire).
3. The degree of freedom provided to the CMHC by the school district to enter into areas of service beyond those that had been originally agreed upon in the initiation of services (a measure of the trust of the school district in the program).
4. The willingness of school administrative personnel to include mental health professionals in the planning of other school programs (based on both interview data and observable practices of the school districts).

The Utility of Mental Health Consultation

The primary question of the research (i.e., determining the impact of mental health consultation programs on school districts) can be stated very pragmatically: Is mental health consultation doing anything that is worthwhile, especially as compared to other forms of services provided by CMHCs? The conclusions of the research, based on the data available, offer strong support for the efficacy of mental health consultation and its considerable utility in the armamentarium of most community mental health centers.

For example, consultees (teachers and other school personnel) were asked to rate their degree of capability in dealing with specific problems related to mental health before and after receiving consultation. The results are presented in Table 1. They have been separated on the basis of exemplary, average, and nonexemplary programs (criteria described above).

The important points implied in this table are:

1. All mental health consultation programs appeared to produce a greater feeling of confidence by consultees in their ability to

Table 1. Percentage of Consultees Rating Themselves as "Extremely Capable" of Dealing with Specific Mental-Health-Related Problems Before and After Consultation

	Exemplary programs		Average programs		Nonexemplary programs	
Ability to deal with	Before	After	Before	After	Before	After
Behavior problems	12%	41%	8%	38%	9%	28%
Emotional problems	15	35	12	38	9	32
Learning disabilities	9	32	17	33	9	31
Attendance problems	3	15	8	13	14	9
Juvenile delinquents	0	6	6	8	2	2
Drug abuse	3	6	4	6	7	12
Dropouts	3	15	6	6	6	9
Quiet–withdrawn students	9	24	8	17	7	16
Race relations	3	3	6	12	5	9
Student unrest	0	6	2	16	5	7
Relationships between teachers	15	24	6	10	9	9
Relationships among school staff	15	26	6	10	5	9
Average change	16%		9%		8%	

handle the student-related (noneducational) problems they faced in the classrooms.
2. The greatest degree of improvement occurred among exemplary programs, with an average of 16% reported improvement for these programs, and the least amount of improvement (8%) occurred in nonexemplary programs.
3. Classroom-related problems (behavior problems in the classroom, learning disabilities, emotional problems, attendance problems, etc.) tended to show the greatest degree of improvement. Schoolwide problems (race relations, student unrest, drug abuse, etc.) tended to show the least amount of improvement, probably because classroom problems were the focus of most of the consultation activities.

Thus, as based on the teachers' self-reports, mental health consultation had positive benefits in the classroom in terms of the teachers' ability to handle a variety of difficult situations that were likely to occur daily.

Consultants were asked to rate the reactions of their consultees to their own consultation efforts. Although this is potentially a more biased rating, the results are consistent with the teachers' evaluations. These results are presented in Table 2.

As can be seen:

1. The exemplary programs had a higher percentage of "enthusiastic" acceptance than the average or nonexemplary programs as

Table 2. Reaction of Teachers and School Personnel Regarding Consultation Efforts, as Viewed by Consultants

	Center rating		
	Exemplary	Average	Nonexemplary
Very enthusiastic	70%	64%	54%
Moderate but broad-based support for program	30	29	33
Limited acceptance	0	7	8
Don't know	0	0	5
Total percent	100%	100%	100%

reported by consultants, and the exemplary programs reported no "limited acceptance."

2. The degree of "limited acceptance" was higher among the average and nonexemplary programs than among the exemplary programs.

Other findings also support this general conclusion. A higher proportion of consultees in exemplary programs indicated they wanted to see "consultation services continued next year" than in average or nonexemplary programs, and more consultees in exemplary programs reported that their consultant was able to "understand the problems and pressures they face in their daily work," again as compared with average or nonexemplary programs.

The primary point of this brief review is that consultation had a positive impact on the direct recipients of the services (consultees), as reported by the consultees themselves, and the better the consultation program the more positive the impact was.

These findings have important consequences for the field of mental health. The true utility of mental health consultation can be placed in proper perspective when the practical economics and leverage that can be obtained through *prevention programs* are considered, as compared with *direct treatment services*. For example, most estimates of the need for mental health services in the United States rely on the 10% figure; that is, at any given moment, at least 1 in 10 Americans is suffering from a mental health problem that is sufficiently disabling to require psychiatric help. And in one of the publications of the Joint Commission on Mental Health and Illness,[4] up to three-fourths of the population report symptomatologies they feel would be improved if they received some form of professional help.

Reports about the nation's mental health problems usually end with a plea for more training and the development of a larger number of mental health workers—psychiatrists, psychologists, social workers, etc.—usually to do what mental health workers currently do (i.e., see patients on a one-to-one basis). Only seldom is there recognition that the number of mental health professionals in ratio to the population is not going to improve significantly and that alternative approaches to answering the nation's mental health needs will have to be developed. An obvious and potentially effective alternative is mental health consultation. It provides the opportunity to reach out to larger numbers of the population and to reach them in a preventive way before they require intensive psychiatric services. If a psychiatrist, for example, can work with five or six people on a consultation basis during the hour in which he normally sees a single patient for personal therapy, his impact for positive mental health could be expanded on the basis of five or six to one (assuming equal effectiveness in both situations). Further, if the individuals he consults with are "caretakers," that is, if they have responsibility for the emotional and social lives of others (as do schoolteachers)—the impact of this psychiatrist can potentially be multiplied another 20 or 30 times. The mental health leverage statistics are astronomical. For each hour a single psychiatrist normally spends in helping a single patient, he could significantly influence the lives of 100 to 150 persons! If these statistics are true, where is the recognition of this powerful mental health leverage? Where is the army of mental health workers eagerly waiting to take up the cudgels for a new cause? And, why has the mental health community generally been so dilatory in assuming broad-scale responsibility for community mental health? *Either mental health workers are guilty of strong professional inertia in not knowing about the utility of consultation techniques, or they do not believe that consultation works.*

Characteristic Differences between Effective and Ineffective Consultation Programs

An important focus of the study was to point out differences that distinguish exemplary from nonexemplary programs. On the basis of data from questionnaires, four primary areas were identified. These are:

1. Executive leadership.
2. Program entry (gaining initial acceptance for services).
3. Qualifications of consultants.
4. Characteristics of style.

Each of these is important to overall program success and is reviewed below.

Executive Leadership

Although it was not a principal focus in the original research design, it became apparent that executive and administrative leadership was a critically important variable separating exemplary from nonexemplary programs. A rereading of the personal interviews with executive and administrative staff of exemplary and nonexemplary CMHCs and the administrators of the school districts they served provides a deeper understanding of the qualities of effective leadership. The interviews are rich in data because they were intensive and semistructured, allowing the discussion to include many meaningful topics of importance to the interviewer or the interviewee. The conclusions derived from this more qualitative data are not limited just to mental health consultation programs. Rather, they relate to a great deal of what goes on in almost all areas of mental health program direction.

The basic conclusion is that a large number of community mental health center directors lack the fundamental executive skills necessary to conduct effective programs in mental health consultation—or even to offer useful programs of direct treatment services that adequately serve the community. Four primary difficulties became apparent in the lack of these basic skills. The problems are often interrelated and tend to compound each other to build an even larger impediment to successful program functioning.

1. *Inadequate Preparation for Administrative Positions.* In interviews and discussions with CMHC directors and directors of programs for school mental health consultation, the vast majority indicate they have not received specific training or preparation prior to assuming their executive or administrative positions. Unlike in business, where technical specialists (such as engineers and systems analysts) traditionally enroll in management development programs offered on an extension basis through universities—or as short, intensive seminars from private companies—CMHC executives by and large do not participate in management development activities. Further, it is also obvious that very few of the 20 center directors (and an approximately equal number of consultation program directors interviewed in the study) had any interest in receiving new knowledge about management techniques to improve their executive abilities. By and large, they had advanced to their current positions by demonstrating professional competence in skill areas totally unrelated to the responsibilities they currently faced. They did not read about techniques of management nor did they seek instruction elsewhere on how to become better managers. In this study, only two of the directors had any background or interest in the art and science of management. This typical pattern is an obvious setting for the continued redramatization of the Peter Principle, according to which every individual rises to his own level of incompetence.

Most striking in a review of the interviews, however, is a general lack of understanding that specific administrative skills are, in fact, required for successful performance in administrative positions. This lack of insight into the executive responsibilities of a program director becomes apparent in the summary by Saul Feldman[2] in the task confronting a typical CMHC director:

> The average CMHC has an annual budget of nearly $1 million. Over thirty percent spend more than that. . . . The average CMHC employs 108 persons and staffs of over 150 are by no means uncommon. Further. these staffs are far more ecumenical than those of the past. Many centers employ people representing 16 different occupations or professional disciplines . . . Many CMHC's obtain funds from ten or more different sources, with different fiscal years. reporting requirements and special needs. Nationwide. no single funding source provides as much as one-third of all the revenue available to CMHC's . . . 85 percent of all federally funded CMHC's consist of several different organizations working together on a written agreement to provide a coordinated program. (p. 5–6)

With these kinds of executive responsibilites, it is obvious that every center director should, by definition, be a superb administrator. The findings, however, suggest that just the opposite is true. Feldman also wrote, "While everyone is in favor of coordination, nobody really wants to be coordinated" (p. 6).

2. *Derogation of Management Responsibilities*. Another prevalent factor contributing to inefficient management practices at CMHCs is the lowly view of "administrators," as seen by a majority of mental health professionals. It became apparent in visits to the centers that status was associated with demonstrated professional skills and mental health expertise in such specialties as psychotherapy, clinical diagnosis, ability to lead encounter groups or conduct family therapy, etc. However, persons who demonstrated administrative or executive skills and who sought these positions were often suspected of being very poor mental health professionals; their desire for administrative positions was considered to represent a retreat from their own professional inadequacies. When negative views about management positions are prevalent, it becomes a self-fulfilling prophesy: it is difficult to recruit the most talented people for these executive positions because of the way they are viewed by the majority and when such talented people are discovered, it may be difficult for them to lead subordinates because of the poor view held of administrative superiors as a result of "built-in" biases.

Others have noted this problem. In an excellent paper by Levinson and Klerman[6] about the mental health administrator, the authors stated:

> In professional circles, the term "administrator" is typically associated with such terms as "paper pushing," "mere detail," and "red tape," and is

> regarded as relatively mechanical and uncreative. In this view, the main characteristics of the administrator are in the image of the anal character: neat, orderly, concerned with control, producing on schedule according to impersonal rules, and demanding production similarly from others.
>
> The term "executive" may evoke another set of images: the "empire builder," "operator," or "politician" who wants to "run things" more to serve his narcissistic needs for power and fame than to further genuine professional goals. The existence of vivid negative images of the executive and the administrator, and the lack of more positive images, reflects the widespread tendency in the professions to conceive of "managerial" and "truly professional" work as antithetical, and to devaluate the former. (p. 54)

These authors describe seven problem areas that are of special concern to the clinician–executive, that is, the person who assumes a leadership position in a mental health organization. The important point is that the majority of consultants interviewed in this study sought a professional identification only and tended to have negative thoughts about persons who assume mental health leadership positions.

3. *The Shibboleth of Individual Freedom.* The third factor working against good administrative and leadership practices in CMHC programs is a vaguely defined belief by most mental health professionals of the efficacy of a laissez-faire world. As clinicians, many psychiatrists, psychologists, and others feel that they are constantly battling those psychic forces that "restrict" the behavior of their neurotic patients. They desire to make their patients more free, more flexible, more creative, and better able to live in the world of external realities rather than internal restrictions. They want to free their patients from the restrictive forces of an overly strong superego or a moral conscience that presumably prevents the development of healthier and more outgoing lives. This attitude also tends to carry over into the personal lives of these mental health professionals, as exemplified by the belief that individual freedom and minimum structure in their own lives contribute to their own positive mental health. Therefore, they tend to resist administrative direction, even at times when they are not aware of such resistance. Typical comments from mental health consultants in the current study are illustrative:

> "The director we have now is great. He lets us do just about anything we want to. He really never interferes with what we're doing; he trusts that we're professionals and are doing a good job."
>
> "I really like it here because I have almost total freedom to do what I want."

"I become very disturbed when people try to put constraints on the things I can do. The best way to ruin a program is to start putting a lot of controls on people."

"The director we used to have was terrible. He supervised what we did very closely and wanted us to turn in reports each month about what we had done. That took a lot of time and I couldn't see that they were worth much at all. Nobody had any freedom to do things the way they thought they ought to be done. Lots of people left. I almost did. Most of the people here now are new."

A paradox exists that is not apparent to mental health professionals who believe this way. Stated briefly, the mental health problems in the nation are massive and can be approached and solved only through systematic and coordinated efforts that focus on the most important of these problems and make the most efficient use of our limited mental health manpower resources; but large numbers of mental health professionals, perhaps the majority, resist attempts to coordinate or direct their efforts because of the perceived danger to their individual freedom and personal mental health or personal life-style. The longer these shibboleths persist, the longer it will be before our major mental health problems are solved.

4. *Lack of Leadership*. Underlying many of the problems of executive and administrative deficiencies, however, is a less tangible problem: a lack of leadership in the direction and guidance of the programs of a typical CMHC. This quality, or rather the lack of it, is less subject to specific instructions and learnings from management training courses because it depends to a larger degree upon the personal dynamics of each individual in an executive position. It is evidenced by the ability to sense the true needs and problems of the community served by a CMHC and to work effectively toward a solution of these problems. In the present study, lack of effective leadership was evidenced in several ways:

a. The absence of a plan of growth for the center that would serve to guide and direct the center's activities in its efforts to provide more adequate mental health services to the community it served.
b. Lack of supervision and review of the quality of work of the permanent and part-time professional staff engaged in consultation (or other services) at the CMHC.
c. No systematic recruitment of new professional staff, especially those whose professional growth was consistent with the requirements of the center.
d. Lack of in-service training opportunities or the opportunity to at-

tend training workshops in mental health consultation for the permanent staff to upgrade existing skills or to develop new skills.

Program Entry

There were a number of factors separating exemplary programs from nonexemplary programs related to their ability to gain access to or entry into a school system. Surprisingly, CMHCs often encountered considerable difficulty in gaining acceptance for their school-based programs—even though the services most often were provided without charge. It appears, on first glance, that most school districts would welcome professional services of almost any type, if they are offered at no cost. However, several areas of difficulty often emerge in the relationships between CMHCs and their school districts.

1. *Joint Development of Plans.* A typical pattern, observed in many CMHCs initiating school-based consultation programs, was to develop a package of services that was considered by the professional staff of the CMHC to be of extremely high quality and what they wanted to offer to selected local school districts. Shock developed among the staff when the school districts turned down the programs, usually because the schools were not involved in the original planning for the program of services. Interviews with school administrators indicate that when they were not invited to participate in program formulation, they tended to become highly suspicious of the ulterior motives of the "shrinks" who have recently contacted them.

The most successful approach observed in the study is based on the CMHC's contacting the senior administrative staff of a school district to indicate the availability of mental health consultation services and requesting a series of meetings to explain the full range of services that could be provided and their implications for the school district. Through these joint meetings, there is an opportunity for school personnel to understand better what it is they could receive, to determine its ultimate utility in the educational process for their children, to decide whether or not such services could, in fact, contribute to the broad educational goals of the school district, and to determine the approximate level of effort or size of program that would be best for the district.

Through these meetings, the school district becomes more comfortable in dealing with mental health professionals and considerably more likely to allow the program of services to be initiated. The most successful programs observed also attempted to sign a contract with the school district, even if all the services were provided without charge. The purpose of the contract was to make a mutual commitment on both sides not only for the approximate level of effort but to make certain that the program was considered an integral part of the ongoing educational process.

2. *Program Relevance.* A critical point related to initial success or failure of many consultation programs relates to the necessity of ensuring that the consultation services are relevant to the perceived needs of the school district. If there is a joint development of plans, as described above, this is usually taken care of during the initial discussions. If this prior planning has not occurred, then the result can be continuing problems for the consultants operating in the school district.

In practice, program relevance means initiating services at the level of interest or perceived needs of the school district. Almost without exception, school districts consider educational goals to be paramount, and any concerns about children's mental health needs are only secondary to educational commitments. Therefore, mental health services must be defined in terms of accomplishing overall educational goals to be most acceptable to educators. In contrast, mental health professionals often tend to be concerned primarily about the mental health needs of children and consider educational problems only as an outgrowth of underlying emotional disturbance. The differences between the two professions (mental health specialists and educators) are subtle but important in practical outcome.

Translated into action, program relevance usually means that most programs of service to school districts must start at the level of case-oriented consultation because the handling or management of problem children is of pressing concern to school districts. For example, when asked what they felt should be the focus of their consultation sessions, 74% of the consultees reported that these sessions should focus "a great deal" on behavior problems in the classrooms, and 54% responded that they should focus "a great deal" on learning difficulties (multiple answers were coded, adding to more than 100%). School administrators were asked what should be used as criteria for judging the success of school consultation programs. Management of classroom behavior problems and academic performance were the most popular choices (mentioned spontaneously by 48% of these respondents). *The most pressing concern of the schools is the educational process and not the mental health of children.*

This distinction is important. In every consultation program rated as highly effective, the consulting staff was providing help to the schools in areas such as classroom management and learning disabilities. There was often a considerable amount of crisis intervention demanded by teachers, since they tended to look to each consultant or educational specialist who came along to take some of the responsibility for managing problem children. Their basic question to consultants, often implied but not stated, was "Do you have skills that I can use." The initial relationship established by the teacher often included presenting the most difficult cases first as a form of testing the efficacy (or magical powers) of the consultant. Unless some useful help or ideas were offered for these problem cases, the teachers in the study often reported that they were "turned off" by their consultants.

As the consultant demonstrated his skills, it was possible to expand into new areas of service and to be accepted in these areas by both teachers and school administrators. This expansion was based upon a feeling of confidence in the consultant's doing useful and pragmatic things. He was accepted as being both professionally competent and personable ("He doesn't act like a shrink"). Thus, over time it was possible to lead into staff development consultation, program consultation, or other variants of consultation services.

3. *Maintaining Communication*. Once a program has been accepted, it is necessary to maintain close communication with school administrative personnel to inform them on a continuing basis of the progress of the program. This includes superintendents, assistant superintendents in charge of special education, and principals of schools where teachers are involved as consultees. Principals are an extremely important group since they are usually concerned about activities within *their* buildings. The primary fear of most educational administrators is that the mental health professional, who quietly enters schools in the district, will be able to obtain confidential information about various problems within the school district and might use this confidential information against school administrators by releasing it to outside personnel (such as PTA groups) or by working with a group of dissidents who are intent on changing the policies of the school district.

This fear is not without foundation, for consultation programs were observed in the study in which consultants disagreed strongly with the views of the school administrative personnel and attempted to take direct or indirect action. Instead of approaching the principals or superintendents to discuss some of their views in a friendly atmosphere, they radiated their feelings to consultees and attempted to develop a confrontation in which teachers were willing to speak up to their superiors about problems discussed in the consultation sessions. Such confrontation attempts usually ended in the abrupt termination of the consultee's services, if not the entire consultation program. Even exemplary programs in the current study sometimes had similar experiences in their past as part of their learning curve on how to initiate and provide school-based services. These exemplary centers indicated that they "got burned" once or twice and they learned from this experience. They now work closely with school administrative staff throughout the school year and make certain that lines of communication at top levels are constantly utilized throughout the year.

Qualification of Consultants

A central issue in the field of consultation is the qualifications and training of the mental health consultant. While the majority of authors seem to suggest that training is an important determinant of consultative success, others question whether training is the only way to develop consultative skills. This latter point of view seemed to be shared by many consultants interviewed in the field visits. There appeared to be a widespread attitude that almost anyone who is adequately trained in mental health can be a successful consultant, regardless of whether or not he has had any specific consultation training. The data from the study support of the conclusions reached by the project staff of the importance of training in effective consultation. Although there is some overlap (some excellent consultants had had little or no consultation training and some well-trained consultants rated poorly), it was generally discovered in the research that those who had received consultation training were more aware of the dynamics of the consultation process, were better received by their consultees, usually had more specific recommendations to offer to consultees, and consequently were usually more successful. This is not to say that formal training is the only way to acquire consultation skills, but this conclusion does provide a challenge to the fairly general attitude that anyone can become a successful consultant. For example, exemplary programs had a higher proportion of more advanced degreed staff than average or nonexemplary programs, as can be seen in Table 3.

Relevant educational experience was also found to be important. The project research staff who visited the 20 sites were asked to nominate consultants whom they felt were particularly outstanding. The review of the backgrounds of these individuals illustrates a point that became increasingly obvious as the project progressed. A large percentage of successful consultants have extensive experience in the school setting. This is an important finding. The majority of the better consultants tended to have:

1. A background in educational psychology.
2. A background in educational counseling.

3. A background in school psychology or
4. Prior experience in the classroom or as a school counselor or teacher.

This finding is directly relevant to the observations of Berlin,[1] Haylet,[3] and Lawrence[5] that the most effective consultants are those who have personal experiences with the situations faced by their consultees. These consultants are less likely to be perceived as alien by the consultees and are more likely to make recommendations that are directly relevant to the consultee's dilemma. The fact that he has a background similar to the teacher's makes it easier for the consultant to establish his credibility with the consultee. The training and skills of these consultants are consistent with the concerns of their consultees, and they are concerned about teachers' problems in clasroom management, learning disabilities, and behavior control in the educational setting.

The specific utility of mental health consultation training can be seen in Table 4. In exemplary programs 20% of the consultants had received formal consultation training, compared with 13% for nonexemplary programs. Perhaps the most striking difference is in the percentage of consultants who reported receiving no training whatsoever. In exemplary programs, this figure was 3% of the consulting staff, while in nonexemplary programs the figure was a remarkable 22%. Also, while the largest percentage of consultants who reported practical experience happened to be in the exemplary centers, the likelihood that some systematic training would take place was greater in the exemplary programs than in the nonexemplary programs.

Neither the length of time an individual had operated as a mental health consultant nor the amount of time he had been employed in the

Table 3. Educational Background (Staff)

	Center rating		
	Exemplary	Average	Nonexemplary
M.D. (Psychiatrist)	10%	4%	8%
Doctorate (Ph.D., Ed.D.)	40	25	13
Master's degree	45	68	67
Bachelor's degree	5	3	0
Other	0	0	12
Total percent	100%	100%	100%

Table 4. Amount of Training in Consultation Techniques (Beyond Normal Academic Training)

	Program effectiveness		
	Exemplary programs	Average programs	Nonexemplary programs
Academic training in consultation (graduate school)	13%	23%	13%
Postdoctoral institute or fellowship in consultation	7	6	0
Practical experience only in consultation	57	50	47
No previous training or practical experience	3	0	22
Other	20	22	18
Total percent	100%	100%	100%

mental health field were predictors of effectiveness in consultation, when exemplary and nonexemplary programs were compared (see Tables 5 and 6). These results are encouraging since they suggest that new programs can meet the same degree of success as programs using more established or experienced consultants.

Table 5. How Long Have You Operated as a Mental Health Consultant?

	Center rating		
	Exemplary	Average	Nonexemplary
Less than 1 year	20%	7%	8%
1–2 years	25	29	29
3–5 years	35	46	42
6–10	10	18	8
More than 10 years	10	0	13
Total percent	100%	100%	100%

Table 6. How Long Have You Been Employed in the Mental Health Field?

	Center rating		
	Exemplary	Average	Nonexemplary
Less than 1 year	5%	4%	4%
1–2 years	20	21	21
3–5 years	35	25	42
6–10 years	20	29	17
More than 10 years	20	21	17
Total percent	100%	100%	100%

Characteristics of Style

Many arguments appear in the literature about the personal qualities and the philosophical approach of a consultant and their impact on the effectiveness of the consultation process. Although these arguments cannot be adequately answered through a study such as this, important insights develop.

The question of whether a theoretic or an integrated consultation philosophy is a useful requirement was investigated through consultants' descriptions of their approach to consultation. Answers were coded as:

1. Based on a recognized theoretic approach to consultation.
2. Broadly derived or eclectic.
3. Similar to usual psychotherapeutic techniques in dealing with individuals or groups.
4. Other or unidentified approach.

The results are shown in Table 7.

The majority (60%) of the consultants reported their approach as eclectic. However, eclecticism was less common in exemplary than in nonexemplary centers. In exemplary programs, 40% of the consultants stated their approach was eclectic, while in the "average" programs it was 65% and in the nonexemplary programs it was 72%. More important, the exemplary consultant was much more likely to use an approach based on a theoretical consultation model. In exemplary programs, 28% of the consul-

Table 7. Describe Approach to Mental Health Consultation

	Center rating		
	Exemplary	Average	Nonexemplary
Based on a recognized theoretic approach to consultations	28%	3%	8%
Broadly based (eclectic)	40	65	72
Similar to usual psychotherapeutic techniques in dealing with individuals or groups	8	12	12
Other	24	15	8
DK/NA	0	5	0
Total percent	100%	100%	100%

tants reported that they adhered to a theoretic–conceptual model, compared to 3% in the "average" center and 8% in the nonexemplary programs.

Consultees were also asked to rate the effectiveness of their own consultants in the group situation or other consultation settings in terms of the degree of acceptance of his ideas by the consultees. This provided a method for classifying consultants as either effective or ineffective. Comparisons of consultants rated as highly effective with those rated as not very effective indicated that the ineffective consultants tended to divide into two groups: those who were overly authoritarian and those who were largely nondirective in their approach. In contrast, the more effective consultants appeared to be highly flexible and adaptive to individual situations by being highly didactic (information giving) at times, especially early in the initial consultation relationship, and gradually becoming more nondirective as they developed confidence in the consultee's ability to solve classroom management problems. Even as they became more nondirective, there was never a conscious attempt to withhold information when such information was requested by consultees.

The list of adjectives used by consultees to describe effective consultants reads like a description of the ideal person. The most frequently appearing words were:

1. Secure.
2. Warm.

3. Friendly.
4. Open.
5. Practical.
6. Competent.
7. Sensitive.
8. Human.
9. Accepting.
10. Nonjudgmental.
11. Able to speak in common language rather than "retreating" into professional jargon.

The more descriptive negative traits that were associated with ineffective consultants were:

1. A sense of personal security, as perceived by consultees.
2. Impractical recommendations that do not fit the classroom situation.
3. Tending to use a professional facade to add authority to recommendations.
4. Considerable lack of social skills, leading many teachers to doubt the consultant's judgment in other areas.

Successful consultants also demonstrated a considerable degree of flexibility that was not entirely anticipated at the beginning of the project, especially since some of the practices employed by the successful consultants were not part of the theoretic structure of any of the major or well-known approaches to consultation. For example, consultants in exemplary programs more often:

1. Focused their sessions primarily on behavior problems faced by the teacher in the classroom (see Table 8).
2. Observed consultees in the classroom setting (see Table 9).
3. Included principals and teachers in the same consultation group (see Table 10).

Consultants from exemplary programs also had more direct contact with cases under discussion, by interviewing children or observing them in the classroom, and they were also more concerned not to offer opinions in areas that were beyond their specific professional competence in mental health.

Finally, perhaps the most important finding of the study is that there are common characteristics that separate effective from ineffective consul-

Table 8. Degree Sessions Have Focused on Behavior Problems in the Classroom

	Center rating		
	Exemplary	Average	Nonexemplary
Great degree	59%	48%	44%
Some degree	29	31	28
Slight degree	6	6	16
Never	6	4	7
NA	0	11	5
Total percent	100%	100%	100%

Table 9. Do You Ever Observe Consultees in Classroom?

	Center rating		
	Exemplary	Average	Nonexemplary
Frequently	35%	32%	17%
Sometimes	25	43	33
Once in a while	10	4	17
Never or almost never	30	21	33
Total percent	100%	100%	100%

Table 10. Do You Frequently Include Principals and Teachers in the Same Group?

	Center rating		
	Exemplary	Average	Nonexemplary
Yes	95%	79%	67%
No	5	18	33
NA	0	3	0
Total percent	100%	100%	100%

tation. Consultation is unquestionably an art, but it comes closer to being an art form that can be consistently passed on from one person to another when it is possible to determine the important characteristics of consultation activities that contribute to success. The sensitivities of an individual consultant, the vagaries of judgment that enter into each consulting relationship, and the qualities of individual personality will always play an important part in the determination of which consultants will be effective or ineffective. However, the probabilities of success of consultation efforts and programs can be greatly enhanced if the techniques and approaches of successful consultants are emulated by others. These include:

1. An advanced degree in a closely related mental health field of psychiatry or psychology, or select educational degrees related to counseling.
2. Specific training in mental health consultation techniques.
3. A flexible and adaptable approach that is neither overly authoritarian nor nondirective.
4. An understanding of or an empathic feeling for the problems faced by the typical classroom teacher and, as a result, the demonstration of a willingness to focus on the problems of classroom management he or she presents for discussion, at least during the early consultation sessions.
5. A personality that is warm and friendly, rather than aloof and professionally judgmental.

References

1. Berlin, I. N. Mental health consultation in the schools: Who can do it, and why. *Community Mental Health Journal,* 1965, *1,* 19–22.
2. Feldman, S. Problems and prospects: Administration in mental health. *Administration in Mental Health,* Winter 1972, 4–11.
3. Haylett, C. H. The evaluation of indirect services and issues of indirect services. *Handbook of community mental health practice,* San Francisco: Jossey-Bass Inc., 1969.
4. Joint Commission on Mental Health and Illness. *Americans view their mental health.* New York: Basic Books, 1960.
5. Lawrence, M. M. *The mental health team in the school.* New York: Behavioral Publications, 1971.
6. Levinson, D. J., and Klerman, G. L. The clinician–executive: Some problematic issues for the psychiatrists in mental health organization. *Administration in Mental Health,* Winter 1972, 53–64.
7. Quinn, R. and Wegner, L. M. *Mental health and learning: When community mental health centers and school systems collaborate.* U.S. Government Printing Office, U.S. Department of Health, Education, and Welfare, No. (HSM) 72-9146, 1972.

II
Specialized Techniques in Mental Health Consultation

5

The Evolving Role of the School Consultant

RAQUEL E. COHEN

Introduction

Mental health workers are increasingly dealing with complex social and human issues within public agencies. They encounter problems of poverty, minority groups, alcohol, drug addiction, and disrupted family structures. Workers interested in the urban school are finding, in addition, that the care of school children with learning difficulties, as a manifestation of psychological and adaptation problems, looms as a large and neglected area.[32] Many people working on new approaches with these children are trying to find new modes of intervention—social work with families, residential care, conjoint family therapy, and group approaches,[5] plus participation in school system programs.[6,8,27,34,46]

These new modalities are paralleling and incorporating many of the broader trends in education and social welfare services today, so that we seem to be moving toward comprehensive care for children within a human services approach. This includes concern for a child's mental health, his physical health, and his educational progress, conceptualized as interdependent systems of influence on his total development.

RAQUEL E. COHEN · Associate Professor, Department of Psychiatry, Harvard School of Medicine.

This chapter addresses itself mainly to the issues raised by the alliance between mental health and school personnel working *together* to develop supportive programs for children with learning difficulties and the accompanying emotional and social disturbances. The terms *mental health professional* and *mental health worker* are used here to identify the professional who focuses on broad aspects of mental health intervention in the school. The concern is for children, from those who are experiencing behavioral difficulties to those who may be more permanently handicapped—intellectually, emotionally, or socially. In general, they can be described as experiencing "learning difficulties" that cause them serious problems in adapting and functioning in school.

The following variables need to be considered in an analysis of the complex phenomenology that singles out a child for special attention by adults in the school environment. In the majority of cases the teacher is the key individual who focuses interest on a specific child. By use of a systems model framework, it is possible to study the interactions among child–teacher–principal–special educational units–school system–mental health system–neighborhood–city. That is, one can conceptualize the forces that, at a given time, become confluent to bring about a "message" from the interaction between the child and the teacher that sets into motion inputs into and outputs from the rest of the interdependent subsystems. When this message translates itself into the "referral" decision, a number of variables operate within the subsystems in a concerted manner. These referrals stem from the teacher's perception and conclusion about the child's learning "difficulties."*

One can also apply the dictionary definitions of *difficulty* to a variety of events and interactions in the classrooms to analyze the factors influencing *the* interaction stemming from both participating individuals. The following areas (as examples of the phenomenology of multivariate interaction) need to be considered in the developing of an understanding of the events so as to plan interventive activities:

1. *Time lapse*. How long have the apparent difficulties been observed by the teacher? Is the problems pervasive or boundaried?

*Definition from *Webster's Seventh New Collegiate Dictionary*, G. & C. Merriam Co., 1967. Difficulty—impediment, the quality or state of being difficult. Difficult—hard to deal with, manage, or overcome. Hard to understand; puzzling. *Difficulty* applies to any conditional task almost beyond one's ability to deal with and requiring skill, perseverance, and patience to surmount or solve. Hardship stresses toil without necessarily implying any effort to overcome or patience in enduring." The word *vicissitude* can be synonymous with *difficult*.

2. *Frequency*. How often do these difficulties appear, in what areas of child's activity, and in association with what factors? What is the level of predictability of occurrence?

3. *Severity*. What is the degree of disruptiveness to the social setting? How does it affect the total learning of the child? How does the intensity of the difficulty affect the child's emotions or vice versa? Are they any indications whether a priori diagnosed areas of learning disabilities, sensory, physical, or emotional factors appear to influence the severity of the ongoing difficulties?

4. *Experience and personality of the teacher*. How able is the teacher to recognize and deal with the learning difficulty, to sustain actively labeled misbehavior from a frustrated child, cope with the many aspects of children's "acting out" when under stress, or recognize signs and symptoms of a child suffering from emotional disturbances?

5. *Classroom factors*. These include the design of curriculum content, physical areas in buildings or "special" rooms where broad flexible approaches of dealing with groups of children will have a direct bearing on the capacity of the teacher to sustain a "deviant" child's activities. The premise appears to be that the broader and more flexible the boundaries of the educational program, the less children will need special programs. The narrower the program boundaries and the more specific the teaching method, the more the teacher will require help with children who deviate from classroom "norms."

6. *System factors*. These include broad social phenomena in the "environment" affecting the schools, such as busing children across district lines, racial integration, and teachers' union strikes. On the other hand, richness of resources and emotional support systems of high quality are forces that will ultimately influence the manifested signals communicated by teachers asking for collaboration with mental health workers. In other words, the teacher's need for "special" help to deal with children who are exhibiting "deviant" behavior can be interpreted as a sign of a disequilibrium in the teacher–child subsystem. Conceptualizing the relationships, behaviors, and activities between them as a subsystem affected by forces stemming from within each individual and from outside subsystems (school–family) is helpful to (a) develop a "stance," (b) obtain relevant data, (c) organize observations and reported data, (d) develop conclusions by approximations that are influenced by continous feedback, (e) identify areas of intervention and collaboration, and (f) modify and develop new modalities of working in schools.

There is a need to reconceptualize the role of the mental health professional working in the schools. The traditional singleness of approaches, either to work with a child or to consult with teachers without awareness of the influences described above, needs reconsideration. Differentiation of roles, patterns of work, skills, and procedures according to objectives is necessary. Both the role and the procedures practiced by mental health ''specialists'' working in schools must be clarified.

Rationale of Participating in School Programs

A mental health professional may wonder how school factors relate to the learning process and how intervention in a school setting will affect a child who is manifesting difficulties in learning because of intrapsychic factors or reaction to a sense of failure. The professional may ponder, too, the degree to which the child's difficulties are ''programmed'' by an environment that provides nonrelevant teaching experiences for the specific needs of the child. Why is the school an important area of intervention for reconstructing the multileveled, disrupted personal and social patterns of a child—patterns that, in turn, affect his learning capacity?[24] What is the meaning of intervening in the school program so that the educational process impinges on a child's functional and educational development?

The material to answer these and other questions has been accumulated from a variety of sources: theory, research demonstration projects, and pilot studies. This chapter establishes models for cooperative planning, the importance of developing supportive programs for teachers dealing with children manifesting behavior difficulties, and the implementation of new approaches to the care of children with manifested learning problems in school settings.

All the fundamental, theoretical constructs of child ego psychology, social and educational innovations in the schools, new roles for teachers and administrators, or new approaches in the field of child psychiatry are not described here. However, findings in all these areas are used to develop this central assumption:

> Planned and programmed incorporation of mental health principles within a school program at the cognitive and affective levels is necessary not only for a child's appropriate personality development and enhanced learning. but also to support and enrich the teacher's function.

It must be kept in mind that, as yet, it has not been definitely ascertained which social factors contribute most decisively to conditions affecting a healthy child's social (or teacher's educational) development.[43,44] Therefore, it is necessary to *concentrate* on the fact that a wide range of social system factors—external circumstances,[25] cultural expectations, the influence of teachers,[23] and opportunities for socialization within the school setting[5]—have a strong influence on handicapping or supporting a child's potential development.

First, attention is directed to the conditions within the setting of the schools where the mental health professional will participate and share his expertise. Then the guidelines are developed that are useful to "map out" the specific areas, both concrete and conceptual, to participate and intervene in the school according to objectives. Finally, procedures and techniques are described that are helpful in developing a cooperative coprofessional role when one is working with educators in the school system.[15]

Characteristics of the Professional Interested in Collaboration with Schools: What Does He Need to Know?

What are the requisite characteristics of the mental health professional who is interested in working with educators in the school setting? He must be a professional who sees the teacher *and* the child interacting as a complex interdependent set of individuals within a field of forces originating from many points in the educational system. He must concern himself with the many aspects of the child's life that encompass immediate and personal influences on the development of his personality.[45] Of these influences, the school is one of the major ones. As is known, the child spends more of his day in the classroom than in any other social system. Thus, the school has an extraordinary effect on emotional well-being. Realizing the impact of this molding potential, the mental health professional should be as concerned with the adequacy of the educational climate as he is with other personal forces impinging on a child's life.[38] Aware of the relationship between learning and the mental health of the child, the mental health professional needs to develop the skills to become a "specialist" in the educational world. He can conceptualize the school system as an organization affected by all the system forces described earlier in this chapter. He needs to identify individual psychological and system environmental factors that can block learning and impede the development of a healthy personality. He must be aware that vulnerable children have limited ability to cope with a variety of intensive or combined factors encroaching on their unfolding patterns of adaptation.

As the mental health professional studies the "environment" of the school system (the interdependence of subsystems, the direction of input and output, the relevant and adequate decision-making mechanisms, the appropriate flexibility of its boundaries), he beings to understand how the school climate is a function of:

1. Tradition.
2. Administrative policies and procedures.
3. The personalities of the various involved educational professionals.
4. Physical plant.
5. The characteristics of the child population mix in terms of ethnic and socioeconomic factors.
6. The local community.
7. The funding base.

This understanding equips him to be an advocate—if he chooses or is asked to take on that role—for the child who is in a developmental *phase* and is vulnerable to suffering from programs that do not individualize his needs. If he is sensitive to the needs of both school personnel and children (each comprising components of interdependent subsystems), the mental health professional can make a significant contribution to a school's mental health program.

In addition to general knowledge, there are specific areas of competence that the mental health worker must develop, depending on the areas within the system where he is participating. He may need up-to-date information about the legal, educational, political, epidemiological, and administrative issues in his school.[19,26,29,30,31,33,47,48] He should be aware of scientific findings in the field of preventive child mental health programs and of research into methods of secondary and tertiary prevention.[9,28,29,32,50] He should know about specialized knowledge and techniques being developed and researched by educators who are accumulating well-documented experiences pertaining to the education of the emotionally, physically, and mentally retarded child.[39] One prominent concern of school personnel with which he should have familiarity, for example, pertains to drug abuse by children and to the use of drugs by physicians for hyperactivity in the young child.

Intervention Procedures

A mental health worker entering the schools should be prepared to expend considerable thought and energy to understand the forces affecting the environment within the system's configuration. *Environment* represents the particular combination of psychological, political, and social forces influencing procedures, policy, and educational philosophy of the school. It is a function of the goals and values of a particular school. It can also be assessed in terms of the assistance and support it gives to the teachers and its potential for stimulating particular types of activities and behavior in children.

Caplan[10] has analyzed the major components of support in the social network necessary to meet task objectives. One can translate his approach into systems language by being aware of the influential forces of the system impinging on the tasks of teachers. These forces provide (or undermine) the support necessary to strengthen the sense of competence, the ability to deal with the challenges of educating children with special needs. These support subsystems promote mastery of educational approaches and offer guidance in decision making and in the solving of expectable problems. Teachers need feedback so as to (1) validate the methods they use to deal with children manifesting learning difficulties and (2) reinforce a sense of achievement based on adequate self-evaluation. Mental health professionals should foster these functions in the school system either by their direct input or by supporting the educational operations that offer these dimensions to the teacher. Invariably a school's environment reveals how the administration leadership guides and supports the activities that go on in its classrooms.

"Special Programs" for Children with Learning Difficulties: Example for Working in a Subsystem

Within as lifelike a setting as possible, necessitating a full range of systems activities, the social environment needs to make available all kinds of opportunities that will stimulate ego organization in the child having learning difficulties and offer him new ways of solving problems. For example, "resource" areas for children with learning difficulties, who need segregated physical space for differing lengths of a school day, should have adequate supplies and a social structure built upon what is appropriate for the reinforcement or remediation of children's learning weaknesses. Success can be achieved only if these children are not isolated permanently but are given an opportunity to participate during maximum intervals in an integrated program with the total child population of a school building. Integrating "special" pupils into regular classes is being increasingly debated within the field of special education.[17] The traditional view, that it is both humane and efficient to protect children with special needs within a special class with a specially trained teacher, is being questioned and abandoned by an ever-increasing number of progressive schools.

Learning, reaction, and socialization activities that involve the child with other people are very important. In these areas, personal failure or success is socially recognized. School activities should support the child in his role as student and reinforce relationships that are appropriate for children to have with their peer group and their teachers. For example, the emotionally disturbed child should be helped to develop his adaptive student role within the school system, while at the same time integrating his socioemotional activities with interpersonal relationships at home.

Basic Components Underlying School Intervention

Mental health workers entering schools also should be prepared for problems related to coordinating pupil health services with mental health professionals operating at different administrative levels.[36,37,38] This can be conceptualized as developing interdependent links between subsystems. In order to prevent duplication, many components of pupil personnel services subsystems need to be integrated into new formats that can deal in a comprehensive and collaborative manner with the child–teacher subsystem. As previously stated, between a school's special services personnel and mental health professionals there tend to be areas of vaguely defined overlapping responsibilities.[40] This can result in poor communication, lack of trust, excessive manipulation, conflicting goals and priorities, and in systems terms, vague input, confused tasks, and erratic feedback. Although professionals working in schools and mental health clinics are concerned about the welfare of an individual child, hierarchical aspects of a school's subsystem can make it difficult for them to ally their efforts with the educators. However, they must work together in order to help the child. Table 1, which delineates the characteristics of their separate functions should help the reader to conceptualize coordination problems.

Table 1. Separate Functions of the Educator and the Mental Health Professional

	Educator	Mental health professional
Goals	To transmit knowledge and skills by educating	To "cure," to strengthen ego function through strengthening coping ability
Focus	On groups	On an individual child or on educational programs
Techniques	Intellectual	Psychological and social
Communication	Cognitive, intellectual	Psychological, emotional
Professional–child relationship	Traditional, distant	Individualistic, intimate
Time spent with child	4–6 hours/day; 5 days/week	1 hour/day; 1–5 times/week
Administrative structure	Hierarchical	Independent (occasionally supervisory)
Accountability	High	Low
Approach	Preplanned, program-oriented	Spontaneous, child-oriented
Social status	Varied	High
Pay	Varied	High
Source of personal satisfaction as a professional	Child's productivity; achievement; competence; intellectual power	Child's well-being; personality; development; ego strength; self-understanding; self-esteem

What are the possibilities for collaboration between professionals starting from such diverse positions?[28] The range of success varies, but if both educator and mental health worker focus on the supraordinate goal of contributing simultaneously to intellectual mastery and personality development, the potential for successful collaboration increases. The most productive contexts for collaboration are those pertaining to ego mastery, coping mechanisms, self-control, interpersonal comprehension, self-confidence, effective and ineffective behavior, reaction to crisis, and issues of self-esteem and self-value in the child. The Joint Commission on Mental Health of Children[32] has established guidelines helpful to schools striving to develop better and more meaningful programs. But, realistically, today's schools are barely able to handle crises without major disruptive aftermath. Although there are economic, political, ethnic, and social variables,[20,22] schools seem to have little time and energy for planning and innovating programs and services for children in alliance with the outside resources in the mental health field.

When mental health programs are well organized in a school, they tend to be integrated into the ongoing activities with the rest of the educational system.[18,49,50] The professionals who staff these programs have easy access to information (subsystem boundaries are flexible) from the teacher or the principal and are sanctioned to enter homes and obtain relevant material from community agencies. But frequently the staff has difficulty coordinating appropriate services for children because their department's administrative policies, communication channels, and boundaries are rigid and nonfunctional, and, therefore, collaborative efforts are thwarted. New professionals are often added to pupil personnel departments guided by powerful teachers' union's edicts, political considerations, or personal preferences without consideration or review of the structure of the existing departments. These forces, originating from outside the school system, should be continually kept in mind. It is possible to see how an array of forces coming from different directions tend to conflict with, neutralize, and in many instances hamper the educational system in the pursuit of its goal to educate the child. Furthermore, there is a special need for the staff of these interrelated school services to help link services between the family and the educator, the health agencies and the school, and the mental health clinics and the community's social service agencies. In most existing programs, this coordination is problematic or absent.

Pupil personnel teams in a school tend to reflect the interest and influences of the administrator, giving community needs low priority. At present, very few personnel units are well integrated into educational programs that emphasize preventive and comprehensive approaches.

Establishing a Collaborative Coprofessional Relationship in the School

Developing Collaborative Rules for Working in Schools

Mental health professionals and school personnel should work out ground rules for collaboration. When he first comes to a school, the mental health professional must define his particular interest, approach, and mode of working. He should be as clear as possible about the level of the program, the type of educational project, or the type of child he is most interested in discussing, thereby indicating to the educators just what they may expect from collaboration with him. These ground rules will define and clarify the goals and aims they share and the procedures they will undertake—for instance, how often and where they will meet and how the mental health worker will set collaborative programs into motion after conferences. In other words, staff must have a clear picture about the mental health professional's function and objectives.

Testing the "Mettle" of the Professional

When first participating in a school program, a mental health professional should view the initial cases as "test cases." School personnel generally use these opportunities to scrutinize a professional's ability and to assess his willingness and capacity to collaborate and communicate within their structure. If the mental health professional realizes that a problem is being used as a means of establishing relationships with school personnel, he will not neglect these first challenges and will address his efforts to the child *and* the needs of the educators. Details of individual children need to be discussed in general terms, with full respect for the rights of the child for confidential and competent diagnosis and treatment. Educators are rarely interested in specific dynamics. Psychiatric material should be kept to a minimum, with elimination of psychiatric or professional jargon.

Techniques Available to the Mental Health Professional

As experiences are accumulated by mental health professionals in the schools, it is evident that there has been an evolution of roles and techniques. Although there are variabilities in interests of mental health workers entering schools (and of educators in accepting their efforts), the resulting interaction can no longer be subsumed only under the umbrella of classical consultation. New techniques have been developed that can be classified according to (1) the degree of responsibility that the professional undertakes; (2) the level of advocacy; and (3) the hierarchical areas where he works. Within each area of collaboration or intervention, a combination of the following techniques will be found useful.[14,42]

Education in Mental Health Principles

It is essential for the mental health professional to realize that the teacher has the most consistent contact with students and, therefore, the greatest potential for effective intervention.[11] Many teachers come to the classroom lacking experience with children whose egos are disorganized and weak. Therapists need to share their knowledge of ego development and adaptational functions, particularly as they relate to a child's concept of self and sense of being meaningful to others. Teachers must understand how children's adaptive approaches and the level on which they communicate their feelings and attitudes relate to the maintenance need of ego integrity. Most teachers need to know which classroom activities promote opportunities for increasing ego organization and which ones do not. Principles of child psychology, special education, and group dynamics can be integrated into the curriculum. A teacher may need help to develop specific skills for communicating with an individual child so that the child is not confused by distortions and so that the teacher is able to carry out effective educational projects.[35] The hope is that when a teacher is educated in the principles of mental health, his repertoire of approaches will be increased.[1,21]

Consultation

In the process of socializing the child, educating him, and coping with his tension, consultation with the educator can be of help.[2,3] The same care of the multilevel process and sequential steps necessary when one is entering a system and establishing relationships should be reproduced in a relatively simpler setting when one is establishing consultation relationships with individuals.[11] A teacher educating handicapped or learning-difficulty children is often confronted with activity and behavior beyond his coping capabilities.[23] A repertoire of techniques must be acquired for working with these types of children. This is core material for the teacher to discuss with mental health personnel. Consultation helps a teacher to increase his knowledge and diminish his feelings of helplessness, consequent anger, frustration, and lack of understanding.

Even though a teacher may become more experienced in handling difficult situations, certain categories of classroom problems often continue that are difficult to handle and for which the teacher would like continuous consultation. The need for consultation (and its value) increases according to the competence of the consultee. As the consultee becomes more aware of the mental health dimensions involved in working with children, he is more likely to benefit from discussion with an expert.

Different categories of consultation between mental health professionals and administrators, special services staff, and teachers have been defined by many descriptive terms according to different authors.[7,11] Distinctions are made by Caplan primarily on the basis of whether the focus of concern is on an individual case or on an administrative problem having to do with a special program or policy. He also distinguishes between those cases in which the consultant's primary job is to give a specialized opinion and recommendation and those in which the consultee is given help in finding a way of solving his own problem.[12]

Collaboration

In collaboration, the mental health professional actively helps a teacher and takes part of the responsibility for dealing with group problems in the classroom or with specific children. It enables the mental health specialist not only to discuss and advise but to participate in implementing a program.[41] He shares the responsibility of resolving problem situations, and he and the teacher work together in ways appropriate to their respective professional training and roles. The mental health specialist may sit in the classroom and participate in some activities. He may be part of group sessions that may be composed of children and teachers or a family group including the child and his parents in an administrator's office. He may see the family and the child in his own clinic and then come to school to discuss the care of the child in the classroom. In collaborative situations, both teacher and mental health professional continually have direct contact with the children or with families, and both contribute to the actual supportive program.[12]

In collaboration, the mental health professional accepts direct responsibility for codetermining what action will be taken, depending on the needs of the child. In this type of working relationship between professionals and the differences between the value systems and goals of mental health workers and educators tend to emerge very clearly. Many of the mental health professional's activities are of a highly specialized nature and have no direct applicability to the school situation. However, his activities must be undertaken in conjunction with what is going on in the classroom. He should understand that he is most likely to enhance the supportive program if he keeps the specific teacher and school system clearly in mind. If the mental health professional is sharing responsibilities for a problem and his expectations for change are not being met, hostility may develop between the professionals. It is important that the mental health worker's sense of a problem's solution be realistic. If he finds that his frustration and anxiety make it hard for him to act as a collaborative ally, he should ask for professional consultation.

Coordination

Coordination includes those efforts that mental health professionals pursue when they endeavor to link together departments or individuals who participate in the educational and supportive program of a given child. For example, there are many occasions when children need special programs that clash with a school's policy and tradition. Individual arrangements may have to be worked out. Understanding of the relations between subsystems enables the mental health worker to design a feasible program. In such cases, mental health professionals can recommend types of settings in which a particular child might function better. Frequently, children benefit from having a different teacher or a different peer group with whom to relate. On these occasions, mental health consultants should work with the administrators whose job it is to form the groups and design the programs within the school.

A school is sometimes unable to understand the functions of different professionals in its own hierarchy as being relevant to the totality of care for a single child. A coordinator can help design a program that meets different needs of children, even though it may seem diversified or superfluous to school administrators. In such cases, an aide or a nurse, for example, who does not ordinarily interact educationally with specific children may be important in collecting all the information and executing the supportive program. There will be opportunities for group meetings, discussions between individuals, and the sharing of responsibility by departments in a school that may not have worked together in the past. Capitalizing on interdependent subsystems allows the mental health professional to guide the efforts of the educators to produce an efficient use of their manpower. This affords the therapist the opportunity to practice both educational and consultative techniques.

Liaison

The principle underlying this concept is that coordinated approaches enhance the development of comprehensive programs and provide follow-through within the health, welfare, and education areas outside of the school boundaries.[11] Liaison techniques have special relevance for low socioeconomic groups, whose needs are varied and are usually not met by the compartmentalized, fragmented, and discontinuous network of services in most communities. The mental health professional should try to stimulate and occasionally establish connections among the services, the educational approaches, and the activities of the school. He should also try to reach as many outside areas of activity as possible: mental health clinics, hospitals, welfare agencies, recreational centers, offices of community legal services, police hierarchies, and the courts, depending on the resources of these subsystems. This is new territory for mental health professionals working with schools, but it is evident that many students who are involved with any of these outside agencies are in need of a variety of resources not found inside the school. Community liaison work is viewed ambivalently by some school mental health workers who prefer to relegate this very large responsibility to school personnel. The potential of the school as a mental health or human services center for deprived and vulnerable children is large, and school personnel must conceptualize their jobs in broader terms. The school is the focus for efforts to reinforce the child's own capacities to influence the total milieu in which he is living. If mental health workers can help to inform school personnel about services available in a community, they can also promote the involvement of school people and parent groups in community planning, particularly when such planning concerns itself with mental health needs. The hope is that a school's active participation in community affairs will come to be respected and requested, contributing, as it can, a valuable dimension to the many programs needed for good child care.

References

1. Berlin, I. N. Mental health consultation in schools as a means of communicating mental health principles. *Journal of the American Academy of Child Psychiatry,* 1962, *1,* 671–680.
2. Berlin, I. N. Some learning experiences as psychiatric consultant in the schools. *Mental Hygiene,* 1956, *40,* 215–236.
3. Berlin, I. N. The theme in mental health consultation sessions. *American Journal of Orthopsychiatry,* 1960, *30,* 827–828.
4. Berman, L. The mental health of the educator. *Mental Hygiene.* 1954, *38,* 422–429.
5. Bettelheim, B., and Sylvester, E. A therapeutic milieu. *American Journal of Orthopsychiatry,* 1948, *18,* 191.
6. Biber, B., *The psychological impact of school experience.* New York: Bank Street College of Education, 1961.
7. Bindman, A. J. Mental health consultation: Theory and practice. *Journal of Consulting Psychology,* 1959, *23,* 473–482.
8. Bower, E. M. *Early identification of emotionally handicapped children.* Springfield, Ill.: Charles C Thomas, 1960.
9. Caplan, G. Mental health consultation in schools. In *The Elements of a Community Mental Health Program.* New York: Milbank Memorial Fund, 1956. Pp. 77–85.

10. Caplan, G. *Support systems and community mental health: Lectures on concept development.* New York: Behavioral Publications, 1974.
11. Caplan, G. *The theory and practice of mental health consultation.* New York: Basic Books, 1970. Pp. 19, 358.
12. Cohen, R. Principles of preventive mental health programs for ethnic minority populations: The acculturation of Puerto Ricans to the United States. *American Journal of Psychiatry,* 1972,, *128,* 1529–1533.
13. Cohen, R. Team consultation in a school system. *College Student Journal,* 1972, *6,* 100–105.
14. Cohen, R. Two for one: Collaboration model. *Mental Hygiene,* 1973, *57,* 23–25.
15. Cohen, R. Working with schools. In G. Caplan (Ed.), *American handbook of psychiatry.* New York: Basic Books, 1974. Pp. 211–219.
16. Coles, R. *Uprooted children: The early life of migrant farm workers.* Pittsburgh: University of Pittsburgh Press, 1970.
17. Commonwealth of Massachusetts, Chapter 766, House No. 6184, 1972.
18. Cowen, E. L., Beach, D. R., Izzo, L. D., Larid, J. D., Rappaport, J. D., Trost, M. A., and Zax, M. *Early diagnosis of emotional disorder in the school setting: A follow-up study.* 1968.
19. Crainford, L. *A national study of Canadian children with emotional and learning disorders.* Canada: The Commission on Emotional and Learning Disorders in Children, 1970.
20. Deutsch, M., Katz, C. M., and Jensen, A. (Eds.), *Social class, race and psychological development.* New York: Holt, Reinhart, and Winston, 1968.
21. Donahue, G. T., and Nichtern, S. *Teaching the troubled child.* New York: Free Press, 1965.
22. Eisenberg, L. Racism, the family, and society: A crisis in values. In S. Chess and A. Thomas (Eds.), *Annual progress in child psychiatry and child development.* New York: Brunner/Mazel Publishers, 1969. Pp. 252–264.
23. Ellis, D. B., and Miller, L. W. Teachers' attitudes and child behavior problems. *Journal of Educational Psychology,* 1936, *27,* 501–511.
24. Freud, A. Psychoanalysis and education. *The Psychoanalytic Study of the Child,* 1954, *9,* 9–15.
25. Freud, A., and Burlingham, D. *War and children.* New York: International Universities Press, 1943.
26. Glasser, W. *Schools without failure.* New York: Harper and Row, 1969.
27. Glidewell, J. C., and Stringer, L. A. Early detection of emotional illnesses in school children. *Journal of Educational Research,* 1963, *56,* 508–515.
28. Glidewell, J. C., Gildea, M. C. L., Domke, H. R., and Kantor, M.B. Behavior symptoms in children and adjustment in public schools. *Human Organizations,* 1959, *18,* 123–130.
29. Group for the Advancement of Psychiatry. *The psychiatrist in mental health education: Suggestions on collaboration with teachers,* Report No. 35, November, 1956, 51–81.
30. Holt, J. *How children fail.* New York: Dell, 1964.
31. Izzo, L. D., and Trost, M. A. Learning difficulties: Early detection and prevention. *Today and Tomorrow in Education,* 1968, *2,*, 3–8.
32. Joint Commission of Mental Health of Children. *Report: Crisis in child mental health: Challenge for the 1970's.* New York: Harper and Row, 1970, pp. 78–80, 250.
33. Kellam, S. G., Schiff, S. K., and Branch, J. D. *The Woodlawn community-wide school*

mental health program of assessment, prevention and early treatment. Brockton, Ill.: Midwest Annual Regional Conference, 1968. Pp. 31–37.

34. Kennedy, W. A. School's phobia: Rapid treatment of 50 cases. *Journal of Abnormal Psychiatry,* 1965, *70,* 285–289.
35. Laycock, S. R. Teachers' reactions to maladjustments of school children. *British Journal of Educational Psychology,* 1934, *4,* 11–19.
36. Mackey, R. A., and Hassler, F. R. Group consultation with school personnel. *Mental Hygiene,* 1966, *50,* 416–420.
37. Mariner, A. S., Brandt, E., Stone, E. C., and Mirmow, E. L. Group psychiatric consultation with public school personnel, a two-year study. *Personnel and Guidance Journal,* 1961, *40,* 254–258.
38. Mensh, I. N., Kantor, M. B., Domke, H. R., Gildea, M. C. L., and Glidewell, J. C. Children's behavior symptoms and their relationships to school adjustment sex, social class. *Journal of Social Issues,* 1959, *15,*, 8–15.
39. Millar, T. P. Psychiatric consultation with classroom teachers. *Journal of the American Academy of Child Psychiatry,* 1966, *5,* 134–144.
40. Mumford, E., Balser, B., and Rucker, M. Ambiguities in a secondary school mental health project. *American Journal of Psychiatry,* 1970, *126,* 1711–1717.
41. Nagler, S., and Cooper, S. Influencing social change in community mental health. In L. Bellak (Ed.), *Handbook of community psychiatry and community mental health.* New York: Grune and Stratton, 1964. Pp. 146–152.
42. Newman, R. G. *Psychological Consultation in the Schools.* New York: Basic Books, 1967.
43. Ojemann, R. H. (Ed.), *School and community treatment facility in preventive psychiatry.* Iowa City, State University of Iowa: Proceedings of the 5th Institute of Preventive Psychiatry, 1965.
44. Parsons, T., and Bales, R. *Family, socialization, and interaction process.* Glencoe, Ill.: Free Press, 1955.
45. Richmond, J. B., and Covert, C. Mental health and educational conference, a report. *Archives of General Psychiatry,* 1967, *17,* 513–520.
46. Roberts, J. I. (Ed.), *School children in the urban slum.* Glencoe, Ill.: The Free Press, 1967.
47. Silberman, C. E. *Crisis in the classroom.* New York: Random House, 1970.
48. White House Conference on Children. *Educational Technology: Constructive or Destructive.* Report of Forum 9, 1970, 1–16.
49. Wilkerson, D. A. Compensatory education. In S. Chess and A. Thomas (Eds.), *Annual progress in child psychiatry and child development.* New York: Brunner/Mazel Publishers, 1969. Pp. 308–318.
50. Zax, M., Cowen, E. L., Izzo, L. D., Miles, H., Telschow, E. F., and Trost, M. A. A preventive mental health program in the school setting: Description and evaluation. *Journal of Psychology,* 1963, *56,* 307–356.

6
Mental Health Consultation for School Administrators

IRVING H. BERKOVITZ

Though the classroom teacher exercises the most direct impact on the child, he lives in a network subject to influence and pressures from many sources including the principal, the vice-principal, the assistant superintendent, the school counselor, the school board, the maintenance crew, the teachers' union, parents, students, and others. Therefore, to offer mental health consultation only to the teacher group may be incomplete, at best, and at times, unknowingly, may increase conflict between teacher and administrator. For example, a consultant who advocates a nonpunitive attempt to understand children's behavior problems, may contradict an administrator's previous policy.[5]

Each school administrator has varying degrees of power and command of subordinates. At times, he also has a sensitive protection of autonomy and a suspicious resentment of influence or interference from the community outside the school. However defensive these administrator attitudes may be, they may have functional value. Schools and schoolchildren are often the targets of all brands of variably motivated change agents,

---

IRVING H. BERKOVITZ · Senior Psychiatric Consultant for Schools, Los Angeles County Department of Mental Health Services. With thanks to L. Eugene Arnold, M.D. and other members of the American Psychiatric Association Task-Force on School Consultation for editorial assistance.

with goals ranging from world peace to a decrease in the incidence of venereal disease, smoking, or eyestrain. The besieged administrator is often at a loss as to which of a multitude of programs to include in the already crowded school day. The mental health professional is just one more vendor in this marketplace.

Thus, it is incumbent on the consultant to obtain understanding, cooperation, or as a last option, benign noninterference from the school's chief administrators. These may be the superintendent, the assistant superintendent, the principal, or the heads of particular departments, such as psychology, special education, and counseling. Most often, the administrator will carefully screen the consultant, no matter how impressive his credentials, before allowing him free access to school personnel. A thorough understanding of the school's organizational structure will help the mental health professional to offer consultation that is productive in terms of the needs of the prospective consultee (e.g., the administrator) and personnel within that school.

The consultant entering a system that has never received consultation may be anxious about meeting the superintendent and the staff for the first time. Hopefully, the consultant will have had instruction in the elements of consultation and ideally will even have been a member of a seminar discussing other consultants' experiences in such situations. This entry-level meeting has elements analogous to (1) a first social visit to the home of a new friend; (2) an interview for admission to medical school; and (3) the first interview with a new patient. In most cases, cordial acceptance will prevail, but at times elements of omnipotent expectation, skepticism, and even paranoia may be present.

In addition to these crucial gatekeeping functions, I feel that the administrator deserves attention as an individual. I will offer the hypothesis that an administrator who is comfortable with himself and his work will more likely respect the autonomy of subordinates, give them more appropriate, useful direction and guidance, better detect crises needing assistance, and enhance his subordinates' operating skill. Moreover, if administrators have a clear understanding and experience with consultation, they can influence a greater number of personnel than any consultant. Certain qualities of good administrative leadership may be inborn, but some may be amenable to improvement with effective consultation. I also presume that sensitive and aware types of leadership will have a more salutory, ultimate influence on principals, teachers, and pupils than will, for example, a repressive, indecisive, insecure administrator. Allowing these presumptions, one could indeed conclude that consultation to administrators is as important as consultation to the classroom teacher or other school personnel.

Evaluation

While this discussion does not concern itself primarily with evaluation, evaluation should be a routine part of every consultation project.[11] In the examples to be cited, mention will be made of evaluation results where these were available.

Gaining Administrative Sanction

It may be that the consultant's best attitude on entry is to let the principal or the superintendent know that he will help advance any program of mental health that he or she is interested in implementing. Teachers are rarely alienated by this open alliance with the principal. In some cases, administrative sanction may already have been obtained by another consultant from the particular mental health agency. Moreover, this first consultant may be maintaining the ongoing sanction with the school system while the second consultant is meeting with teacher–principal groups, etc. However, when one consultant is operating satisfactorily with a group of consultees, it is all too easy to ignore the state of mind of the sanctioning administrator and later be startled by some overt or covert interference, including nonrenewal of saction.

If some of the school personnel have previously experienced unsuccessful or poorly handled consultative encounters, these will be uppermost in the mind of the administrator. If not discussed openly, residual feelings may prejudice this crucial entry phase. The consultant, if he feels some of the more mistrusting elements have not been resolved, may find it advisable to schedule further meetings with the administrator and/or his staff, so that there can be an optimum entry.

In the interest of maintaining sanction, periodic revisits, with the sanctioning administrator, may be desirable two or three times a year to inform him (without violating consultee confidentiality), to neutralize distorted negative reports, or to reorient and determine the appropriate needs of the consultees and the consultation procedure.

If the consultant feels that the administrator(s) could profit from and would be interested in further discussions, he should decide where proper priorities may lie. For example, it may seem more strategically useful to spend consultative time with a group of 4–6 assistant superintendents or 10–12 principals, than with 15–20 teachers, if one is allowed that choice. Ideally, if there is a sufficient number of consultants and a sufficient budget, consultation could go on with all three of these groups. If there is limited manpower and budget, however, it may be necessary to choose the most strategic, receptive group for consultative input, depending on the overall goals of the consultation program.

Characteristics of Some Administrators

Mention of certain general characteristics of administrators may be useful; any generalities about such a large group of diverse individuals are, of course, subject to exception. While the education of the student is certainly of importance to the administrator, many other considerations often assume necessary preeminence, for example, budget, personal promotion, intrastaff rivalries, community pressures, and union negotiators. Therefore, the traditional individual-client, case-oriented type of consultation is not always the most relevant area of interest. Case material consisting of situations encountered in administrative practice would be more appropriate.

The consultant may need a special interest in or experience with organizational theory and practice to engage the interest of and be most useful to a group of administrators, especially above the level of principals. The intrapsychic focus of the clinically trained mental health specialist may at times seem to be of less relevance.[7] Principals, being closer to the child and the parents, do find value in discussing concepts and issues related to child behavior and/or family relations.[10] They also may be interested in how to deal with their roles as leaders helping teachers to improve performance, feel secure, deal with different children, etc. Interviewing technique to help in personnel selection or dealing with parents is of interest as well.

Types of Consultation to School Administrators

These may be schematically outlined as follows:

1. Consultation with principals.
   a. In sessions including faculty.
   b. In conference about a child.
   c. In guidance committees or on pupil service teams.

   d. In groups for principals around crisis issues or issues of child development, administrative management, communication improvement, and/or increased personal awareness.
2. Consultation with vice-principals.
3. Consultation with department heads.
4. Consultation with superintendents. In communication-oriented, administrative-style workshops, with or without academic credits.
5. Consultation with *assistant superintendents*.
   a. In school district groups.
   b. In communication-oriented, administrative-style workshops.
   c. In ongoing minimally structured discussion groups.
6. Consultation with *school boards*.
   a. In groups with other boards.
   b. In groups with district personnel.
7. *Program-centered* administrative consultation.

In addition, in these procedures there may be variables of site, frequency, and length of meeting, as well as sponsorship by mental health, educational, and/or academic agencies. These variables will be discussed.

Consultation with Principals

The principal may at times be an *active participant in consultation meetings with teachers at his school,* especially in an elementary school. The average elementary school of 15–25 classrooms is like a small family in which everyone knows each other, cliques develop, social contacts outside of working hours frequently occur, and a certain stability of teacher group and student population may prevail. The mood or esprit will be set by the principal. Some will be repressive, insecure, and remote, while others will be enlightened, encouraging autonomy and innovation in their teachers, as well as working harmoniously with community members and pupils.

Those principals who welcome a consultant to their faculty frequently join the discussion group either to monitor influence on their teachers or to share the wisdom of the guest expert. This participation can be useful unless a competitive relationship with the consultant should develop. This possible rivalry must be kept in awareness by the consultant as much as the relationship with the teachers themselves. The principal can intimidate, block, neutralize, or allow independence of the consultant in discussion with the teachers analogous to what he may allow the teachers communicating among themselves. Whether or not to expose or confront any of the more negative roles, should these occur, must be carefully evaluated since the consultant is a guest in the system and can be easily ejected. Yet, to be rendered impotent or ridiculous will not further the development of that consultant or possibly any other future consultant in the school district. If serious conflict should develop, it may be best to discuss this away from the view of the faculty group with the principal alone and possibly with a sympathetic superior school administrator included.

Shearer[14] describes the principal's important influence and contribution in the *psychiatric evaluation of a child with teacher*, school mental health person, and consultant:

> The principal is less likely to become involved with the withdrawn child. but the class funny boy. the acting-outer. the class or community scapegoat or reject, he knows well. He requires no assistance with the majority of these cases. but when he does and referral is made. the nature and extent of this previous involvement can be crucial in formation of the proper handling of the given child's difficulties. If the involvement has been more than superficial the psychiatrist should be alert for transference and countertransference problems. (p. 48)

Shearer brings attention to an "important consideration—the narcissistic injury to the principal," when the "warm fatherly (or motherly) approach" to difficult children is unsuccessful.

Shearer concludes:

> Perhaps the greatest impact the consulting psychiatrist can have on mental health in the schools is the open recognition he gives the teacher and principals that their intuitive approach to the vast majority of the problems of their charges is sound and helpful. (p. 52)

Another type of format is like a case conference. In the school setting this is often termed a *guidance committee* or *pupil service team*. In many elementary schools this type of group will meet weekly (or less often), with the principal as an active member and the consultant as a resource person. More often a school person is the leader of the meeting rather than the consultant, which helps to encourage school personnel's decision making rather than dependence on the expert.

Personnel attending the meeting may include school psychologists, counselors, social workers, child welfare and attendance workers (or other personnel who serve this function), the teacher of the involved child, the vice-principal, or other personnel involved with or interested in the discussion of the child. Occasionally parents may be invited to attend. In these meetings the school behavior and the total life situation of the pupil under discussion are considered in fairly detailed fashion, with recommendations arrived at for changes in school program and/or obtaining outside professional examinations or treatment.

This type of conference is most likely a case-oriented type of meeting and may not significantly influence the school milieu as much as other types of consultant activity. However, it does provide a valuable clinical service for the number of children discussed, and occasional suggestions may arise concerning aspects of the school milieu involving other pupils as well.

In addition, those teachers who attend may experience some beneficial changes in their attitudes to children in the classroom. The principal in this type of meeting may well identify with the leadership style of the consultant as well as expand his own knowledge of child development.

In a few instances a principal has invited the *consultant to sit in his office* while he handles matters on the phone; interviews parents, children, or teachers; and otherwise manages the affairs of the school. This may become a one-to-one tutorial relationship between two colleagues. The expense of using a consultant for one person in the system rather than for a larger number of persons can be questioned. Yet the principal's strategic position and influence on so many other individuals may justify the investment.

Consultation with a group of principals, not including faculty, may often have to precede the entry of a consultant into discussion with the faculty. It seems to help for the principal to test and observe the consultant in the company of his peers and to experience some small or large sample of the consultation process before allowing the consultant to influence his own faculty. Such a group consultation meeting with principals may come about because a consultant comes to a district and convinces the appropriate administrators of the value of such a meeting, or because a group of principals feels the need for a consultant, or because of a crisis.

In 1956, Berlin[5] wrote:

> my previous experiences had shown that reduction of tensions in administrators around specific problems seemed to make it possible for them to better help their teachers. (p. 216)

Therefore, he decided to meet with about 20 principals in a group. He found that

> The principals were somewhat tense and anxious about meeting with a psychiatrist, fearful that what they might say would be analyzed and that they

> would be exposed and found wanting in the presence of their peers. . . . The group would have preferred formal lectures on child development, diagnosis of emotional disturbance, and specific or detailed directions about how these could be handled. . . . Most principals were not interested in listening to other case presentations or in joining in the discussion after each presentation from which some general influence could be drawn. Staff problems, such as I naively hoped would be discussed, were never mentioned. (p. 217)

What happened in 1956 might not necessarily occur now, 20 years later, considering a different cultural attitude about and familiarity with mental health services. Yet, occasionally it may still occur depending on the approach used by the consultant and the makeup of the consultee group. On the other hand, Berlin found that consultation with the high school principal in his own administrative staff arrived at a greater degree of involvement, "greater unification of the staff and greater freedom to explore differences."

Altrocchi[1] reports similar initial difficulties with consultation to administrators in groups:

> If group cohesiveness is lacking, the case-seminar method of group consultation may not be effective. For example, in group consultation with the principals of schools scattered over a large rural county, there was a defensive tendency on the part of some group members to regard the problems presented to the group as idiosyncratic to other schools and not characteristic of their own. Consequently, it became necessary for the consultant to focus upon specific informational content rather than on the cases introduced by the group members. (p. 133)

In Oak Park, Michigan, Cutler and McNeil[8] conducted what seems to have been a more satisfying series of seminars for all the principals in the system. Frank discussion and lack of personal defensiveness characterized these sessions, which were centered around (1) personnel practices, interviewing, and educational supervision; (2) the philosophic foundations of educational administration; (3) time studies of principals' activities; (4) definition of the role of the principal in the system; (5) the principal as disciplinarian and mental health worker; and several others. Morale problems of the principals themselves were touched upon, as were community relationships and the utilization of special services. In an evaluation of the attitudes of the participants before and after these seminars, it was found that there was an increased awareness in several of the administrators of their specific roles in the child management process. Striking was the finding that many of the administrators started out wishing to be less directive and forceful than teachers, but as the consultation progressed, they moved to an increased desire to be directive and forceful, which was considered a more appropriate level of managerial behavior. This fear of being an appropriately firm but not autocratic authority was a frequent finding in work with principals. It would seem that in the face of the many pressures from all sides, it is tempting for a principal (or any authority) to withdraw into a policy of "no decision" with occasional arbitrary, autocratic outbursts and a tendency to blame other groups for difficulties.

An example of *crisis-related work with principals* is reported by London and Perlswig.[10] (Cf. Shearer.[14]) In response to central administrative concern about increasingly difficult ethnic issues, five volunteer discussion groups, each consisting of one or two psychiatrists and four to eight principals, were formed. These group meetings lasted 2 years, were separated from the official school administration, were entirely voluntary, were offered without fee, and were conducted after school hours. The principal who developed these meetings had expected that the consultants would "help the principals to understand themselves better."

The meetings were planned in the form of a seminar of coequal professionals from differing disciplines meeting biweekly for 2-hour sessions. In order to emphasize the coequal status, a principal in each group was asked to moderate the discussion. There was no agenda and the principals were essentially open, articulate, and eager for a friendly and mutually supportive collaboration. The consultants insisted that the principals "find educational answers" and resisted assuming the role of experts in the school setting. One of the most important contributions of those meetings was that of providing an opportunity for the principals to share ideas and information with each other, as well as with the consultants. At first, the consultants' participation was "more in the role of intelligent laymen seriously interested in schools." As time went on, the principals became intrigued by the consultants' recurrent question, which was unfamiliar to them: "How did you come to do this?"

> Gradually, we began to make use of the substance of our psychiatric knowledge. Certain clinical concepts, such as *limiting goals, setting limits, and consulting among colleagues* could be applied to the principals' situation. . . .
>
> In contrast to the behavioral science tradition of consultation among colleagues, there was no effective form in which principals could share their common concerns . . . because the principals did not have a concept of limited goals integrated within their professional equipment, they were not prepared to meet the new challenges placed on them. They were likely to attempt too much or too little. . . .

> The principals showed orientation toward action that interfered with reflective thinking and frequently led to premature resolutions of difficult problems. . . . Their isolation from fellow principals also favored an action-orientation. because consultation among colleagues does tend to promote reflection and dissipate unnecessary feelings of urgency.
>
> The principals felt resentful because the consultants refused to conform to their expectations of consultative role and the consultants frustrated them with many questions and few answers.
>
> Because the principals were relatively unfamiliar with concepts of separation. deprivation. childhood sexuality and aggression. they were too often at a loss to deal effectively with problems of children. They tended to react to the manifest behavior (the restlessness. lack of concentration. masturbatory activity. dirty notes. and manipulative behavior) only as moral and training problems rather than as possibly reactive symptoms of stress. (p. 10)

A somewhat similar consultative experience not occasioned by any crisis was reported in Pittsburgh by Ruben[12] during a 13-week seminar with a group of 10 principals, 4 elementary and 6 secondary. This seminar used books and articles written by educators, psychologists, and psychiatrists, some of which were "highly critical of current educational practices." Two films were shown to the group; one dealt with the use of behavior modification techniques in helping autistic children in a mental hospital and the other was a film "that made a strong plea for society to humanize schools." In some sessions, role playing was used, especially to help the principal experience "how it feels to be a black parent and then a white parent."

> Since all agreed to keep confidential any problems that were raised. an atmosphere of trust and altruism quickly developed. . . . The participants helped each other look at the causes of the problems and recommended solutions. . . . The principals began to talk about why some students were truant. Some agreed that a safe smoking area should be created. Others began to see that students who drank wine and beer on school premises were in need of help rather than suspension. Teachers who caused problems with students were seen as troubled human beings who needed help and perhaps needed to be praised for some of the good things they were doing with students. It became apparent that superintendents needed help to deal more humanly with their principals. and parents needed to be viewed as important partners in their children's learning experiences and not as enemies of the school. The group discussions opened the way for greater understanding of these problems. (p. 5)

In answer to an evaluation questionnaire at the end, the principals commented that they were more sensitive to others' feelings, more tolerant of opposing views, more aware of their relations with others, more objective in looking at teachers and their problems, and more confident of their ability to work effectively with students, teachers, and parents.

The Personal Awareness Approach with Principals

The previous examples can be seen as relevant to the clinical knowledge of the psychiatrist–consultant. Other kinds of consultation may involve the personal awareness or group dynamics models, in which concepts of group forces and roles may be more relevant than concepts of individual psychodynamics. While this approach may deal ultimately with the same consultee factors as dealt with in theme interference reduction and consultee-centered consultation,[7] it does not use a client-centered focus and deals more immediately and directly with the consultee. While this may become therapeutic, it is *not* formal psychotherapy of the individual consultee. At the most, it may approach a type of confrontation. It remains closer to the work sphere than to the family or personal sphere.

In a *medium-sized school district* of Los Angeles County, a psychiatrist consultant met with eight elementary school principals who came to his office weekly for a 1½-hour group discussion. Let us call this district "Long Branch."

These discussions were more personally oriented. When consultation meetings occur off school grounds, especially in a clinical setting, a more personal emphasis will usually occur. For example, in one particular meeting one of the principals presented his difficulty in being firm with teachers of his school who chronically came late in the morning. The "hot seat" and role-playing techniques were used to help him understand and possibly alter his presented difficulty. Another meeting dealt with one principal's mannerism of constant smiling. Concerning this therapeutic orientation, Altrocchi[1] states:

> Considerable clinical sensitivity may be required in deciding when to slow down or, instead, to deal directly with affective expression by a consultee . . . on rare occasions, a brief excursion into a consultee's personal problems may be termed appropriate because of the centrality of the problem to the role of the particular professional group. Such emphasis of the consultee's private life should only be pursued if the consultee has the requisite strength to deal with his problems, commands the respect of the group, and provides the initiative for discussing his personal problems "as a case in point." (p. 132)

Without passing judgment on the advisability or inadvisability of the more personal approach, an outstanding element in the Long Branch meetings was the *consistent conscientious attendance, dedication, and involvement of the eight principals* for almost every week of 2 school years. This degree of involvement certainly speaks for some felt value and probable gain from the process. Unfortunately, measured changes were not available.

In response to a questionnaire various significant reactions were reported. In answer to the question "What's the most important thing you got out of these sessions?" the following responses were submitted:

> "Improved ability to listen to and communicate with others."
>
> "Becoming more aware of how I can cause myself depression about problems I haven't solved."
>
> "I believe I take more time to help children with problems and am less quick to make judgments."
>
> "I spend more time thinking in depth about some of the teachers' problems."
>
> "Yes, my evaluations and dialogue with teachers, parents, and students have become more responsible on my part, which has led to more open communication with all concerned."

Communication-Oriented Staff Development Approach

In a smaller school district (eight schools), 12 personnel—the 8 principals, 1 curriculum coordinator, 2 assistant superintendents, and the superintendent—participated in yet another variety of highly involving experience.[3] Let us call this district "Las Matrinas." The superintendent had requested an interpersonally oriented type of consultation since he had had previous experience with a similar type of consultation. He had become superintendent 1 year prior to the request for consultation and felt the need to improve communication with his administrative group. The consultant was a psychoanalyst who had had personal experience as a medical school administrator and who had conducted workshops for management in the business area. The consultant first met each administrator individually and solicited agenda suggestions for a later combined group meeting. These suggestions were then combined anonymously. The group meeting was not held at the consultant's office, as in the previous example, but at a hotel meeting room near the school district. The participants desired some distance from the daily school setting but not a clinical orientation. The following brief consensus was then circulated just prior to the first group meeting:

In-service Sessions for Administrators
(1970–71)

The administrators have recommended two major goals for in-service training for the current academic year with an *almost* uniform priority given to sessions with a strong process focus as a first step. Such sessions would aid administrators in the further development of communication skills, have a strong human relations–group dynamics focus, and be concerned with such issues as conflict resolution, personal growth, building trust, leadership training, and team building.

As a second step many specific issues were identified as areas to be explored and discussed after progress has been made in the elements designated in step one. A partial list of such issues is as follows:

(1) The buildling of a continuum from kindergarten through 12th grade.
(2) Clarification of roles—relationship of specific positions to the total district.
(3) Grading.
(4) Work overload.
(5) Definition and philosophy of middle school program. (p. 22)

The following frequency and length of meeting were determined according to the wishes and schedule of the group and the consultant at each meeting.[9]

1. The first three meetings occurred on each of three consecutive days. The first day's meeting was three hours, second and third meetings, six hours each.
2. The next two meetings occurred two and one half months later on two consecutive days. The first day's meeting was four and one half hours long; the second, seven and one half hours.
3. The next meetings began one month later and occurred at a frequency of approximately nine days apart as follows: March 1, three hours; March 10, ten and one half hours; March 22, four and one half hours; March 30, four and one half hours.
4. The last two meetings for the school year occurred one month and two months later and were four and one half hours each in duration.

It will be noted that in the Las Matrinas example, the *entire* administrative staff of the district was involved. In Long Branch, less than 10% of the district's administrative group was involved. Therefore, in Las Matrinas, one would expect a greater impact on the total system as well as on individual schools. In the meetings themselves much attention was devoted to an impasse in understanding between two or three of the administrators. After 2 years of consultation in Las Matrinas, several of the administrators reported changes in styles of relating to each other and to their staffs.

In the second year of the program the administrator group requested that a videotape be made of the usual business meetings for evaluation during the meeting with the consultant. They hoped thus to critique themselves in order to carry over the gains in communication to the more usual school meeting. Evaluation was done by interviewing consultees 3 years later. Overall response to consultation was favorable. Of those surveyed, 71% expressed moderate to strong satisfaction, and only one person was clearly dissatisfied. There was a trend for persons who had been long-time members of the district to show a higher level of satisfaction than persons who were relative newcomers. Many consultees, particularly principals, reported incidents with teachers, parents, or children that suggested that consultation at the administrative level was diffused to the level of the schoolchild and the community.

Nearly all participants mentioned beneficial changes, such as smoother administrative decision-making processes, improved communication, and increased self-awareness and understanding of others. Many persons recommended extension of the communication group model to school-level staff so that teachers and administrators could become a better working team. Several of the participants mentioned some unanticipated benefits. One was that consultation gave an opportunity for administrators new to the district to see their fellow staff members in a free and open setting.

Some verbatim comments were significant[15]:

> It is easier to telephone my colleagues regarding a question or a need that arises. Our relationship is direct and informal. Without consultation. I might have to spend more time in face-to-face meetings. or use up time in preparation and warm-up before getting to an issue with one of the persons I work with. . . . I no longer ignore the input from others or try to skirt their objections . . . I feel free to take a tough, hard line with my teachers, but even so I am getting few requests for transfers . . . I can take criticism more easily. As a result. I developed rap sessions with my staff. and I found that my staff perceived me differently from how I perceived myself. Partly as a result of this. I have involved my staff in decisions affecting the school. for example the selection of teacher aides. I like to think I would have done this anyway. but it is possible that it was facilitated through consultation. . . . I was a new principal at a school. When I first arrived there were some days when as many as 18 or 19 students were lined up outside my door awaiting disciplinary action. Now there are none. I have taught my teachers to become better listeners. . . . Reading scores in my school have increased from 26% to 62%, partly as a result of better teacher and principal interaction . . . I am better at handling emotionally distraught children. and allow them catharsis and expression rather than try to still their feelings. . . . As a result of my leveling

> with teachers and comparing philosophies of child management, we've become better able to work together. One of my teachers has changed to become fairer in her treatment of problem students. She seeks discussion and explanation before reacting punitively. She has become a more reasonable person.

In *another district* (of 10 schools) the assistant superintendent was instrumental in providing the availability of the consultant to the principal group and himself, with occasional attendance by the superintendent. Concurrently, the same consultant, assisted by one other psychiatrist–consultant, met for 15–45 sessions with each of seven elementary school faculties every other week.

The participants provided the following evaluation after 3 years of these programs[3]:

> General benefits which seem to have resulted include:
> (a) Greater sensitivity to feelings of others;
> (b) Improved communication skills—particularly the ability to listen;
> (c) Awareness of the behavior norms which operate within groups;
> (d) Greater acceptance of different attitudes and values;
> (e) Ability to retain greater perspectives and behavioral congruency in conflict situations;
> (f) Increased willingness to discuss personal feelings and attitudes in an open manner. (p. 23)

Consultation with Vice-Principals

The vice-principal often has a more difficult role than that of the principal. His authority is less clearly defined. He may be assigned tasks avoided and not wanted by the principal, for example, disciplinary problems or interviewing difficult teachers or parents. Moreover, the vice-principal may often be a part-time teacher in the classroom and have received no administrative training.

This group, therefore, is generally less reflective and more solution-oriented than the principals and, probably, also the teachers. Little has been written of consultation primarily to this group of administrators. Often they will be included in consultation to groups of teachers or at times principals.

In Los Angeles County, the Department of Mental Health, in collaboration with the Office of the Los Angeles County Superintendent of Schools, offered several 3-hour meetings to groups of vice-principals from many districts in the county, involving psychiatrists and other mental health professionals as consultants. These meetings involved much question-and-answer dialogue, some interpersonal exercises, role playing, and discussion of problem areas. These were well received and requests were made for a regularly scheduled series.

Consultation with Department Heads

These key personnel, such as chief psychologist, head counselor, and chief of special education, often sit in on consultation meetings with their department personnel, if these are going on. At times, this may not be desired since their presence may inhibit freer discussion by subordinates. This has to be decided on an individual basis. If the department head is to be excluded, individual meetings with the consultant may be necessary from time to time to avoid angry and/or suspicious feelings. Occasionally, consultation is possible with a group of department heads recruited from several school districts or from within a large school district.

Consultation with Superintendents

While the principal is certainly one of the most crucial school personnel influencing teachers, parents, and children, the administrator above the principal also carries important influence. This influence can express itself in determining policies to be followed in the district and/or providing support programs for the principals, whether these be encouragement, consultation, materials, extra teachers, or other services.

The superintendent usually meets the consultant on the first entry of a consultation service into the district. This meeting may consist of a handshake and a brief discussion of 5–15 minutes or a more extended conversation with the superintendent and his staff in which the consultation and the consultant are thoroughly evaluated, as described earlier. In most cases, unless the consultant actively seeks out the superintendent to maintain sanction, especially in larger districts, the two will not meet again. In a few cases, especially in smaller districts (less than 15 schools), the superintendent and the consultant may develop a mutually productive relationship.

Since the superintendent's attitudes carry wide influence in a district, it was decided in one program to offer assistance to the superintendent group.[3] This had several purposes:

1. To determine type of influence on a school system by entry at the top level of administration.

2. To offer help to the lonely executive at the top.
3. To open districts not yet aware of or receptive to mental health consultation.
4. To help facilitate consultation already proceeding by allowing the superintendent to see its scope, values, and limitations.

Method

The workshop, consisting of three parts, lasted from 9:00 A.M. to 2:30 P.M. It began with a "minilab," in which half of the group had the task of talking with each other on a feeling level, while the other half observed. Then, outside and inside groups changed places and repeated the exercise. During the second half of the morning, the groups combined to discuss what was learned from the minilab as well as the implications from the experience for the superintendent's role. At lunch, some of the same discussion continued while the consultants and individual superintendents had time to become better acquainted.

In the afternoon session, a simulated game was used. At the conclusion, the methods of interaction used by individuals and the implications of these for the end results, as well as the effect on other participants, were discussed.

Combined responses, from all superintendents, to the structured section of the evaluation were:

1. How interesting was the experimental day to you?

Exceptional	2
Considerable	18
Average	4
Some	4
Little	0

2. How valuable was it?

Exceptional	1
Considerable	11
Average	10
Some	3
Little	3

3. Do you think the experimental day should be offered for other superintendents?

Yes	23
No	4

4. Would you like to continue the same form of open discussion with this group?

Yes	21
No	5

The unstructured responses reflected more personal reactions. Some participants expressed appreciation for the opportunity to discuss the unique problems of the superintendent with those who also faced them, for example:

> "To meet with others in similar positions of responsibility and pressure without a structured agenda was worthwhile;" and "More chances for superintendents to 'let down' among their peers would seem to be a good thing."
>
> "I find myself more aware of the nonverbal communication occurring in conference with staff and others. This awareness has added to the input for decision making," or "awakened interest in how others see me."
>
> "I feel that given a second go-around we could better utilize the expertise of these consultants." (p. 24–5)

Because of the generally positive reactions, a series of discussion meetings was scheduled for the 1971–72 school year. Three 3-hour meetings were held at 3-month intervals. Initial attendance was 9–10 of the original 28. This number decreased gradually and fell to 3 by the third meeting. While press of duties was certainly involved, loss of interest must have occurred as well, especially with meetings spaced 2–3 months apart. Discussion in the meetings had centered on how to balance work and personal life, whom to trust as a confidante, how to deal with community pressures, levels of personal satisfaction, and stress of the superintendent's role. There was a desire for "answers" by some. No special procedures were used in the three 3-hour meetings other than unstructured discussion. There was little personal revelation other than in two cases in the first meetings. These two superintendents did not return to later meetings.

Consultation with Assistant Superintendents

Meetings with some assistant superintendents may have occurred already when a consultant enters the district and initially meets the superintendent and his staff. In larger districts (over 25 schools), the assistant superintendent may be the person designated to maintain communication and liaison with the consultant. In these cases, discussions with assistant superintendents may be superficial or routine, but in rare cases a relation may develop in which significant issues and policies are discussed and valuable exchange takes place.

When a district has such a strategically placed administrator strongly in favor of the consultation program, it would seem to have a very secure duration. However, there may be the factor of overt compliance but covert resentment in some principals.

In large school districts (over 50 schools), communication between the various assistant superintendents is usually incomplete. They tend to run their own departments and meet usually only in business or budget meetings.

On the basis of the experience with the superintendents described previously,[3] a workshop entitled "Human Interaction Problem Solving for Assistant Superintendents" was offered in 1971–72. In the announcement, it was mentioned that a similar type of workshop had been appreciated by superintendents. This may have encouraged greater interest from the assistant superintendent group. Out of a group of 131 assistant superintendents in 95 school districts, 60 responded to the invitation. These were divided into three smaller groups. The format of the meetings was the same as for the meetings with the superintendents a year earlier.

Results of the evaluation from the assistant superintendent group were positive. Above-average satisfaction was indicated in all areas evaluated, and approximately two-thirds asked that continuing meetings be made available. Four were scheduled at an interval of every 2 months. A group of 10 or 12 regular attendees developed. As the group continued to meet, the problems discussed were increasingly specific. Several continued in the 3-hour discussion meetings every 2 months in 1972–73. The following year, the group requested monthly meetings 8 months of the years. A wide assortment of district and personal items were discussed in an open format.

Comparison of Consultation with Superintendents and Assistant Superintendents

According to the three psychiatrist consultants, all of whom had served during both series, several factors were apparent from the two sets of meetings. It was agreed that the problems that had been discussed were common to all groups, with the role-related difference that:

1. Superintendents were the most aware of their isolation.
2. Assistant superintendents had to deal with the situation of having a person superior in command.

Discussion by assistant superintendents was more spontaneous and less guarded than in the superintendent group. There seemed a greater need and willingness to enter into open communication. Issues of dealing with teachers and principals were more fully discussed. However, less readily discussed were issues of dealing with the superintendent. When this issue did enter the discussion, several expressed the dilemma of working with a superior whose career in the district might be shorter than theirs, whose awareness of problems in the district might be more limited, and who was not always willing to trust or depend on the particular assistant superintendent. The issues of loyalty and honesty, job preservation and/or advancement recurred several times. Several of the initial group have since become superintendents and said that the consultation meetings had helped them to relate in a more open way with their staffs.

Combining Academic Credits and Consultation

In some consultation programs, it has been possible to arrange academic credit for the experience. This feature will be valued by some educators who wish to receive credit for salary raises or to meet district requirements. There is a risk of increased passivity in some consultees, who choose an easy credit or other incomplete motivation. Yet some programs may gain stature and attendance when sponsored by a respected academic institution. Such a "course" developed for superintendents[16] was described in the university brochure as follows:

> Workshop for School Superintendents
> in Effective Communication Training
>
> The goal is to help superintendents communicate more effectively with staff, community, school members and self.
>
> *The First Seminar* will deal with affective communications, applicable to interpersonal relationships in the school organizational structure. Especially to be considered will be the overt and covert expression of anger and hostility, trust, warmth, and love.
>
> *Seminars Two and Three* will more specifically relate the affective concepts presented during the first seminar to the following areas of superintendent function:
>
> The superintendent and staff relations, especially the leadership role, supervision, delegation of authority, team building, decision-making, group-process skills, negotiation, and evaluation.
>
> The superintendent and the community, including dealing with aspects of

confrontation, community advisory councils, and mobilizing effective support for school programs.

The superintendent and self, including effective functioning compatible with self-esteem: With whom can the superintendent talk as a confidante? Facilitating and encouraging honest feedback; feeling good about oneself in one's job; criteria for self-assessment; clues for self-improvement.

Seminar Four (Action application of the above materials). This will be a discussion of experiences of mental health consultation which have been provided for all categories of school personnel. These embody some of the concepts described above, e.g., the superintendent as a facilitator and expeditor of effective organizational functioning for subordinate staff, and use of available community agencies. Audio-visual resources will be considered.

Enrollment in the course consisted of 12 superintendents and 3 assistant superintendents. As a part of the initial meeting, each was asked to submit a description of current problems puzzling them in their daily work. Discussion then centered on alternative methods of dealing with some of the issues. Evaluation obtained from two-thirds of the group showed considerable interest in the series: they felt that it was of value and that it should be offered to the other school administrators. The following statements were submitted in response to the question: "Have you noticed any differences in the way you work as a result of this experience?"

Have become more aware of individual behavior of participants in groups with which I work. More sensitive to nonverbal as well as verbal communication. More understanding as to why people may take the positions they do in discussions. More listening—less talking on my part.

Covert Administrative Problems Complicating Consultation

Most often, as in the previous examples of consultation with administrators, a problem focus is not initially stated, or fully realized, until after some period of consultation has occurred. It may be desirable, therefore, to keep in one's mind, even in the first meetings with an administrator, that there may be a covert, systemwide problem underlying some of the issues that consultees bring up for discussion. For example, the following occurred in one district[2]:

Initially, the superintendent had anxiously requested that the consultant could meet only with the guidance director. The director then told him that a

> particular school had requested consultation. The director then informed the principal of the school that the superintendent had assigned the consultant there. This director was determined to make improvements in the district!
>
> The director also kept knowledge of consultant activity from a powerful assistant superintendent who might have vetoed the service. After one year, teacher and counselor anxiety about lack of administrative support became apparent to the consultant. He requested administrator participation which put the guidance director in a difficult position of having the previous actions exposed. If better administrative involvement had been insisted on initially, possibly the progress of the consultation services might have been smoother. But there also might have been an early veto of services. The consultant ultimately withdrew in frustration, but the consultation did resume a year later with a different consultant. Coincidentally, by this time there was a new superintendent and a new guidance director. Even without optimum initial sanction, apparently, a useful consultative experience had occurred. (p. 350)

A surprising example of concealed difficulty occurred during consultation to a district of 12 schools. The assistant superintendent had requested the use of a consultant seemingly out of a desire to make use of currently available services. The consultant then scheduled individual meetings with each of the 12 principals to determine their needs. He soon discovered that the principals almost unanimously were annoyed, anxious, and working less efficiently because of unsettled feelings concerning the behavior of the superintendent. The superintendent was involved in a romantic affair with a woman of the community who was active in a school-support organization. One of the principals in the district had been fired a few years earlier for a similar action.

The meetings with the consultant relieved some of the angry feelings of the principals. The following year, attempts to continue consultation to the principals as a group were not successful. It may have been that relieving the tension of the crisis was sufficient and meetings for ongoing consultation were not desired. After another 2 years, the administrative group was involved in problem-oriented consultation unrelated to the previous crisis. Different consultants were involved.

Consultation to School Boards

School board members have only rarely been involved in mental health consulation. There may be several reasons. They are not usually in schools, or relating to children and school personnel, at times when a consultant would meet educators. There has been a tradition of separation of board members from ongoing association with district personnel, other than with the superintendent and his staff. Some districts have legal restrictions on such association. Boards are considered groups for action and decision making rather than reflection. Boards are often only part time or are newly installed and incompletely informed noneducators who represent community interest or political points of view. Various districts do provide some brief orientation or in-service training experience to board members.

It would certainly seem of benefit for school boards to meet with a mental health consultant to consider the mental health aspects of serving as a board member, the educational process, or the dynamics of their interaction with school personnel, community, and each other. Regional or state school board organizations may bring together members from various districts to discuss germane issues, for example, the special problems of boards of larger city school districts. At such meetings, there could well be some input from mental health consultants.

In one school district (14 schools), the 5 board members, 6 central staff (including the superintendent), and 13 principals did meet with a mental health consultant, "To open up communication, increase understanding, increase mutual trust, and confidence among these three groups." This consultant, a clinical psychologist experienced in consulting to all categories of school personnel (but not in the district of the consultee board), happened also to be an elected member of the school board in a neighboring district. Not all consultants to boards can or need to possess this special credential.

In the words of the consultant, the first meeting of this group went as follows[13]:

> At first, participation in the total group tended to be rather guarded, particularly on the part of the principals. However, in all of the sub-group sessions, principals became open and serious, getting at the most central issues. People were not trying to be overly polite or to avoid touchy issues. They exchanged perceptions, really listened to each other, drew the other person out and came to know each other as human beings. They saw the connections between people's actions and their past experiences. They saw each other's weaknesses, nervousness, their capacity to make mistakes and to recover from them. They felt the concern of each other for themselves. So they came to see the others as pretty nice, reasonably capable human beings rather than as robots, callously playing a role.
>
> The word "family" was spontaneously used to describe the group several times during the evening. At the same time, one board member cautioned that we must be able to speak out frankly for children or for the rest of the

community and should not build such loyalty to the family that we neglect others or lose objectivity.

Program-Centered Administrative Consultation

Yet another type of consultation with administrators is called *program-centered administrative consultation*[7]:

> The consultant is invited by an administrator or by a group of administrators to help with a current problem of program development, with some predicament in the organization of their institution, or with the planning and implementation of organizational policies, including personnel policies. He is expected to come into the organization, study its problems, assess the significance of the relevant factors, and then present a report containing his appraisal of the situation and his recommendations for dealing with it. (p. 223)

It can be seen that this type of consultation occurs when the administrative group becomes aware of a problem and calls for help.

Caplan described a dilemma that he related to program-centered administrative consultation, but it well may be relevant to all consultation with school administrators:

> The nature of the program or policy problem is likely to be such as to demand knowledge and experience in the fields of organizational theory and practice, planning, fiscal and personnel management, and the ramifications of general administration, in addition to the clinical area. This requires that the mental health consultant equip himself with this additional knowledge if he wishes to offer his services as an administrative consultant, even if he tries to restrict his operations to the "human relations" aspects of administration. (p. 224)

Different from the previously described consultee-centered consultative procedures, Caplan feels that

> Because program-centered administrative consultation is usually a relatively short process of a few days to a few weeks in duration, the consultant is operating under considerable time pressure, and he cannot afford to move at the slow speed that is likely to be comfortable for a staff which is confused and is struggling with communication blocks, or is relatively ineffective because of reduced morale associated with the problems that stimulated the request for consultation.
>
> It is important to realize that his consultee is not the staff group, but the administrator who called him in. His relationship with this consultee must be

> a coordinate noncoercive one. . . . This administrator must be free, and must feel free, to accept or reject part or all of the consultant's recommendations.
>
> On the other hand, the consultant's relationship to the administrator's subordinates is not coordinate. In order to accomplish his mission, he must have authority to move freely within the organization, to obtain information, and to require the participation of its staff in his efforts, whether or not they agree with his plans and methods. Of course, in most instances he will be well advised not to throw his weight around and behave in an authoritarian manner, because this will arouse resistance and prevent him from obtaining the willing cooperation of the staff.
>
> It is not part of the role of an administrative mental health consultant to allot blame for an administrative impasse or failure; but although he could communicate his observations and suggestions carefully and in system terms so as to reduce to a minimum the possible harm to individuals, he should objectively and honestly analyze difficulties and recommend remedies that replace areas of organizational weakness by opportunities for strength. (p. 227–28)

Since the consultative experiences described above have taken place, many additional old and newer challenges have assailed school administrators, e.g., achieving ethnic balance in schools, militant parents, teacher strikes, violence and crime on school campuses, and decreasing school financing.

The stresses involved in the administrative role seem to have increased (perhaps also in all educational roles). As a result, the effects of these stresses on health, job satisfaction, and job performance have become the focus for consultative services to administrators.

The consultative formats described above did often achieve useful assistance to stress reduction as well as to changes in administrative styles. However, varied approaches and continuous exploration of innovative techniques are needed to develop consultative modalities which can meet the needs of the majority of administrators as well as other school personnel.

Summary

Meetings with school administrators are useful to the improved work performance of the particular individual administrators as well as a necessary step in the obtaining of sanction to work with teachers and other school personnel.

The work pressures that burden administrators and the crucial influence that administrators exert on other school personnel by their leadership style, as well as formulation of regulations, justify granting them high priority as prospective consultees. This priority will be deserving especially if one wishes to maximize the impact of consultation being given to any particular school system. If the school system is large (e.g., 50 schools), effective consultation with administrators may be more difficult. The consultant to administrators should have some familiarity with, empathy with, and tolerance of organizational dynamics and pressures. Consultation to administrators will undoubtedly have ultimate value for children in schools. The teachers will benefit from better administrative support, which will improve their sensitivity and comfort in providing services to children.

References

1. Altrocchi, J., Spielberger, C. D., and Eisdorfer, C. Mental health consultation with groups. *Community Mental Health Journal,* 1965, *1,* 127–134.
2. Berkovitz, I. H. Mental health consultation to school personnel: Attitudes of school administrators and consultant priorities. *The Journal of School Health,* 1970, *40,* 348–354.
3. Berkovitz, I. H. and Thomson, M. Mental health consultation and assistance to school personnel of Los Angeles County. Office of Los Angeles County, Superintendent of Schools, Downey, California, 1973.
4. Berlin, I. N. Some learning experiences as psychiatric consultant in the schools. *Mental Hygiene,* 1956, *40,* 215–236.
5. Berlin, I. N. School child guidance services, retrospect and prospect. *Psychology in the Schools,* 1966, *3,* 229–236.
6. Caplan, G. *Principles of preventive psychiatry.* New York: Basic Books, 1964, Chapter 9.
7. Caplan, G. *The theory and practice of mental health consultation.* New York: Basic Books, 1969, Chapter 10.
8. Cutler, R. L., and McNeil, E. B. *Mental health consultation in schools: A research analysis.* Ann Arbor: University of Michigan, 1966.
9. Goodhart, G. Personal communication.
10. London, N. J., and Perlswig, E. *Urban principalship in crisis* (unpublished), 1967.
11. Mannino, F. V., and Shore, M. F. The effects of consultation. *American Journal of Community Psychology,* 1975, *3*(1), 1–2'.
12. Ruben, A. G. *Humanizing school principals.* Bulletin of the National Association of Secondary School Principals, 1972.
13. Sarchet, J. Personal communication.
14. Shearer, M. The principal is often overlooked. *Community Mental Health Journal,* 1968, *4,* 47–52.
15. Smith, P. Personal communication.
16. Thomson, M. Personal communication.

7

Mental Health Consultations to Welfare Agencies

ALEXANDER S. ROGAWSKI

Introduction

Epidemiological studies of psychiatric disorders have repeatedly shown that in most populations low social and low economic positions are associated with higher rates of psychopathology.[1] The disadvantaged status contributes to the intensity and frequency of all social indicators of impaired mental health. Welfare workers, who are called upon to assist these segments of the population,[2] often have only limited professional and technical preparation to cope with the mental health needs of disturbed clients and their troubled families. This alone would make it desirable for welfare staff to have easy access to support and consultations by mental health professionals.

There are other reasons as well. A recent position statement of the Group for the Advancement of Psychiatry on *The Welfare System and Mental Health*[3] describes the adverse effects of current welfare practices on the mental health of many people affected by the welfare system: recipients, workers, administrators, and even the citizenry at large.

ALEXANDER S. ROGAWSKI · Professor and Director, Division of Social and Community Psychiatry, University of Southern California School of Medicine; Coordinator, Mental Health Consultation Services, Central Region, Los Angeles County.

Community psychiatrists should be expected to regard the welfare system with its opportunities for early intervention as an ally in preventive efforts on behalf of a high-risk population. They should be eager to establish consultation relationships with welfare agencies. This, however, is not the case.

In general, consultation services have become more available during the past two decades because of the development of community psychiatry and the creation of community mental health centers. Yet, as Glasscote[4] recently pointed out, personnel of community mental health centers have been wary of moving into the field of consultation even though it was one of the five originally required "essential" services.[5] He ascribes this fact to the staff's lack of specific experience and training. Consultation services for welfare agencies are even less frequent. Relatively few mental health professionals work consistently in this field. Mannino and Shore[6] do not list a single paper on welfare staff in a recent review of 35 studies on the effects of consultations. This is the more surprising since some of the pioneering papers on mental health consultations were based on experience gained with welfare staff.

Over 65 years ago, in 1909, Adolf Meyer[7] anticipated the development of comprehensive community mental health care. He recommended that psychiatric facilities establish collaborative relations with other care providers in the community. Welfare workers were specifically included in his plan, but it took a long time before mental health professionals began to pay attention to welfare agencies. In the late 1940s, Jules Coleman[8] was among the first to report on his work with welfare agencies. He described the mutual benefits in these words: "Social work has needed the contribution of the psychiatrist because of the wide prevalence of emotional disturbance among its clients and psychiatry has needed the assistance of social work in finding and meeting the community responsibilities."[9] He also proposed a new model of consultation that is "basically worker oriented rather than client oriented,"[10] and resembles closely Gerald Caplans "consultee-centered" consultation.[11,12] A thorough review of the literature reveals only a small number of additional papers on welfare consultation.[13]

There are many reasons to account for the relative scarcity of consultations to welfare agencies:

1. Many mental health professionals do not realize that the welfare system provides more than mere financial support and is involved in many social services. Even though these functions have been curtailed since the

federalization of the adult categorical aids (SSI, formerly ATD, AB, OAS), they are still available on demand. Furthermore, the category of Aid to Families with Dependent Children (AFDC) has not been federalized, and welfare agencies perform many family and child welfare services, including protective services for actual and potential victims of child neglect and child abuse, child placement, homemaker services, referral, and information.

2. Most mental health professionals come from a middle-class background and have no personal experience with the welfare scene. With the exception of students of social work, they rarely receive instruction on welfare issues and welfare operations. They are likely to develop prejudicial attitudes about welfare based on sensationalistic and politically inspired newspaper stories. Thus, they are unfamiliar with the system and with the great dedication of most welfare workers, who attempt to improve the lot of their clients against enormous odds. Furthermore, professionals prefer to talk to colleagues in their own field and in the hierarchy of human services, welfare occupies a lowly status.

3. The problems of welfare clients are often so severe, complex, and chronic that mental health professionals feel that nothing can be done to relieve them unless the realistic circumstances could be drastically changed. Actual experience of working with welfare clients fortunately does not bear out such pessimism.

4. Mental health professionals are also antagonized by the complex and confusing bureaucracy of the welfare system. There are continuous changes in policies and practices, staff transfers and "reorganizations" that reflect shifts in political power, legal decisions, and administrative needs that make it difficult for outsiders to keep pace with the state of operations.

5. On the other hand, welfare administrators, although needing help with problems affecting their clients and their staff, are often reluctant to call upon mental health professionals. They fear that consultants unfamiliar with the system will complicate their task rather than relieve them. Communications between the mental health system and the welfare system are often strained and mutually frustrating.[14,15] If the members of either system do not understand in what ways their counterpart can help them and what the other's limitations are, their expectations will be unrealistic and the transaction will end in frustration and anger. The ultimate victims of such miscarried efforts will be the welfare clients and the welfare workers.

Establishment of a Consultation Relationship

From the foregoing it should be evident (1) that a collaborative relationship between mental health and the welfare system is highly desirable and (2) that it must be built on mutual understanding to fulfill the purpose of improving services. In an attempt to further such development, the Group for the Advancement of Psychiatry published a companion paper to the position statement cited above,[3] *The Psychiatrist and Public Welfare Agencies.*[16] In this report, greater psychiatrist involvement in welfare systems is advocated and a model of intervention is described that has proved its usefulness.

The literature contains many excellent descriptions concerning the establishment of a mental health consultee relationship,[12,17,18] and the reader is referred to these sources with regard to general principles and practices. Here we shall focus on some problems encountered in work with welfare agencies.

The first step toward a rapproachement between the welfare and the mental health systems must be taken by a representative of a public mental health agency, preferably its director. This person has to present to the welfare director the benefits of mental health consultations and submit a plan for the provision of such services to obtain administrative sanction. Thereupon the actual consultants have to arrange for preliminary meetings with the agency staff to become mutually acquainted, to learn about workers' problems and needs, and to agree on a format for the services with a clear understanding of their purpose and the mutual responsibilities of the participants.

Who is to pay for the consultations? The problem of funding has been one of the reasons for the underutilization of consultation services. Welfare budgets are tight and specifically allocated. Occasionally agencies can divert some in-service training funds toward consultation. Even these sources seem to have dried up at present. In the opinion of this author, the mental health establishment has a vested interest in mental health consultations and should underwrite its expense. If the mental health skills of welfare personnel can be strengthened, many welfare clients will not be referred to the mental health system as patients. Mental health consultations should be seen as primary prevention and should be supported by public funds just as preventive measures in public health are.

The Los Angeles County Department of Health, through its Division of Mental Health Services, has provided consultations to the Los Angeles County Department of Public Social Services for 15 years. Two service models were used simultaneously. Permanent staff of regional mental health services have been available for ad hoc consultations in crisis situations. In addition, a large pool of mental health consultants were recruited from local private mental health practitioners, psychiatrists, psychologists, psychiatric social workers, and nurses who were remunerated on a fee-per-90-minute-session basis. These special consultants were oriented, trained, monitored, and evaluated. An appointed coordinator responded to requests by individual districts, arranged for liaison, and maintained the cadre by recruiting new consultants. For many private practitioners, the opportunity to consult with welfare was a welcome break from their office routine, and it became an important personal and professional growth experience. This model can certainly be established in other communities with due adaptations to local conditions.

Federally supported community mental health centers, of which there were 505 in March, 1975,[4] have been legally required to offer consultations[5] but have frequently failed to do so. They have been pressed for funds and have used staff time primarily for revenue-producing activities. Recently additional federal legislation has been passed that provides for special consultation and education grants. Thus the fiscal outlook for consultations is currently much brighter.

Finally, the possibility should not be excluded that in some localities a mental health professional demonstrating his skills on behalf of welfare clients may be invited by the staff to participate in a welfare staff in-service training project and may employ the consultation model for this purpose.

The Mental Health Consultant

The views presented in this paper are based on the writer's experience as a consultant, program planner, and coordinator to a large urban welfare agency and as an educator of several generations of mental health consultants over a period of 15 years. It is entirely possible that the experience of other workers in the field may have led them to a different conclusion, and no claim for universality of these views is made.

In our opinion, the success of a consultation program depends to a significant degree on the person providing the service, on the clarity of his conceptions, and on his preparation for a task that requires a rethinking of one's professional skills and modification of their application. In addition to clinical proficiency, a mental health consultant must be able to feel comfortable in a nonclinical setting where he cannot protect himself with the trappings of his professional status. He must be able to engender confidence in an atmosphere of monitored warmth and must never forget that he is dealing with colleagues on an egalitarian basis and not with patients. He should be armed with a basic conceptual model of mental health consultations, with theories and practices that should be tested and updated with growing experience. He should have a working knowledge of the welfare setting, its history and legislation, its policies and practices, and should be familiar with the local working conditions of his agency before he ever agrees to conduct the first consultation. The two GAP reports, No. 85[3] and No. 94,[16] cited before may serve as useful introductory guides. A careful study of Gerald Caplan's lucid and comprehensive writings on mental health consultations[11,12] is also highly recommended, although a consultant will eventually develop a model suitable to his personal style, corresponding to his experience, and adapted to the setting in which he works. Caplan's model can help him not to stray from the role of the mental health consultant into related professional roles of supervisor, psychotherapist, or teacher. All these roles resemble each other in some aspects and at times overlap with the role of the consultant, and yet it is essential that the consultant be aware what his basic function is to avoid damaging his relationship with the consultees and thereby his special usefulness. At all times, a consultant must keep in mind that he stands administratively outside the consultee's system and must not make recommendations that are the prerogative of supervisors or administrators in the agency. He is never responsible for the consultee's clients or program. This responsibility is fully retained by the welfare staff, who have the right to accept or reject, fully or in part, whatever plan or recommendation may issue from the consultation.

A welfare consultant—unlike, for instance, a consultant to the school system—carries the additional burden of dealing with a system that seems in continuous flux as a result of internal and external pressures. A school consultant can reasonably expect that the staff in his system will remain relatively constant and that whatever changes will take place in the school will take place slowly over a period of time. The welfare consultant will find major reorganizational changes and shifts of personnel from month to month. The cloud of constant change accounts for part of the apprehension and frustrations of the staff. The consultant is well advised to scan the morning paper for a story on welfare before he goes to his consultation session, because it may explain some aspects of the climate in the agency. His constancy and stability may be an important part of his value to the consultees as he reminds them that human nature is less likely to change as fast as bureaucratic arrangements.

The Consultee-Centered Group Consultation Model

The aim of the traditional case consultation is to arrive with the consultee at a method of remedying a deficiency in the client. In the consultee-centered consultation, the aim is to improve the work ability of the consultee, not only with regard to the presented case but hopefully with all similar cases. For this reason, consultee-centered consultations are especially suitable for purposes of primary prevention because they attempt to enhance the mental health skills of significant care providers in the community who become front-line allies of the mental health system.

In the experience of this author a modification of Gerald Caplan's consultee-centered case consultation conducted with a working unit of welfare workers and their supervisor turned out to be the most satisfactory model.

At first, because there was such a discrepancy between the number of welfare workers and the number of available mental health consultants, we decided on group consultations. What was started out of sheer necessity proved to be a most useful design with many advantages over the individual consultation method. The consultant was able to meet the worker, who presented a case in his habitual work milieu, and had the opportunity to observe that the presenter's work efficiency was often less affected by intrapersonal process than by tensions in the work unit. Since these people spent more time with each other than with their families and developed unconscious attitudes toward each other resembling child–parent and sibling relations, we soon began to refer to the work unit as *work family*. The group process was not only diagnostically helpful but it reinforced the impact of the consultation in unit meetings and in aftersession, informal discussions among the participants. Supervisors often reported that members of the unit, other than the presenter, seemed to benefit equally if not more from the consultation since their receptivity was not interfered with by performance anxiety.

The highly complex and sophisticated technique that Caplan developed to conduct consultee-centered mental health consultations cannot be presented adequately here, and the reader is referred for specifics to Caplan's text.[12] Suffice it to say that the consultant needs to assess the nature of factors interfering with the consultee's optimal work efficiency from the way the case is presented. On the basis of his assessment, he intervenes in such a manner as to reduce the interference and thereby improve the worker's efficiency to manage this and similar cases.

Here we wish to stress only a few important points.

Throughout the consultation only the case is discussed. To the sensitive consultant the worker betrays some of his internal interfering problems by stressing a similar constellation in the client's case. This phenomenon is referred to as the *parallel process,* a term that Caplan borrowed from the description of the supervisory process by Ekstein and Wallerstein.[19] While the consultant seems to address himself to the parallel constellation in the client's problem, he actually influences the corresponding interference in the worker. The method using indirection and metaphor is subtle, but when it succeeds, there is an immediate responsive anxiety reduction in the consultee that bears out the correctness of the intervention. The method is proposed by Caplan to avoid the consultee's resistance, which a direct interpretation or confrontation might arouse.

This author has found that the method may be so subtle that it sometimes fails to reach the consultee altogether. While the parallel process is an excellent method to determine the factors that interfere with a consultee's efficiency, experience has shown that many consultees can be faced quite openly with an explanation of their difficulties. They do not react with resistance and in fact are often appreciative if the explanation is given tactfully and without condescension and protects the consultee's dignity in the presence of his supervisor and peers.

The beginning consultant, especially when he is primarily a psychotherapist, often has difficulties abstaining from dealing exclusively with the client's problems. He must remind himself that he cannot assume that he can "treat" a client effectively through a rather brief contact with the welfare worker, especially since most cases selected for the consultation are complicated cases that have frustrated the efforts of one or several caseworkers. At best, the consultant can hope that his intervention will help the worker to function better and that the worker then may find better ways to manage present and future cases.

Caplan's method heavily stresses personality factors in the worker as causes of reduced proficiency. Group consultations have clinically demonstrated that often the trouble lies equally in interpersonal problems between the worker and other staff. The worker who has been asked to present a case to the consultant may be just the "designated patient" who has been elected to deflect from other tensions in the work unit. Furthermore, much of the reduction in work efficiency is simply the result of unending frustrations brought about by working in both a rigid and an unstable bureaucracy, hampering the workers' efforts to help their clients.

Therefore, we often had to modify the standard technique and resort to clarifications of the worker's role under given circumstances, how conflicting policies of the system could be observed and yet interests of the clients safeguarded. We had to assist consultees in the discussion of methods of problem solving and alternatives of resolution of a given problem, and this approach proved to be effective. Consultees were often upset simply because the complexity of their clients' problems confused them, and in such cases, a meaningful structuring of a case problem resulted in a marked reduction of an anxiety that had reduced the consultee's ability. The overriding goal of our efforts was to ensure that the consultee left the consultation with a feeling that the questions he had posed to the consultant had been answered in some form and that he also seemed to feel better about his work. And when we saw a consultee return to a problem case that had caused him to despair with renewed vigor and enthusiasm, we took this as an indication that in some fashion we had been helpful.

In the following case presentations, we wish to illustrate clinically some of the principles we have presented.

Case Illustrations

(A) The "Parallel Process"

The social worker, a young woman with a recent master's degree in social work, presented the case of a family consisting of a 31-year-old divorced mother, five children ranging in age from 9 to 15 years of age, her 39-year-old Lesbian companion, and the 47-year-old grandmother. The worker considered the "confusion in sexual identification" the major problem of the family. She wondered whether a Lesbian couple could be entrusted with the care of young children or whether these youngsters, who showed signs of serious emotional disorders, should be placed in a foster home. The worker admitted that she felt angry at the mother, who had shown herself repeatedly an unsuitable and rejecting parent. She wondered whether her anger might be due to some uneasiness about homosexuality. The mother had asked on several occasions that one or the other of her children be placed in a home or in an institution. The worker felt unable to make a definitive move in this direction. In the course of the consultation, the client's homosexuality turned out to be a factor of lesser importance compared to her other behavior. In fact, the mother's Lesbian companion turned out to be the most reliable and responsible member of the group. She showed concern for the children, took care of them, supported them economically and emotionally, and visited them whenever they were in a hospital or temporarily placed in a home. The mother had attempted suicide on three occasions. She had abandoned the four children suddenly for several years when, on the spur of a moment, she moved across the country, away from a violent, abusive alcoholic, and bisexual husband. During their separation, she had never written her children or contacted them. One day, just as impulsively, she went back and kidnapped them from her in-laws on a whim and without advance preparation. Periodically, she assaulted one or the other child, threw them out of the house, burned all their belongings and toys, but then changed her mind and insisted that they return home. She behaved sexually exhibitionistically in front of the children without concern for the effect on them. Understandably, the children showed numerous symptoms of neglect, indications of severe emotional disorders, and psychopathic behavior ranging from violent acts and fire setting to sexual acting-out and elopements. Only during a period when the older children had been placed in foster homes did they show a semblance of normal behavior.

In this example, the "parallel process" is manifested in the worker's unconscious identification with the ambivalence of the client, who could neither accept her children and care for them nor give them up permanently to offer them the chance to grow up in a stable setting. During the 8 years this family had been clients of the agency, 19 welfare workers had worked with them. They alternatingly tried to unite the "family" or attempted to save the children by removing them from the mother. The same inconsistency paralyzed the present caseworker. She could not make up her mind whether to initiate placement procedures or to keep the children with the clearly unfit mother. The caseworker's confusion about her role was masked by the assumption that "the confusion about sexual identity" was the main problem.

The consultant played down the sensationalistic aspects of the sexual situation and focused instead on the client's ambivalence about her role as a mother. In response, the caseworker declared that she had lost her uncertainty about the steps she had to take to save the children from complete ruination. She said, "I have not felt free to go ahead with my plan. I have not been the worker that I usually am and that I like to be." She appeared greatly relieved that she felt able to proceed with a clear conscience.

This brief summary does not reflect the richness of the presentation and the liveliness with which the workers and their supervisor participated in the consultation.

There seems to be no better way to learn consultation techniques than to participate in a group consultation, first as an observer, later as a coconsultant, and finally as a consultant monitored by a senior consultant. Following the consultation, preceptor and preceptee can discuss the hidden dynamics of the consultation and the rationale for the intervention. This method has been used for 12 years by the Division of Social and Community Psychiatry of the University of Southern California School of Medicine to instruct senior psychiatric residents in the theory and practice of consultee-centered mental health consultations to welfare agencies.[20]

If a preceptor is not available, much can be gained if one records a consultation on videotape or sound tape and replays it several times in order to analyze the group process and learn from one's interventions.

(B) Combining "Parallel Process" with Some Direction

A 16-year-old girl requested placement with a foster family because she could not stand living with her restrictive family. In the preceding 6 years, she had run away from home on more than 20 occasions and at times involved the welfare authorities in her fights with the family. Usually she stayed away with friends, but for only a few days. She notified her family of her whereabouts and then returned home.

The welfare worker who presented her case was a young man in his mid-20s who feared that the client was seriously emotionally ill. He felt strongly that she ought to be placed with a foster family for her protection. He presented his plan to the girl's father, who accused him of meddling and told him never to come back. By threatening the father with expensive court procedures, he regained access to the home but was unable to change the father's stand. He requested the consultation to learn a method to render the father more cooperative.

During the consultation, the worker could not specify why he considered the client emotionally ill. She was an attractive young girl who rebelled against her father because he did not allow her to wear short skirts to school. He also refused to allow her boyfriend to come to the house, and this was the reason she had run away the last time. The worker described the father as an authoritarian tyrant who had so cowed his wife and his younger four children that they all agreed with him that the source of all troubles was the oldest daughter. She had always been unmanageable and differed from the other family members, who were said to be quite unattractive in every respect, including appearance.

The consultee's descriptions of the family and his fidgety behavior whenever he mentioned his client indicated that he was at least unconsciously attracted to the young woman. He saw himself as her defender against the ogre father.

He behaved quite similarly to the father, who saw himself also as the guardian of his attractive daughter and who sought to protect her against other suitors. Father and welfare worker were involved in a power struggle in a competitive effort to "save" her.

The consultant pointed out that the father had caused some of his daughter's behavior by setting himself up as an adversary of her boyfriend. If he would permit the young man access to his house, his daughter would have fewer reasons to run away. The hidden purpose of this intervention was to indicate to the worker that he too had placed himself in the role of adversary of the father by trying to separate him from his daughter. The worker accepted the consultant's explanation, but he was unwilling to reconsider his plan of removing the daughter from her family. One of the other workers, a mature woman, indicated that the girl did not seem to behave so unusually for a 16-year-old. She seemed to express concern for her family since she always told them about her whereabouts. It seemed like a gross exaggeration to refer to her as a "runaway." The consultant was not going to interpret that the exaggerated description of the girl's plight was due to the worker's need to see himself as a "knight protecting a maiden in distress." Instead he complimented the worker for having gained access to the home, albeit with threats, which was perhaps the only way to get the attention of an authoritarian man, as the father seemed to be. But since he was frequently meeting with the family, he could help the father to abandon his hostile stance. He could show him that he could help his daughter better and keep her home by allowing her boy friend to come to the house. The worker laughed and said, "I guess you want me to be a Kissinger." He obviously had understood that he could serve his client better by being a mediator than by intensifying the strife in the family. And by this time he had dismissed his original plan of removing the daughter from the home.

If there was any lasting change in the worker it was the experience that one may serve clients better by helping them to resolve problems rather than by driving them into the role of the adversary.

(C) Role Clarification

An ambitious welfare worker who was pursuing a master's degree in public administration while continuing to work full time at her agency, a woman in her late 20s, reported that she felt frustrated over the case of a young woman client who had come to the attention of the agency because her baby had suffered a hairline skull fracture under unclear circumstances. Allegedly the client has stumbled walking downstairs with the baby in her arms. There was a suspicion of child abuse and the worker was to supervise her for several months. The baby was the woman's first child after several years of marriage. Because of the baby, the couple had moved to a somewhat larger apartment, and as their expenses increased the husband, a television repairman, had accepted a second job. This left the young woman at home alone with the baby for most of the day. On weekends, the husband was so tired that he slept most of the time. The woman complained bitterly about her lot and the lack of understanding from the husband. The worker attempted to help her by suggesting that she attend a secretarial school to increase her independence and also to have some outside stimulation during the day. The baby was entrusted to the care of a friend. At first, things seemed to improve because the client enjoyed the change. But the husband was unhappy about the new arrangement. He wanted his wife to be a housewife and a mother to their baby. He felt that he was working hard to make this possible. Soon, there were arguments, which grew more and more violent. One day the husband called the worker because his wife had suddenly disappeared, leaving the baby unattended at home. After several hours, she called from a gas station and explained that she had been desperate about the turmoil at home. The worker requested a consultation because she felt she had to solve the marital disturbance and she saw no way out of the dilemma.

The consultation revealed that the worker was an ambitious person who felt women should become independent by educating themselves and by achieving a career of their own.

The personal ambition projected on the client made the worker neglect her primary function to focus on the safety of the baby. She had never included the husband in any discussion with the client and had encouraged plans that did not include considerations for his needs. An explicit discussion of her primary role responsibility to protect the interests of the child made her see the situation in a new way as a problem to be solved by the entire family rather than by mother and worker alone.

Summary

Mental health consultations to welfare agencies are an important aspect of primary prevention, since welfare workers deal with a high-risk population and current welfare practices often affect people involved with the system in an adverse manner. Although advocated as part of comprehensive mental health planning since the early years of this century, relatively few mental health professionals are engaged in consultations with welfare staff. Organizational and funding patterns are available to enable publicly employed and privately practicing mental health professionals to participate in welfare consultation programs. This paper describes the qualifications of a mental health consultant, some principles of establishing a consultation relationship with welfare agencies, and a workable consultation model. Three cases are presented in a condensed form to illustrate the consultee-centered group consultation method.

It is hoped that this brief presentation will arouse the interest of mental health professionals to become involved in this challenging and gratifying form of application of their professional skills. The references can guide the reader to a more extensive and detailed treatment of the subject.

References

1. Dohrenwend, B. P., and Dohrenwend, B. S. The problem of validity in field studies of psychological disorder. *Journal of Abnormal Psychology,* 1965, *70,* 52.
2. Herrick, H. *Mental health problems of public assistance clients.* Sacramento: California Department of Mental Hygiene, 1967.
3. Group for the Advancement of Psychiatry. *The welfare system and mental health,* Report No. 85. Group for the Advancement of Psychiatry. New York, July, 1973.
4. Glasscote, R. The future of the community mental health center. *Psychiatric Annals,* September, 1975,, *5*(9), 69–81.
5. U.S. Congress. Public Law 88–164. Mental Retardation Facilities and Community Mental Health Centers Construction Act of 1963. Washington, D.C.: U.S. Government Printing Office 1964.
6. Mannino, F. V., and Shore, M. F. The effects of consultation: A review of empirical studies. *American Journal of Community Psychology,* March, 1975, *3*(1), 1–21.
7. Meyer, A. The problem of the State in the care of the insane. In *The collected papers of Adolf Meyer* (vol. 4). Baltimore, Md.: Johns Hopkins Press, 1952.
8. Coleman, J. V., and Apteker, H. H. Division of responsibility between psychiatrist and social worker in a foster home agency. *American Journal of Orthopsychiatry,* 1944,, *14*(3) 511–520.
9. Coleman, J. V. The contribution of the psychiatrist to the social worker and to the client. *Mental Hygiene,* 1953 *37,* 249–258.
10. Coleman, J. V. Psychiatric consultation in case work agencies. *American Journal of Orthopsychiatry,* 1947, *17,* 533–539.
11. Caplan, G. *Principles of preventive psychiatry.* New York: Basic Books, 1964.
12. Caplan, G. *The theory and practice of mental health consultation.* New York: Basic Books, 1970.
13. Rogawski, A. S. *Mental health programs in welfare systems.* In Silvano Arieti (Ed. in Chief), *American handbook of psychiatry,* vol. 2, Part 4: G. Caplan (Ed.) *Community psychiatry.* New York: Basic Books, 1974.

14. Wittman, M. Some problems in the development of cooperation between mental health and community welfare programs. *Mental Hygiene*, 1963, *47*(4), 641–648.
15. Wittman, M. The social welfare system: Its relations to community mental health. In: S. E. Golann and C. Eisdorfer (Eds.), *Handbook of community mental health*. New York: Appleton-Century-Crofts, 1972. Pp. 127–135.
16. Group for the Advancement of Psychiatry. *The psychiatrist and public welfare agencies*, Report No. 94. Group for the Advancement of Psychiatry, New York, November, 1975.
17. Beisser, A. R., and Green, R. *Mental health consultation and education*. Palo Alto, Calif.: National Press Books, 1972.
18. Haylett, C. H., and Rapoport, L. Mental health consultation. In L. Bellak (Ed.), *Handbook of community psychiatry and community mental health*. New York: Grune & Stratton, 1964. Pp. 300–318.
19. Ekstein, R. and Wallerstein, R. S. *The teaching and learning of psychotherapy*. New York: Basic Books, Pp. 300–318.
20. Rogawski, A. S. Teaching consultation techniques in a community agency. In Mendel, W. and Solomon, P. (Eds.), *The psychiatric consultation*. New York: Grune & Stratton, 1968. Pp. 65–85.

8

The Ambivalent Consultee

The Special Problems of Consultation to Criminal Justice Agencies

STANLEY L. BRODSKY

Consultation may be conceived of either as a consistent, firm, and reliable technique that applies well in almost every setting or as a variable, occasionally tenuous, flexible approach that is dependent on the individual problem and the agency concerned. At one end of this dimension, the consultation process may be considered as a concrete mold into which the problem and the process is poured. The problems that exist in one agency and one setting will repeatedly take similar forms as problems in other agencies. The products of increased independence and goal achievement of the consultee are consistent; the mold itself, while sometimes varying in size, reflects the same shape of knowledge and experience.

At the other end of this dimension, consultation may be considered as a sweater slipping over the body and the particular nature of the consultee. At its best, it is an attractive fit and functions usefully to improve the consultee's state of being; at its worst, the fit is ill, overly loose or overly

STANLEY L. BRODSKY · Professor of Psychology, Associate Director, Center for Correctional Psychiatry, University of Alabama.

tight, and the aims of consultation are not achieved. While rack-bought consultation will work well in some cases, it is the custom tailoring and careful fitting that makes the difference in successful application.

The transition from off-the-rack clothes to a custom fit is not easy. Our position is that consultation to criminal justice agencies and administrators calls for a form of custom tailoring, and in this chapter we seek to describe the nature of the customer and some of the methods of shaping our professional garments appropriately.

Special Characteristics of Criminal Justice Agencies

While traditional methods and approaches to consultation described elsewhere in this volume are applicable to criminal justice agencies, the special characteristics of these agencies call for considerable adaptiveness on the part of the consultant. Essential to the success of such consultation is an awareness of the operating psychology and sociology of the agencies and of the conflicting, often competing, pressures placed upon them.

Secrecy and Image Enhancement

Two major identifying characteristics of criminal justice agencies are their needs for both secrecy and the enhancement and maintenance of a positive public image. Police departments, court agencies, and correctional agencies are under close public scrutiny. They are frequently the subject of criticism for presumed unjust procedures and for not serving the interests of the powerless, the poor, and various minority segments of the public. This charge is not new. It has been heard intermittantly for at least 150 years in the United States and considerably longer in other countries. This has produced an extraordinary sensitivity to attack from without, as well as to criticism from within, on the part of criminal justice agencies and has led to the development of techniques designed to insulate them from many forms of public and internal scrutiny.[18]

Once such agencies have moved into secrecy and image enhancement, it is analogous to putting a finger in each end of a Chinese finger-tube. The more one tries to pull them out, the more the tube tightens up. The agency process of withdrawing into deeper secrecy, privacy, and protective mechanisms results in rules' being published that require all agency personnel to receive formal approval before being interviewed or speaking about departmental matters. A senior officer becomes the sole point through which all "public relations" information is channeled. And the tube is tightened through imposition of additional bureaucratic structures. Official secrecy policies reinforce tendencies among line personnel to disclose little about themselves and their work to news media and the public. In this manner, an important postulate of agency self-protection emerges. It is:

> Take care of your own. Never discuss internal problems with outsiders.

The maintenance of an opaque window vis-à-vis outsiders is particularly true with behavioral scientists who want to work with or study the agency. Most police departments and correctional agencies feel they have been exploited by researchers or graduate students from the behavioral sciences and the mental health professions. Countless tales circulate among such agencies of university researchers who present themselves as colleagues or helpers and who leave, having contributed nothing to the agency, and subsequently arouse a furor of public scorn through their writings or public statements. Sometimes research, the reports of which are critical of an agency, is conducted with minimum agency awareness of the possible negative impact. The fury of a woman scorned is minor compared to the outrageous indignation of the justice agency that has been tricked or exploited.

Individual Motivations

A myth has developed that employees of justice agencies are attracted to their work because of internal needs that coincide with job demands related to authoritative directing and controlling of the actions of others. The presumption is that these employees are seeking an ideal fit between job requirements and personal needs.[8] The stereotypic belief is that, because of persistent and lifelong hostility to others, they seek and find a socially appropriate vehicle for aggressive expression in law enforcement or correctional work. However, the best research evidence fails to support this belief.

The motives for employment are primarily related to such mundane factors as a desire for job security or a family tradition in correctional work, and there is no reason to conclude that there is more maladjustment among policemen[7,20] or correctional officers[6] than among members of other occupational groups of similar education or income backgrounds. And changes also take place after employment. For example, Niederhoffer[13] has reported increased cynicism and decreased idealism over time among police.

Role Conflict

Justice agencies serve the purpose of maintaining control over the behaviors of large numbers of people through direct and indirect ways. Arresting, watching, and confining individuals are all direct methods of regulating the actions of citizens. Indirect methods occur through the imposition of threats of consequences, severity of penalties, likelihood of being apprehended, and the stigma of being a client of the justice system.

This social control function is in apparent conflict with the stated and felt functions of most mental health professionals, who see themselves as acting on the behalf of their clients. For the novice consultant, the difficulty in "joining forces with the enemy" is very great. The police, for example, are seen as restrictors, while mental health professionals often see themselves as liberators.

Special Problems of Consultation to Criminal Justice Agencies

The predominant loyalty and responsibility of the justice agency is to the community and to societal norms and laws.[2] This broad, relatively diffuse societal focus presents a problem for some consultants.[4] The distillation of such concerns appears in the periodical *Rough Times* (formerly *The Radical Therapist*) in which work by mental health professionals with police, courts, or prisons is often seen as collaborating with agencies of injustice and class oppression.

Imposed Consultation

A deterrent to a productive outcome is that consultation is sometimes imposed on justice agencies from within or without. It occurs frequently from within when an administrator holds the fervent belief that his subordinates need a behavioral consultant and contracts for such a service. The imposition from without occurs largely when a funding agency, a superordinate body, or an independent study group dictates or urges it.

Coerced consultation is never initially welcome. The fact that it is undertaken at all reflects the fiscal well-being of justice agencies and the large number of consulting firms seeking a share of this largesse.

Whose Side Are You On?

It can be equally troublesome for the consultee if the consultant takes an active and empathic interest in the welfare of the prisoners or offenders. Justice agencies' employees often speak metaphorically of the "war on crime" and the offenders as "the enemy." It is not unusual for them to ask, "Whose side are you on?" This writer has been introduced to groups of police trainees as one genuinely on the side of law enforcement to indicate both that he was highly valued and to suggest that he was not presenting himself as a softhearted psychologist who is sympathetic to law violators.

This antagonism toward the client diminishes as one rises higher up the administrative ranks in justice agencies. However, even among upper-level administrators, there is a skinned-knee sensitivity to identification with prisoners and offenders. The sensitivity has grown as court actions and citizen groups have improved client rights. Justice agency staff experience a simultaneous diminishing of their own rights. The staff frequently view the problem as a zero-sum game in which every gain for the offenders is a loss for them. Only the most progressive and secure agencies do not show this felt competitiveness with client rights.

The mental health consultant can count on having ascribed to him or her highly empathic attitudes with the offenders before the consultation process is initiated. With considerable accuracy, it is known that many psychiatrists and psychologists address themselves to the needs and problems of the offenders rather than those of the agencies they serve. A not unusual posture is that presented in Sanford's book *Sanctions for Evil,*[16] in which the highest priority is assigned to the protection of victims (including law violators) from bureaucratic and harmful agencies. As the "Whose side are you on?" question becomes expressed in many ways, the initial challenge is to require of the consultant that he or she not be a spy with personal agendas that are benficial to offenders.

Consultation to Mental Health Professionals Within Justice Agencies

The prior discussion applies to consultation with criminal justice administrators. However, consultation is also frequently offered to mental health professionals within criminal justice settings. These people are, by and large, enormously deprived of professional stimulation. One observes repeatedly a "long lost brother" syndrome when consultation is offered to them. There is a startling and mutually positive sense of being in touch with others, of being able to talk about shared experiences, and an overwhelming feeling of renewed friendship.

Little mental health consultation is offered within criminal justice settings, although the amount is increasing. Conrad[5] has written that the mental health worker's major role in the prison is that of crisis resolution. The mental health professional is typically stereotyped into the role of convincing the prisoner who is threatening to jump from the water tower to come down and of otherwise dealing with suicidal, psychotic, or maladjusted prisoners. Given a number of prisoners on the verge of some equivalent dramatic act, consultation has traditionally taken a back seat to direct service.

Consultation to Administrators

There are sharp differences between criminal justice and mental health administrators. Most criminal justice administrators have little professional competence in behavioral skill areas. Typically, they are career administrators who have risen up an organized, competitive career ladder based in part on managerial skills. The exceptions to this are a few people who are political appointees who have no skills in either administrative or professional areas.

Among the larger group who are professional administrators are individuals who value management and administration highly. While mental health administrators may believe in the "shibboleth of individual freedom" (see Chapter 4), the criminal justice administrators hold overly to the belief in effectiveness of tight controls, detailed direction, and task-oriented leadership. While a consultant may try to make mental health administrators tighten up, the consultant to criminal justice administrators often will encourage them to loosen up.

Consultation as an Evolutionary Process

Most of the persons consulting to criminal justice agencies did not start out as consultants. Rather they began with other roles, dealing particularly with training, personnel selection, or research tasks; they have gradually acquired more of a consultant's role and less of specific problem-solving responsibilities. The role change may be considered an evolutionary process.

The most frequent origin of the evolution is from training. Most states have required training programs for their law enforcement personnel; some have required training programs for probation, parole, and correctional officers and for other criminal justice personnel. These training programs have explicit mandates that psychological training will be offered. Often the training is described as "handling the mentally ill offender" or "interpersonal skills training."

Schwartz and Liebman[17] identify training and selection activities themselves as substantive consultation areas and consider Caplan's definitions of consultation as "restrictive and unrealistic." The present author does not include part-time direct service in training and selection as consultation.

A second major form of initial work is in selection activities. With police departments more than with other justice agencies, there is an emphasis on screening out the mentally unfit. In Tennessee, a psychological testing and mental health screening leads to a certification that the selected person is sane. The certification of sanity is not required for politicians, psychologists, or other professions; its presence for police even in one state indicates the value placed on positive adjustment in police officers.

When these training and selection activities are perceived favorably, and when the consultant is interested in broader impact, then there is usually some mutual exploration of consultative involvement. The agency administrator will often pull the trainer aside after a training session and chat about other agency difficulties. If this process is jointly felt to be favorable and productive, there tends to be a formalizing of this consultation relationship. It is now labeled *consultation,* regular appointments are established, and agency problem-solving is explicitly identified as a goal. The consultant may or may not maintain the original training or selection role. Some do; others pass it on to colleagues. However, it is the explicit redefinition of the role and the problems that makes up the evolutionary skills. A contrast is necessary between the earlier direct service and the subsequently developed consultant role in terms of targets, goals, and methods.

In the process of establishing credibility, one of the most important steps is having visible and prominent success. If this occurs in the early contacts, the consultee and others will repeatedly introduce the consultant in terms of this first success, such as in solving the problems of the guards' falling asleep in the towers, or reducing personnel turnover, or increasing input of officers into shift and vacation scheduling.

Consultation to Law Enforcement Agencies

Some observers of mental health–police working relationships are pessimistic, believing that joint efforts are futile and unsuccessful. In this spirit, Schwartz and Liebman[17] report that "mental health professionals and police personnel are blessed by a state of mutual ignorance which often ensures that attempts at collaboration are doomed to failure." While such prophecies of doom by mental health Cassandras are sometimes fulfilled, an equal potential exists for states of mutual bliss and achievement. In the attainment of these positive goals, issues of consultees' autonomy and dependency are confronted.

Law enforcement agencies are attentive to maintaining their autonomy and independence from outside intrusion. It is paradoxical, therefore, that one of the hazards of consultation to law enforcement agencies is the high degree of potential dependence upon the consultant in the decision making. Once the credibility of the consultant has been established strongly, law enforcement administrators tend to show great eagerness in allocating enormous responsibility to the consultant. The acceptance of such responsibility is usually viewed very cautiously by consultants. In law enforcement settings, initial acceptance of a medium amount of responsibility provides a good basis for further agency development and consultation, as part of "sliding in" from peripheral to central consultation roles.

An informal consultation arrangement usually arises with the full-time psychologist working with a police department. The psychologist almost always is hired to fill highly specific service functions. These may include diagnostic testing as part of personnel selection, on-the-job or recruit training, or evaluation of particular departmental practices. For these psychologists, the offering of consultation is irregular, informal, and often surreptitious; which means that neither an explicit agreement with the department head nor an official job description includes consultation duties. Consultation is smuggled in, in the sense that it is added to other ongoing activities.

The "myth of the displaced object" refers to the belief that agency problems external to the consultee are the exclusive target of the one-on-one consultation. There are many situations in law enforcement consultation in which this myth is difficult or undesirable to maintain. A powerful example of discarding the displaced object myth is present in Peter Runkel's book *The Law Unto Themselves*.[15] Runkel was a psychotherapist working on a police department project. Frequently, police officers would see him in his office about personal matters by talking about a job-related issue. At that time, Runkel had the option of pursuing their job effectiveness and what it meant for contact with citizens or pursuing their personal feelings more extensively. His decision was to offer a short-term, intensive, therapeutic experience for the officers—a practice quite in contrast to the model of what is consultation.

Mann[10] described a less personal problem-oriented consultation effort in his book *Psychological Consultation with a Police Department.* Mental health information and crisis management consultation were provided to Austin, Texas, police officers, particularly at the time of shift changes. The goal of widespread use of the consultation services and attitude changes by line police officers was not achieved, although high-ranking officers reacted with enthusiasm to the program. The objectives were achieved of increasing both the number of referrals by police and the number of interventions into family disturbances.

In a related project, Bard[1] and his colleagues trained 18 New York City police officers in skills as family crisis intervention experts. Following the training, students enrolled at the graduate center of the City University of New York met on a regular basis with the trained officers. The role of the graduate students was to offer consultation and aid in crisis resolution. Bard reported that it was of considerable value for the students in learning the nature of police work, while of mixed but overall positive value to the officers in improving their skills.

Police departments have high rates of divorce, suicide, ulcers, hemorrhoids, indigestion, and headaches,[9] a list of symptoms that makes police sound as if they are "before" persons in advertisements for new medicinal products. Given this array of symptoms, the role of the consultant in setting up stress-relieving circumstances in the agency is of particular significance.

Law enforcement administrators and officials are firmly committed in belief, systems, and actions to a quasi-military command and formal structure in their departments. They maintain three different types of relationships with persons around them:

1. Relationships with superiors. These are characterized by deference, polite suggestions, and careful maintenance of appropriate behaviors.
2. Relationships with subordinates. These are characterized by direct orders, definitive statements, and postures of authority.
3. Relationships with peers. These are characterized by the greatest openness, camaraderie, and ease.

Law enforcement administrators go through a testing and targeting procedure with new persons with whom they come into contact. The consultant is tested, through simple examination of credentials, working affiliations, and attitudes toward police and through interpersonal testings. Then the behaviors and roles of the consultee are adjusted according to the results of the preliminary testing.

The task of the consultant, with the foresight of imposition of command structure, is to establish and maintain a position "one step to the side." By actions, he or she should assume neither superordinate or subordinate roles nor genuine peer and friendship roles, although there may be elements of all of these.

Consultation to Correctional Agencies

Two major issues around which consulting to correctional agencies and administrators revolves are the felt lack of autonomy by administrators and the low trust–high control syndrome in which prisoners and outsiders alike are distrusted and efforts are expended to control their behaviors by the prison or parole agency. Persons who administer and plan correctional programs often report that they experience little independence and few choices in the operations of their departments. It is indeed true that the number and types of persons coming into correctional agencies are controlled by the courts. There is no option available for refusing certain types or limiting the entries. In most states there is a similar process in output. Independent parole agencies determine who will leave and who will remain, although the recommendations of the correctional administrators are often taken into account. It is the intermediate stages between offender entry and exit that concern correctional decision-making.

Limited Autonomy. Even within the correctional process itself, administrators often see a number of strong and inflexible constraints. First, many of the rules and regulations affecting their decisions and planning are determined by outside groups, by legislation, or as the result of class action suits and other court procedures. Second, there are prison organizations, formal and informal, that limit their degree of freedom, including guard unions, which actively seek to influence policy and administrative decisions within the institutions. To a lesser extent, the prisoner and ex-prisoner unions and organized lobbying societies have a similar effect; however, the prisoners' informal organizations create the greatest inertial resistance to program change and planning.

One theme cutting across much correctional consultation is reflected in the personal and organizational outcry, "My God, what can I do?" Consultation thus takes the form of exploration of the genuine alternatives that are available and the risks involved in the pursuit of these alternatives.

A second consultation approach and theme deals with the clarification of goals and the methods of achieving these goals. In correctional settings, the warden, the superintendents, or the senior administrators are rarely rewarded or encouraged because of low recidivism rates; indeed, no warden to this writer's knowledge has ever been fired because of a high recidivism rate. However, there are a great many wardens and administrators who have been released, transferred, or demoted because of prison riots, stabbings, or escapes. Thus, the pressure on the correctional administrator becomes more to avoid violence or prison eruptions than to achieve constructive results.

Participatory Management. Within correctional settings, there is an extraordinary reservoir of potential talent among officers, inmates, and colleagues. One of the ways of dealing with the limited alternatives and of avoiding incidents is for the consultee to develop means of mobilizing this talent in a shared pursuit of common goals. The National Advisory Commission on Correctional Standards and Goals[12] has identified such participatory management as a significant and standard procedure to be followed in the operation of correctional institutions. The nature of correctional facilities brings about a low trust–high control syndrome. In any setting in which line level staff and residents repeatedly experience limited freedom and close behavioral supervision, feelings of being controlled and seeking to avoid such control emerge. The consequences are a pervasive distrust and fear of manipulation. At the administrative level, the fear is that the staff and the inmates alike consistently act to achieve the goal, "How can I get out of this?" The typical short-run managerial solution has much face validity but few long-run payoffs; the manager seeks to maintain personal control and inspection of all operations and personnel. A goal often defined early in correctional consultation is the achievement of high inmate and staff morale and lessening of tight upper-management restrictions. Participatory management serves this function as well.

Mental Health Professionals in Prisons. Like the administrative staff and the prisoners themselves, mental health professionals employed in correctional agencies feel the need to obtain freedom and to delineate their own roles. Most prison mental health departments have identified formal goals of evaluation of all prisoners and treatment of the most troubled and troubling offenders. Inmates are evaluated repeatedly: as they enter, as they progress through confinement, as they are placed in jobs or in minimum-security locations, as they are considered for transfer to other institutions, and as decisions are made for release or parole. Most correctional psychologists and social workers are aware that their tools and skills are only minimally related to the decisions being made. Rather than the use of individual assessment results, many such decisions are based on immutable characteristics, such as offense type or age. In other decisions, the intuitive judgments of the administrator, based on experience and personal values, are the chief criteria. Many mental health professionals have ethical concerns about whether institutional and release decisions should be based on psychological factors. If the punishment is to fit the crime (rather than the criminal), then the personal characteristics of an individual should not be used to his disadvantage or to loss of privileges within the institution. Consultation with these mental health workers is often directed toward their roles as institution consultants and change promoters.

The Prison Clinician as Consultant. Dealing with the most severely disturbed persons in a number of institutional settings may be pursued through community mental health plans and programs. Mental health staff frequently engage in staff training so that the line officers themselves can be positive influences. As the mental health workers wander around the institution, their constructive effects can be likened to those of the psychiatrist–protagonist in Bradbury's "The Man in the Rorschach Shirt."[3] In that story, the hero travels through buses and beaches, with people looking at his wild, imaginitive shirt designs and projecting their own needs and desires on it. The projection and subsequent discussions result in psychological maladies' being healed, without the concept of healing ever mentioned. The correctional mental health worker similarly receives many projected needs or unfulfilled desires. One formal organizational structure that enhances this process has been the changing of the job requirements and titles. What formerly was called the department of mental health or the psychiatric unit in several institutions has been retitled a human resources center or a life skills center.

The limitations of a prison setting are sometimes so binding or overwhelming that very modest consultation goals must be set. In maximum-security prisons, prisoners and staff operate under detailed time schedules and restrictions on movement. These oppressive prisons seem especially offensive and inhumane to the consultant who only visits the setting; regular employees are less sensitive to oppressive conditions. The consultant often finds the consultee grappling with whether to try against high odds to change the correctional milieu, to adapt to it, or to leave. The extremes of harmfulness to prisoners in the maximum-security setting often produce extremes in the consultant's personal judgments of needs for change. This makes geniune consultee self-determination of goals more difficult to achieve.

Ambivalence in the Consultation Relationship

The justice agency consultee brings an extraordinary degree of ambivalence to the question of consultation. Such consultees will often have strongly felt needs for assistance and perspective. In spite of the public denial of difficulties, administrative and job-related problems are openly admitted by consultees to colleagues. The search for assistance is persistent and wide-ranging. Perhaps only the chaplaincy has as many persons so actively, eagerly, and attentively seeking out continuing job-related knowledge.

There is great ambivalence about entering consultation on the part of criminal justice administrators. Given the special nature of the problems that beset the relationship of the criminal justice agency, the mental health professional, and the consultant, such ambivalence is probably not surprising. Role conflicts center continuously between the helping and the controlling activities in criminal justice agencies. In corrections settings, this process is recognized as the treatment–security dichotomy. The conflicting demands in law enforcement have led Niederhoffer and Blumberg[14] to characterize police as the "ambivalent force."

A second course of ambivalence arises from the difficulty in neatly assigning superior, inferior, or peer roles to the consultant in his dealings with various people. In the earliest stages of consultation, the consultee may cautiously approach, test, withdraw, avoid, and defer as part of the structuring of mutual role assignments. The criminal justice consultee typically believes in disciplinary approaches to managing annoying or recalcitrant behavior, and he is sensitive to any indication that the mental health professional believes in permissiveness or an "understanding approach to handling behavior problems."[19]

Another source of ambivalence is the cognitive provincialism in consultees. While many occupational groups feel that their work experience is unique, the insistence is especially strong among justice agency employees. Some typical comments are illustrative:

> "You never know what true responsibility is until you have sat on the bench for five years."
>
> "No one understands what it means to be a correctional supervisor or to work in a prison. Walking past hundreds of locked cells and men every night does something to a man."
>
> "If you have never worked in policing, then there is no way you can ever appreciate what it is like being a cop."

The most effective way for dealing with this ambivalence and experiential provincialism is through direct experience in the justice field. It is a serendipitous finding that a number of mental health professionals have had experience as probation or parole officers, police, or correctional officers. While building trust and rapport are the *sine qua non* of the justice consultation process, the establishment of goodwill proceeds much faster with this experiential affirmation of the consultant's worth.

The belief that this is so has led in part to the development of graduate studies in criminal justice psychology. A half dozen universities—Nebraska, Alabama, Florida State, Hahnemann Medical College, John Jay, Middle Tennessee State—have offered criminal justice curricula for clinical psychology graduate students. An equal number of settings have specialty training for psychiatric residents. Over 50 graduate programs in social work have related programs as well.

The ambivalent consultee is often joined by an ambivalent consultant. However, the potential for high impact and mutual reward is high, and the change from ambivalence to affirmation is a common and exciting process.

References

1. Bard, M. *Family crisis intervention.* Washington, D.C.: U.S. Government Printing Office, National Institute of Law Enforcement and Criminal Justice, 1971.
2. Bittner, E. *The function of police in a modern society.* Washington, D.C.: U.S. Government Printing Office, NIMH Crime and Delinquency Monograph, 1971.
3. Bradbury, R. The man in the Rorschach shirt. In R. Bradbury, *Sing the body electric.* New York: Doubleday, 1967.
4. Brodsky, S. L. *Psychologists in the criminal justice system.* Urbana: University of Illinois Press, 1973. Pp. 43–50.
5. Conrad, J. Research for decision-making in corrections. *Proceedings of the Ninety-ninth Congress of Corrections,* Minneapolis, Minn., 1969. Pp. 317–323.
6. Goldstein, B. *Screening for emotional and psychological fitness in correctional officer hiring.* Washington, D.C.: American Bar Association Commission on Correctional Facilities and Services, 1975. 19 Pp.
7. Gotteson, J. *Psychological factors in police selection.* Hoboken, N.J.: Stevens Institute of Technology, 1970.
8. Kelling, G. The person–role fit in policing. In W. Kroes (Ed.), *Stress-reduction in law enforcement.* Washington, D.C.: U.S. Government Printing Office, National Institute of Occupational Safety and Health, 1975.
9. Kroes, W. Stress reduction in police. Paper prepared for a Conference on Stress Reduction in Police. National Institute of Occupational Safety and Health. Cincinnati, Ohio, May 7–9, 1975.
10. Mann, P. A. *Psychological consultation with a police department: A demonstration of cooperative training in mental health.* Springfield, Ill.: Charles C Thomas, 1973.
11. Mitchell, G. T., Banks, T. L., and McLemore, L. B. Police conduct and the black community: The case of Jackson, Mississippi. *Journal of Political Repression,* 1975, *1*,, 97–110.
12. National Advisory Commission on Criminal Justice Standards and Goals. *Corrections.* Washington, D.C.: U.S. Government Printing Office, 1973.
13. Niederhoffer, A. *Behind the shield.* Englewood Cliffs, N.J.: Prentice-Hall, 1967.

14. Niederhoffer, A. and Blumberg, A. S. *The ambivalent force: Perspective on the police.* Waltham, Mass.: Ginn and Company, 1970.
15. Runkel, P. *The law unto themselves.* Ann Arbor, Mich.: Planaria Press, 1972.
16. Sanford, N. (Ed.). *Sanctions for evil.* San Francisco: Jossey-Bass, 1971.
17. Schwartz, J. A., and Liebman, D. A. Mental health consultation in law enforcement. In J. R. Snibbe and H. M. Snibbe (Eds.), *The urban policeman in transition.* Springfield, Ill.: Charles C Thomas, 1973. Pp. 555–580.
18. Shellow, R. Active participation in police decision-making. Paper presented at the Annual Convention of the American Psychological Association, Washington, D. C., 1971.
19. Sokol, R. J. Consultation with police: Some problems and conceptualizations. In J. R. Snibbe and H. M. Snibbe (Eds.), *The urban policeman in transition.* Springfield, Ill.: Charles C Thomas, 1971. Pp. 592–610.
20. Sterling, J. *Role concepts of police officers.* Gaithersburg, Md.: International Association of Chiefs of Police, 1973.
21. Warren, M. Q. The psychologist as action researcher. In S. L. Brodsky (Ed.), *Psychologists in the criminal justice system.* Urbana: University of Illinois Press, 1973. Pp. 51–60.

9

The Special Problems of Consultation with Local Churches

KENNETH R. MITCHELL

The local church in many communities plays a significant part in the delivery of front-line mental health services, in a wide variety of forms. The fact that it does so in the mid 1970s represents a reversal of what the observers predicted 10 years ago. In the mid 1960s, enrollments in theological seminaries were faltering; those who did enroll, moreover, made it clear they intended their theological education to equip them for almost anything but pastoral leadership in a local church. Now, however, seminary enrollments are significantly on the rise, and the local church is often identified by students as the place they want to work, because it seems to be "where the action is." Local parishes and congregations make serious efforts to be communities of mutual care and support, where both ordinary and exceptional people can find help intended (and in many cases carefully designed) to meet felt needs.

These encouraging developments are not without their problems. Although church and clergy provide forms of mental health service, they do so from a unique base that must be recognized by any mental health

KENNETH R. MITCHELL · Director, Division of Religion and Psychiatry, The Menninger Foundation.

professional consulting with pastors or church groups. Although counseling activities and crisis ministries are assuming increasing importance in the life and work of pastors and their churches, they are by no means all that the pastor does. Religious rituals, preaching, sacraments, moral exhortation, and other practices exist side by side with these mental health activities, and they may either augment or undercut the ministries connected with mental health concerns.

In addition to the problem created by this multiplicity of activities, a second problem arises from the fact that the forms of work having direct connection with mental health concerns have a history and tradition entirely their own. Pastoral care and counseling, crisis intervention, and other "healing ministries" are a part of what in ecclesiastical tradition is called "the cure of souls," the history of which has been exhaustively traced by John T. McNeill.[4] The contemporary training of ministers and other religious figures in mental health settings sometimes has the effect of alienating them from these traditional roots and of tempting them to see themselves as mental health specialists without a clear professional identity. For clergy to operate effectively, it is important that they remain in contact with those roots and with pastoral tradition.

The mental health professional who provides consultation to pastors needs to be aware of these special factors influencing the consultation. I have identified these factors as "problems"; in addition, however, they lend to consultation an intriguing aspect that may make the consultant's work more interesting and more challenging, if also more problematic.

Special Issues for the Pastor as Helper

The pastor of a local church is a person consulted with great frequency by those experiencing troubles of various kinds. As he works with them, four special issues may color that work to a large degree. For the consultant working with the pastor, these issues also assume special importance.

The Scope of the Pastoral Task

The kinds of problems brought to ministers by those who seek their help vary widely. Some people who approach the minister would be identified by a clinician as potential patients: persons whose usual defenses against unwelcome experience have almost completely broken down, whose thought processes are gravely disordered, or whose emotional balance is precarious. On the other hand, they may be persons whose mental and emotional processes have not been pushed beyond tolerable limits but who now face an external situation that they do not believe they have the equipment to handle. Many of them will be seeking vocational or marital guidance. The pastor's case load runs the gamut from marital counseling to brief psychotherapy and from quick crisis intervention to long-term pastoral care. The pastor may be called on to extend simple support during a time of difficult waiting or in the context of a hard decision that must be made. He may offer specific, direct guidance. He may offer a focused and contracted counseling process. On occasion, he is thrust into a crisis situation in which quick and forceful intervention is necessary to avert a tragedy or to pick up the pieces after one.

The Pastor's Level of Preparedness

The pastor's level of preparedness to engage in these ministries varies greatly. Some ministers and nuns have participated in clinical pastoral education, a demanding educational process in which their work is examined by a supervisor in an institutional setting, usually a mental hospital, but often a general hospital or a prison. This training is usually as psychologically sophisticated as postdoctoral clinical training for psychologists or psychiatric residency programs and is equally intense and demanding. Clinically trained clergy may usually be counted on to have absorbed relevant psychological principles and to be reliable workers. But there are many clergy who have not had such training. The qualifications *demanded* of clergy in our society do not include clinical pastoral education, even though all clergy *do the kind of work* for which that form of education is designed to prepare them. Clinically trained or not, the pastor functions as a counselor. This poses an interesting problem for a potential consultant.

In addition, the pastor may be engaged in the supervision of a wide variety of care-giving ministries in the church. Many local churches engage in some form of extension ministry carried on by members of the church and supervised by the pastor: coffee house ministries, street ministries, day care centers, and schools. None of these is necessarily a clinical setting, but in each one mental health problems may emerge to confront the pastor with the need for specialized action and knowledge.

The Minister's Special Public

The minister's base of financial support may have a profound but subtle impact on the way he or she works. To serve a local church as a minister means to accept a salary paid by the congregation and often controlled by a board or committee of the local church. Fees are usually not paid to the minister on the basis of service rendered, nor are ministers supported by the public as a whole, as might be the case in some European countries with a religious establishment. Rather the minister is supported by a special public of relevance, which has first call on his services and sometimes demands exclusive call on those services. Within the congregation as a whole, support for a clergyman or clergywoman is usually based upon the ministry of public worship and preaching. Even those who make heavy use of the pastor's services as a care giver or a counselor may nonetheless base their contribution to the church and thus to the minister's financial support on his effectiveness in the pulpit.

Effective intervention by the minister in a crisis situation or in a counseling situation may be compromised by this factor. The minister is likely to know whether the person seeking help is a peripheral church member or a heavy financial contributor or a member of a powerful board or committee. If the help seeker is peripheral to most of the church's life, the minister may feel free to use his or her own judgment about effective forms of help. But if, on the contrary, the help seeker is financially or politically influential in the church, the pastor may shape intervention to meet the expectations of the help seeker and to give the kind of help demanded, whether or not that form of help is effective. From one point of view, this may seem hypocritical or corrupt; it is cited here as a factor with which the consultant needs to be acquainted. In any case, the help seeker is likely to be a member of the pastor's special public of relevance and therefore to have a relationship to the pastor with special meanings built up over a period of time. In some cases, this may even mean that the pastor is reluctant to engage in interventions that he would otherwise consider useful and effective. The pastor often needs considerable support from a consultant before he *can* do what he believes he *should* do. The consultant, therefore, needs to explore carefully with the pastor the nature of the pastor's prior relationship to help seekers.

The Right of Initiative and Access

Another important distinguishing factor in pastoral work is the so-called right of initiative and access. This factor is no longer the exclusive property of the pastor, but historically it is the pastor who has not only the right but the duty to initiate a helping relationship without being requested to do so by anyone. When the pastor senses that someone is in trouble, usually in his own congregation but perhaps outside it, he is enjoined by his professional obligation to move into the troubled situation even in the absence of a clear request for his services. In most other helping professions, such behavior would be unethical, a form of ambulance chasing. But for the pastor, not to engage in such behavior is a dereliction of duty.

It is interesting to note that, just as a few other helping professionals are permitting themselves to experiment with visits made on their own initiative, pastors have become somewhat frightened of using this traditionally sanctioned mode of work. Consultation with pastors can legitimately support the use of the pastor's right of initiative and access. It makes the pastoral office a superb opportunity for interventions, and for the development of relationships, without intrusiveness.

Celibacy

A special situation exists for celibate clergy and religious,* as well as for those who consult with them. In the Roman Catholic tradition, the choice to enter the priesthood or the religious life (which involves a choice for celibate living) is made when many identity issues have been worked on but before intimacy issues become a serious developmental consideration. My own observations of this situation, reported a few years ago,[2] convinced me that intimacy problems have a peculiar power for clergy and religious. Their earlier vocational choices have foreclosed the intimacy struggle prematurely, and thus, like other repressed material, this struggle returns in a variety of forms, some direct and some disguised. In our experience in the Division of Religion and Psychiatry at The Menninger Foundation, this does not mean that celibate clergy are unfitted for marital counseling. What it does mean, however, is that in all forms of extending help, the management of distance becomes for the celibate person a highly problematic issue. Father Smith may have serious trouble in keeping himself objective enough because he tends to become overinvolved with parishioners, but Father Jones, despite his intention to help, keeps such rigid distance from his parishioners that they perceive him as having no capacity for empathy. The consultant alert to this issue may be enabled to offer especially perceptive help.

*Within the Roman Catholic tradition, the word *religious* is used as a noun (both singular and plural) to refer to men or women who have taken monastic vows. It is thus a collective noun referring to monks, nuns, and priests who are members of particular religious orders.

Summary

These issues—the breadth and scope of the pastoral task, the great variation in levels of preparedness of ministers, the minister's attachment to a special public of relevance, the right of initiative and access, and, in some cases, celibacy—are a few of the special issues that may color the work of clergy and religious helpers. These should remain in the back of the consultant's mind, and there may be occasion for their explicit expression within a consultation. Whether specifically mentioned or not, awareness of these issues needs to be part of the consultant's armamentarium in mental health consultation with ministers.

The Pastor's Identity

Mental health consultation to pastors must be based on an understanding of the particular identity and theoretical base that combine to inform the minister's work. What tasks do pastors have, and how do they organize themselves around those tasks? How do they conceive their work overall?

One traditional answer to this question is a conception called the *offices of the ministry,* a series of discrete tasks, each of importance but without a clear overarching theory. This conception dates from the work of Richard Baxter[1] and includes preaching, pastoral care, moral exhortation, administration of the sacraments, scriptural study, teaching, and administration. More recently, Seward Hiltner[3] has provided the beginnings of an overarching theory: *pastoral theology.* Hiltner has pointed out that the overall work of a minister may be understood if it is viewed from three perspectives: communicating, shepherding, and organizing. Whatever the minister does, each of these three perspectives is always present in every pastoral act. Thus, while the minister is in the pulpit (communicating), he is also concerned with the well-being of the parishioners (shepherding) and with the overall health of the congregational body as a group (organizing). When he is in his study, engaging in a counseling process, the shepherding perspective may be uppermost in his mind, but he is still responsible for message, tradition, and health of the church.

This perspectival view may help differentiate the consultation process with the minister from consultation to a mental health professional on the one hand or to a school system or a court of law on the other. For the teacher, attorney, or judge, mental health concerns are important but peripheral to their primary task. For the mental health professional they are central. For the minister, unlike either of these other groups, mental health concerns are temporarily central within the context of counseling or crisis intervention, *but* the minister is also concerned with many other aspects of his work, deriving from the other perspectives mentioned above, and the impact of these other concerns will not be immediately clear to the consultant. Rather than merely guess at these other concerns, the consultant needs to assess clearly and openly with the pastor the influence other aspects of his task may be having on the work considered in consultation.

Consultations with Clergy

The consultation process with clergy and religious workers offers to consultants many interesting opportunities but also presents some important challenges.

One such challenge arises in connection with the scope of the consultant's work in a local church. On the one hand, the consultant may be faced with a series of counseling cases, sharply focused on characteristic clinical problems. On the other hand, however, the kind of material brought to the consultant may be far more vague than that, and it may be very difficult for the consultant to make a clear determination of what is being required of him. The eager but inexperienced pastor may experience considerable difficulty on focusing the kind of material he wishes to bring for consultation, and if one works with lay workers in the church, the presentation may be vaguer still. Thus, particular sensitivities and skills are required for the consultant as he attempts to put a framework around the kinds of work being asked of him.

Similarly, the consultant accustomed to working within a psychological frame of reference may be confronted with broader social questions. Many churches are essentially groups of middle-class and upper-middle-class persons attempting to extend some form of ministry to minority groups. In addition to the psychological struggle involved in working with minority groups, there are many ethical and social issues that arise, and the consultant is likely to be treated by the church personnel as an expert in all these areas. A sensitivity to the sociological makeup of the church itself, as well as to the sociological makeup of the groups the church is attempting to serve, is extremely useful to the consultant.

The usual distinction between supervision and consultation is an important one to remember, both for the consultant and for the pastor. Those pastors who have undergone clinical pastoral education will be accustomed to the supervision relationship, in which the supervisee is not a finished professional and is seeking a new skill or status. Similarly, the mental health professional, when working outside his own field, can sometimes be trapped into regarding the professional in another field as a nonprofessional. It is easy for either the pastor or the consultant to slip into the supervisory style that fosters more dependency than is necessary or desirable. In contracting for the consultation (and at many points thereafter!), the consultant may need to be careful to define the relationship as a coequal one between two professional persons. This leaves the consultant free to make very specific and direct suggestions and the pastor equally free to accept them, reject them, or simply chew on them.

Obviously, the consultant may hold philosophical or religious views that are significantly different from those of the pastor or the church. As he becomes involved in a relationship with a minister or a church worker whose religious views are quite different from his own, it may become important for the consultant to identify the important differences and to speak clearly from his own perspective, at the same time equally clearly according respect to the views and positions of the pastor or the church worker. The pastor is going to have to work from within his own perspective; without the respect and support of the consultant, the pastor may become confused. It is in the long run unwise for the pastor to attempt to do some of his work from within his own theological perspective but to feel that he must abandon that perspective and attempt to be a half-baked psychologist or a pseudo social worker.

The consultant will sometimes find himself dealing with case material that could arise from practice in an outpatient clinic or an emergency walk-in service or from some other customary locus of clinical practice. Some of the material in consultations with clergy, on the other hand, provides an unusual, and therefore intriguing, challenge in which the consultant may be obliged to make translations of his consultation skills. In the material that follows, I intend to provide the reader with some concrete examples of both kinds of work.

The Range of Cases

In one particular week in the spring of 1975, the following cases were brought to me for consultation. In this section, I will not go into great detail about the cases, but simply present them as they came to me, in order to indicate some of the kinds of case material that is regularly brought.

Father Brown, a Roman Catholic priest working as a hospital chaplain, was asked by a friend of his who was a pastor in a local Roman Catholic parish to work with Mr. King. Mr. King, discharged after 13 years of mental hospitalization, now lives a marginal existence. He has a relatively steady job and an equally steady girl friend. He still has many ideas of reference, occasionally hallucinates, and has severe difficulty in making decisions. Father Brown is just beginning his pastoral care activities with Mr. King and comes to consultation for the purpose of trying to decide upon goals for the relationship. During the course of consultation, Father Brown adopts two goals: to keep Mr. King out of the hospital, if possible, and to provide a means for keeping track of Mr. King's condition. Since Mr. King is irregular in keeping his appointments at the outpatient clinic of the hospital, Father Brown decides to establish a relationship with the psychiatrist who sees Mr. King in the outpatient clinic, so that hospitalization, if necessary, can be facilitated.

The Reverend Mr. Young is the pastor of a small church. One of the families in his church has entered family therapy with an independent therapeutic agency (or psychiatrist). The family consists of Mrs. Thomas and her three children; Mrs. Thomas is divorced from her husband, who lives in the community. The family therapy process involves Mrs. Thomas and the three children but does not involve the father. The family therapist has asked the Reverend Mr. Young to engage in an individual counseling process with one of the daughters in the family, who is thought to be potentially suicidal. The family therapist wishes to bring the divorced father into the family therapy meetings, but the daughter says that if this is done she will commit suicide. Mr. Young seeks consultation to determine means of helping Brenda Thomas to accept the presence of her father in family therapy sessions, a proposal about which Mr. Young himself has serious doubts.

Sister Hall, working in a local Roman Catholic parish, carries a heavy load of marriage counseling cases. In preparation for her consultations with me, Sister Hall usually writes a note about the material on which she would like consultation. One such note reads: "Mr. and Mrs. Williams get very little emotional satisfaction from one another and are unable to ask each other for what they need. They are angry, resentful people who balk at the thought of dealing with the hostile feelings they have for each other as well as at the thought of dealing with the tenderness they feel. They intellectualize a great deal." In the consultation hour itself, she asks, "In the light of the tremendous capacity that Mr. and Mrs. Williams have for intellectualizing, how can I keep them working on the issues of their emotional exchange with each other?"

Pastor Green is a Congregationalist minister who also seeks a consultation concerning a marriage counseling case he is carrying. He has had his first interview with Mr. and Mrs. Bell, whose differences in their levels of sexual interest are plaguing them. Pastor Green believes that if the difficulties are truly sexual ones, he is not the appropriate person to offer help. But he is not at all convinced that the sexual problems are the real problems, and he seeks consultation for the purpose of separating the sexual problems from the interactional problems that he suspects underlie the difficulties that were the ticket of admission for Mr. and Mrs. Bell. As an outcome of the consultation, he decides to engage in a time-limited 6-week process with Mr. and Mrs. Bell to try to make a clearer determination of the nature of the underlying issues. Meanwhile, he also decides to investigate the possibilities of direct treatment for their sexual dysfunction.

The Reverend Mr. Peters is both the pastor of a small church and the chaplain of a well-run retirement residence. Three nights ago, Mr. Peters received a telephone call from the night nursing supervisor at the retirement residence. One of the patients in the medical unit had been found walking the floor in a nightgown, moaning and crying. The staff, despite their experience, found themselves deskilled by the behavior of Mrs. Miller. They noted that the chaplain had a good relationship with this elderly lady and asked if he would come and help the staff to manage the incident. He did so; what's more, he sat down as a consultant with the staff after the incident and helped them to work through their feelings about Mrs. Miller and to understand why they may have been deskilled by her behavior. Now he brings the entire incident to a consultant, to review it and to ask if there were issues hidden in this incident that he might have missed.

Father Long is in the eighth month of his service as chaplain of a children's unit in a mental hospital. He has also become involved with an emergency telephone answering service in the community. He took a call in the middle of the night from a very depressed lady who had been referred to him by the telephone service. For a half hour, he worked with the lady over the telephone and then suggested that she should come to see him the next day. She turned up on time, but now Father Long is wondering how much of a chance he was taking with a potentially suicidal person by letting her end the telephone conversation. In fact, he discovers that he did the right things in this case, but at the time he did it he had not the slightest idea why.

These vignettes illustrate activities that are all ordinary activities on the part of ministers and religious. A mental health consultant working with clergy might expect to have such material brought in for consultation. Most of these cases, of course, might just as easily have come from a social worker, from a nurse, or from others more directly concerned with mental health. One of them, the case brought by the Reverend Mr. Peters, turns out to be a consultation about a consultation that he had extended to nursing personnel. With that one exception, the cases are ordinary instances of pastoral care and counseling. Let us consider the possibility of some less usual types of consultation.

Innovative Consultations

In the course of ordinary pastoral care consultation, a minister mentioned to a consultant that a very distraught lady in the congregation had been upset by something the minister had said in a sermon. The consultant wondered aloud about the actual content of the sermon, and the minister brought out the manuscript for the sermon he had preached the preceding Sunday. Although the manuscript seemed interesting and, from a psychological point of view, innocuous enough, the consultant wondered about the minister's style in delivering the sermon. As a result, the minister and his consultant decided to set up a series of consultation sessions focusing on the psychological aspects of the sermon.

It can be very desirable to discuss a pastor's preaching. There are, to be sure, cautions to be observed. The minister may feel—is in fact often taught to feel—that sermons should be criticized only from theological or homiletic points of view. The consultant, from his or her vantage point, may find the theological aspects of the sermon strange and unwieldy, philosophically or theologically contrary to the consultant's own beliefs. Many consultants might, moreover, shy away from dealing with sermons for fear of working in an area where they themselves have little expertise and where the pastor seems more like the expert.

Over against this, the consultant needs to recall that preaching is a highly complex activity and particularly that it involves many psychological facets. As Hiltner suggested,[3] preaching contains within it, or should contain within it, the shepherding aspects of ministry, that is, the aspects of ministry most closely related to mental health concerns. Second, preaching is an interpersonal activity designed to move its listeners, to have some kind of an impact on them. And finally, as the consultant in the illustration realized, the ideas that take shape in a preacher's mind or in his manuscripts are not always the ideas that come across to the congregation, because the minister's delivery alters the impact of the words.

With these factors in mind, the consultant was able to be of great help by reviewing with the minister an audio recording of the sermon, listening with the pastor for the emotional effect it had, and encouraging the pastor to consider the difference between intention and actuality. Later, they were even able to consider together a videotaped recording of a worship service. In engaging in this kind of consultation, the consultant would have to be prepared for the pastor to use theology as an intellectual defense. But how different is that from the defenses to be expected from a child care worker, a telephone volunteer, or some other consultee?

The administrative or organizational work of a minister may also be subject to consultation. A Lutheran pastor brought to a consultation group his difficulties in carrying out a calling program with inactive church members; the program had been designed by the governing board of his church. As he described the difficulties, a woman in the group noted that the phrase Pastor Van Dusen used in referring to the people on whom he was supposed to call was "the delinquents." When this was called to Pastor Van Dusen's attention, he replied that this was the standard terminology in his denomination. The consultant—in this case, his peers under the guidance of a consultant—suggested that he examine this word, whether it was standard terminology or not. As he did so, he began to recognize the contempt that was built into the word. He gradually became a little less defensive and was finally able to talk about his resentment of a program invented by his board of trustees and dumped on him by them. Examining these two factors enabled Pastor Van Dusen to consider the possibility of dealing with his church board in a different way and to make his calls with considerable greater comfort.

This vignette illustrates not only the possibilities of consultation concerning administrative work but also the usefulness of group consultation. The group in question in this vignette met regularly every Monday afternoon, with each member given the opportunity to present an example of his or her work for consultation. I have known of a similar group that met every Wednesday morning for an extended breakfast. They had hired a psychiatrist taking training in community psychiatry as their consultant, thus providing themselves with expert help and also providing the psychiatrist with an opportunity to engage in community psychiatry consultation on a regular basis.

In the illustration given, the case material that was presented looked at first like pastoral care material, with the pastor essentially asking, "Why am I having difficulty in making pastoral calls on people who are not coming to church?" The consultation group quickly perceived, by focusing on an emotionally loaded word, that one key issue was the pastor's relationship with his church board, whose ideas of pastoral calling were considerably less sophisticated and psychologically informed than the pastor's own ideas.

Let us pause for a moment to review the vignettes in this section and the preceding one. In the preceding section, I listed a series of vignettes having largely to do with the minister's practice of pastoral care and counseling. In terms of Hiltner's definition of the three perspectives that are present in pastoral theology, the dominant perspective in those vignettes was the shepherding perspective. Where the shepherding perspective is dominant in the minister's activities, the material may resemble clinical material brought for consultation by other mental health workers. In the other two vignettes listed in this section of the paper, the communicating perspective is dominant in one and the organizing perspective in the other. The point of Hiltner's theory, however, is that all three of these perspectives are always present in any particular piece of pastoral work. The consultant who worked with the minister on his sermon, and the peer group consultants who worked with the Lutheran pastor on his relationship to his church board, ferreted out those places where the shepherding perspective came into play, despite the fact that other perspectives were actually dominant in the work the minister was doing. It is thus by means of lifting up the shepherding perspective for examination that the consultant with mental health skills can be of particular use to the pastor.

A Consultation Process

In presenting the record of a single consultation session, I hope to bring to bear the ideas discussed in this essay upon a particular piece of work by a consultant and a pastor.

Pastor Marks brought to Dr. Reed his concerns about his first interview with Miss Marian Bing. Miss Bing was a member of the pastor's church, attending worship services twice a month. She participated in few of the church activities. He had known Miss Bing slightly and had wondered about her relationships to the people around her. At 27, she was a markedly overweight young woman, bearing on her face the scars of adolescent acne. Her aunt, Mrs. DeBray, was a very active member of the church. Mrs. DeBray had been widowed at about the same time Miss Bing's parents were killed in an automobile accident, when Miss Bing was 8 years old. She had adopted Miss Bing and had reared her. Now, however, Miss Bing had recently secured an apartment of her own.

It was Mrs. DeBray who called the pastor and asked him to begin a counseling process with Miss Bing. The pastor was properly alert to the meanings of a third-party referral and was therefore reluctant to accept an appointment made for Miss Bing by her aunt. The aunt, however, was a strong-minded woman, quite dominating, and had in fact been the chairperson of the nominating commitee that had nominated Mr. Marks as pastor of the church. The pastor rightly assumed that it would be quite difficult to refuse to accept the appointment made for the young woman by her influential aunt. Upon discovering that Miss Bing had supper with her aunt each Friday evening, the pastor decided to use that knowledge and paid a call on Mrs. DeBray on a Friday evening when he knew that Miss Bing would be present. He had also guessed that Mrs. DeBray's real concern had to do with her own resistance to the separation that Miss Bing had recently achieved by moving to an apartment of her own. He therefore turned to Miss Bing during the conversation, asking how she liked her new apartment. This question immediately elicited a negative response from Mrs. DeBray about Miss Bing's apartment, and the two women became angry with each other in short order. It did appear that one of Marian Bing's great problems was achieving separation from her aunt, and before the call was over, the pastor had suggested to Miss Bing that she might want to talk further with him about that.

In bringing this material to consultation, Pastor Marks was quite concerned about what he perceived as a tendency to be manipulative. On the one hand, he felt quite secure in assuming that a direct refusal to Mrs. DeBray would jeopardize his position in the church, alienating him from a significant part of his base of support. On the other hand, he wanted to be in a position to offer Miss Bing an opportunity to discuss her problems and to make her own choice to consider a counseling relationship with him. He had in fact accomplished what he set out to do, without either alienating Mrs. DeBray or offending her niece. But he thought that the indirectness of his tactics revealed the manipulative strength within himself. In the early part of the consultation hour, this was not immediately apparent. What the consultant was able to pick up was that Pastor Marks described Mrs. DeBray in two quite separate ways: first, as a dominating woman who made direct demands on those around her; but second, as a manupulative woman who worked rather indirectly to get what she wanted. The consultant pointed out to Pastor Marks that these two images needed some reconciling with each other, and it was then that Pastor Marks began to consider the possibility that it was he himself who had engaged in manipulation. He began to raise the question whether he could have dealt more directly both with Mrs. DeBray and with Miss Bing.

He wondered, moreover, what the impact on him had been of Miss Bing's generally unattractive and unhappy appearance. Had he already sensed the possibility that Miss Bing was an unhappy young woman, deeply conflicted over her recent decision to separate from her aunt and thus needing support in maintaining her newly found independence?

The consultant thus had to deal not only with the usual issues accompanying the initiation of a counseling relationship, particularly where a family member was exerting pressure for her own purposes, but also with the pastor's concerns about his use and possible misuse of the right of initiative and access. The consultant was aware of this tradition in pastoral work and was therefore able to help Pastor Marks focus on this use of pastoral tradition but to connect it with the pastor's hesitation to defy Mrs. DeBray directly. From the point of view of counseling, it was an ordinary enough case, but it carried within it a number of special features deriving from the special position and tradition represented by the pastor.

Broader Issues

I have written this chapter largely from the point of view of consulting with the pastor in the local church. It is largely through the pastor that the consultant has contacts with local churches. But the pastor is not the only person working in the local church with whom a mental health consultant may have fruitful contact. Churches that engage in a wide variety of outreach ministries, including coffee houses, youth clubs, and educational programs, staff all these activities with a corps of volunteers. Supervision of these volunteers may be directly in the hands of the pastor, or it may be conducted by a committee in the church. If some member of such a committee, or some volunteer working in one of these ministries, happens to be an educator or a mental health professional, he or she may have been exposed to the concept of consultation or may have used consultation. In that case, that person may make the initial request for consultation for this kind of work. More often, however, it is the pastor who has had some experience with consultation and who may suggest that the coffee house project or the telephone ministry project secure the services of a consultant.

It is characteristic, but not necessarily universal, that such projects are well intentioned but unsophisticated. In a local church of my acquaintance, there is a "Board of Stewards," whose task is to call on isolated, lonely, or shut-in members of the congregation. The pastoral advisor to the Board of Stewards (which is composed entirely of women) is a young woman who is the assistant pastor of the church. She herself is sophisticated in counseling techniques and has made excellent use of clinical training in mental hospitals. A member of the board with whom I am very well acquainted told me in a recent conversation that several members of the board simply could not accept the ideas put forth by the Reverend Miss Black. Miss Black had apparently been trying to help the board understand some of the principles of empathic listening, but some of the older board members insisted that it was always wrong to encourage lonely people to talk about their loneliness, because that allowed them to focus on the negative aspects of their experience, and "after all, what they need is cheering up." Later I learned from Miss Black that she had indeed experienced the meeting of the Board of Stewards as a great strain, and we engaged in some brief consultation concerning ways in which she might help members of the Board of Stewards to be more effective callers.

Nine years ago, when a tornado had devastated the community, this same church (many of whose members had been affected by the tornado) put together an emergency committee to try to meet the needs of those who had suffered some kind of loss. In that case, the pastor had drawn on the resources of mental health professionals who were also members of the church, not as primary callers on those who had suffered loss or damage but as consultants to the committee. These specialists, of whom I was one, engaged in a brief intensive training session for volunteers and then served as debriefers when the volunteers returned from their calls.

Thus, a mental health professional may be called on to serve as a consultant in a wide variety of forms of ministry that do not focus directly on the work of the pastor but on the work of the committee and volunteers within the church. The same principles of consultation of course apply, but in these cases, the consultant is dealing with volunteers who are unsophisticated both in pastoral tradition and in the principles of psychodynamics, human growth, or other concerns of mental health professionals. This by no means implies that such volunteers are inept. What the consultant will in fact usually find is that there are large areas of high if untutored expertise, balanced, however, by other areas in which there is no experience or information at all. Such work can be a fascinating challenge to the consultant because it requires the willingness to explore carefully what knowledge and experience the consultee actually possesses and to gauge the consultation accordingly.

Summary

Mental health consultation to the local church primarily involves consultation with its professional staff, who may have a wide range of training and experience. It may also involve consultation to volunteer individuals or groups within the church who are carrying on some special form of ministry. The relationship and the interaction between church tradition and psychological concerns, sophistication and unsophistication, highly professional and highly unprofessional stances provide the consultant with an intriguing, sometimes difficult, and often unusual opportunity to assist people who often function in our society as front-line mental health workers, whether they are aware of that function or not.

References

1. Baxter, R. *The reformed pastor*. In E. A. Park (Ed.). *The preacher and pastor*. Andover, Mass.: Allen, Morrill and Wardwell, 1845. (Originally published, 1656.) Pp. 227–350.
2. Mitchell, K. R. Priestly celibacy from a psychological perspective. *Journal of Pastoral Care*, 1970, *24*,, 216–226.
3. Hiltner, S. *Preface to pastoral psychology*. New York: Abingdon Press, 1958.
4. McNeill, J. T., *A history of the cure of souls*. New York: Harper & Bros., 1951.

10

Consultation to Complex Organizations in Transition

The Dynamics of Change and the Principles of Applied Consultation

RALPH G. HIRSCHOWITZ

The task environments of contemporary organizations are complex, volatile, and increasingly uncertain. Regulatory pressures, market exigencies, and competitive pressures generate inescapable demands for change. In consequence, a critically salient issue confronting contemporary complex organizations is the management of transition. Since the leader's personality, values, and style* significantly influence his and the organization's adaptive behavior, this chapter focuses particularly upon consultation to the leaders of complex organizations under conditions of transition.

**Style* is used here as synonymous with "ways of doing business." The concept of style encompasses the characteristic ways in which the leader conducts himself, his mode of decision making, and the *process* by which he interacts with his external and internal constituents. The image he projects, the norms by which he lives, and the values he communicates determine how the leader's people view him, their view of themselves, and the organizational image communicated to the external world.

RALPH G. HIRSCHOWITZ · Assistant Professor of Psychiatry. Harvard Medical School.

The mental health consultant in complex organizations pursues public mental health goals: the prevention of adaptive casualties and the promotion of healthy coping capacities in the population under the organization's influence or control. The thrust of the consultant's population-oriented endeavors is fourfold:

1. To identify and modify psychological "pollutants" in the organizational environment.
2. To "immunize" people against psychological hazards that cannot be modified or prevented.
3. To strengthen the "hygienic" properties of the psychological environment.
4. To strengthen people's capacities to cope with diverse adaptive challenges.

In the history of administrative mental health consultation, few descriptions of consultation to industry are recorded. Many mental health consultants hold to familiar ground by confining their efforts to human service organizations. This may be associated with the preservation of a self-image of the clinician–consultant as "clean"—and a related stereotype of the business executive as "dirty." The shift in consultation from care-giving agencies to business organizations requires a major leap. The leap requires that the "myth of dirty hands" be relinquished and demands new conceptual maps, ease with businessmen, and an understanding of their language and the unique demands made upon them. For consultants whose primary background has been clinical, mentors to model and teach this more robust consultation have rarely been available. Such consultation in times of transition demands a grasp of such processes as:

1. Influencing the patterns by which an organization adapts to change.
2. Ensuring that people's relevant psychological needs are met as the pace of change accelerates.
3. Strengthening organizational support systems.
4. Creating "immunization" programs to prepare for anticipated change.
5. Teaching coping skills.
6. Introducing "psychological cost accounting" in the planning of change.

Intrinsic to this approach is appreciation for the leverage opportunities presented by the crises of organizational transition. Crisis theory is applied by the promotion of interdependencies, capitalizing on transition's temporary heightening of people's ministration and mastery needs. The principles by which organizational crisis intervention and administrative consultation are meshed have been elaborated in earlier publications.[10,11]

Psychological Cost Accounting

In the translation of crisis theory into a language congenial to business executives, psychological cost accounting has been introduced as a tool for the planning of change. Psychological cost accounting roots the choice of change strategies in analysis of their projected psychological and political costs and benefits. The consequences of alternative strategies are assessed for groups in all the relevant environments of the organization. Relevant groups that might need to be considered are consumers, local environmentalists, stockholders, regulatory agencies, media, and the executives' primary constituents, employees. Psychological cost accounting produces strategic plans that minimize the likelihood of adaptive casualties and maximize cohesion, coherence, and commitment.

The Hazards of Organizational Consultation

Organizational consultation makes great intellectual and personal demands upon the consultant. An adequate grasp of integrated conceptual models is a *sine qua non* for the task. Models encompassing multifactorial approaches to organizational diagnosis should permit organizations to be compared with one another and consultant intervention to be evaluated against clearly stated diagnostic parameters.

For all consultants, mastery of their roles is imperiled when there is selective filtering and compression of data into a monistic theoretical frame. A stance that is atheoretical or inadequately theoretical inevitably disposes to premature problem closure; since problems remain undiagnosed, solutions generate further problems in their wake. Some of these hazards in consultation are evident in the proliferating literature on organizational consultation. Much of the writing is strong on ostensible problem-*solving* intervention but weak on problem-*diagnosing* theory and evaluation. When theory is limited, tolerance for ambiguity low, and the need for action high, cognitive Procrusteanism is likely to occur. Organizational search then becomes selectively restricted to reconnaissance of behavioral fields for data that permit the reduction of complex problems to elegant—but invalid—formulations. These formulations then justify the application of precast technical solutions. Solutions then, insensibly, no longer function as *means* toward problem-solving *ends* but are pursued as ends in themselves. The consultant unconsciously diverges from teaching what the consultees need to learn in favor of their learning what he needs to teach.

Experience in the training and supervision of mental health consultants indicates that the search for anxiety-assuaging "What do I *do?*" techniques is common early in the trainee consultant's ascent of a mental health career ladder. The tendency toward impulsive action is curbed by vigorous supervision in which habits of reflection are taught and clinical causal–analytic "diagnostic" thinking extended to organizational macrosystems. In effective training programs, additional safeguards are provided when trainees are accepted into consultant training only when sufficiently seasoned as therapists. They should have learned to regulate their own anxieties, curb their rescue fantasies, and avoid the *furor therapeuticus* that otherwise impels the young consultant to *do* before he diagnoses.

When the consultant's conceptual guide maps are inadequate, he fails to define processes at *all* the organization's relevant interfaces: between the organization and its external environments as well as those between, and within, its internal subsystems. As diagnosis moves with higher power focus to illuminate intergroup, interpersonal, and intrapersonal strains, analytic demands of a high order are placed upon the consultant. In differentiating symptom from overall problem, he uses Sapir's "multifocal lens" to move back and forth between the macroperspectives of the organization in dynamic interaction with its task environments to microperspectives of the personality patterns and adaptive styles of the organization's leaders.

The effective consultant operates on a clinical diagnostic paradigm, rotating his lenses to monitor functional and dysfunctional interaction between interdependent parts, suprasystemic wholes, and their larger environments. Systematic diagnostic scrutiny characteristically embraces dimensions such as:

1. The historical evolution of the organization's mission, image, distinctive competencies, structure, function, and style.
2. An "environmentalist," low-power focus upon the external

groups and forces that affect, and/or are affected by, the organization.

3. Analysis of the organization's boundary-spanning and boundary-scanning activities and the quality of its environmental "intelligence" and planning functions.
4. Exploration of the interplay between interdependent subsystems in the organization.
5. Patterns of integration and differentiation.
6. Modes of adaptation.
7. Leadership.

From the Steady to the Unsteady Organizational State: The Threat of Consultant Role Obsolescence

The wisdom of many seminal contributors to organizational consultation was recorded at a time when our social and organizational worlds were steadier, more predictable and certain, than now. Consultation models that evolved in response to relatively steady environmental conditions often fail therefore to fit the unsteady state of contemporary organizational environments. Most of these are characterized by proliferation, uncertainty, and volatility.

As Emery and Trist[6] have compellingly suggested, the "texture of organizational environments" has evolved from "calm" to "turbulence." In consequence, leadership—and consultation—can no longer assume that the leader's primary role is that of equilibrium-maintaining steermanship. Given the certainty of continuing uncertainty in organizational environments, adaptive leadership requires frequent proactive shifts in direction, jettisoning the obsolete and promoting the new. Leadership must both steady—and unsteady—the organization.

In helping contemporary executives achieve leadership, today's consultant therefore requires a sophisticated appreciation for this steady–unsteady oscillation in times of social, organizational, institutional, and individual *change*. The consultant, like his consultees, must be ready to jettison steady-state assumptions when unsteadied by adaptive demands. When the models he has learned and practiced under steady-state conditions do not fit an unsteady environment, his models need renovation. In achieving this renovation, the consultant must therefore understand the change imperatives confronting complex organizations. Without this information and a model for the adaptive mastery of change, the consultant is like an explorer who enters a foreign land without a map, a translator, or a compass. A discussion of the change demands upon organizations—and a model for their adaptive mastery—therefore follows.

Organizational Change Imperatives

From Calm to Turbulence: The Shift of Our Time

Emery and Trist[6] have characterized the past few decades' shift in organizational environments as evolving from calm, "placid-clustered" to volatile, "turbulent" environments.

The placid-clustered environment is characterized by a general lack of organization within its constituent components, high predictability, and a ready acceptance of transactions initiated and regulated by the organization. By contrast, a turbulent environment is pluralistic, dynamic, and unpredictable. The turbulent environment is uncertain and volatile, and the organization tends to lose control of such an environment. In the placid environment, the organization can maintain great constancy because the environment adapts to the organization; in conditions of turbulence, the adaptive demand is upon the organization. The organization must adapt to such differentiated sectors of contemporary environments as consumers, environmentalists, regulatory agencies, competitors, and fluctuating monetary policies. Unable to control or manipulate a turbulent environment, leaders must develop adaptive strategies based on sophisticated environmental scanning and planning processes.

The evolution from placid constancy to turbulent uncertainty has occurred simultaneously in the entire society and all its component institutions. Movements rise and fall and new ideologies burgeon. The consequent shift in social values and individual expectations multiply the demands upon organizations. Adaptive struggles to find new ways of managing the business ensue.

The Changing Society

Change imperatives emanate from many sources. Examples are:

1. Shifts in demographic patterns.
2. Inflation, recession, and their consequences.
3. The rise of consumerism and its differentiation into consumer movements.

4. Continuing pressures for citizen participation from minority groups, including women and the young.
5. New definitions of citizen rights and entitlements.
6. Environmentalists' demands to curb pollution and improve the quality of the natural environment.
7. Pressures to curb psychological pollution and improve the quality of human life in organizations and institutions.
8. Growth in the power and influence of multinational corporations.
9. Changing family patterns.
10. Technological change, with its "global village" and "future shock" implications.
11. The energy crisis.
12. Realization of the exhaustibility of natural resources.
13. Insistence upon the social responsibility of organizations.
14. Growth in the number and influence of governmental regulatory agencies.
15. The specialization of work with prolongation of the period of education in preparation for occupational roles.
16. Change in the national ideology.
17. Changes in employee expectations and definitions of rights and responsibilities.

Against this backdrop, the organization needs to be in responsive touch with such relevant sectors of its task environments as consumers, suppliers, and regulatory agencies, while maintaining a wary eye upon competitors and emerging sociotechnical trends. In mounting strategies to adapt to these multidifferentiated external environments, it must sustain the working interdependence of its constituent units. This regulation of the organization's internal human environment is crucially dependent upon adequate awareness of the evolving expectations of employees.

The Revolution of Rising Expectations: Employees, the New Constituency

Employees are mounting change demands from inside the organization. Spurred by the articulate interest group advocacy of minority group members, including women and the young, employees are negotiating their needs with unaccustomed militancy. In consequence, organizational leaders are being exposed to pluralistic value orientations and articulated expectations from which they were previously insulated. The new breed of employee lays claim to interactive participation not previously encountered. He does not display the automated obedience and ritualized deference behavior of previous generations and is likely to talk up, questioning and challenging authority. Some employees are asserting that information and participation is a *right* of organizational membership.* The right of individuals to exercise *informed* choice is being simultaneously affirmed in other social arenas, reflecting the movement described by Lodge[13] from America's traditional veneration of the rights of *property* toward the rights of *membership*.

In consequence, as the sentiments of organizational subordinates become known to superiors, leaders, made aware that they are out of touch with their internal constituents, begin to question their communicational and interactional patterns. Often, these are inadequate to register the diverse changes in *both* the external and the internal environments of the organization. Some leaders deny that significant changes in citizen, consumer, or employee expectations are occurring at all. However, trends are clear and ignored at some peril. In a 1975 commencement address at the Harvard Business School, Lodge† summarized the trends:

> We are moving from the world of the old ideology to the new one and we are not going back.
>
> A lot of what is happening is inexorable. In some areas, we have a choice. It is crucial to see the difference, so we can make the choices and not fight the inevitable.

While many executives lag in response to inexorable trends, enough executives have exercised leadership for the essential ingredients of adaptive leadership to be identified. Studies of the adaptive leader show that he is both *proactive* and *interactive*. He has learned to respond nondefensively to *external* constituents, building respect and extending credibility as he moves; he does business by reciprocal negotiation. The lessons learned with consumerists, environmentalists, and regulators are applied in interactive engagement with his *internal* constituencies.

While organizations with proactive, interactive leaders are likely to be effective and adaptive, those with *inactive, reactive, or preactive* styles lag behind the needs of their multiple constituents and are not adaptive. Often, the consultant's primary task is to heighten leader awareness of the need for proactivity and interactivity—and to make it happen.

*A recent study of "all youth" by Yankelovich[19] ranks "participation in job decisions" as second only to health care as a perceived "entitlement."

†See also Lodge's[13] discussion of "the changing society."

A case example of the costs and consequences of laggardly, reactive leadership follows.

The Reactive Organization: A Case Study

The longer established the organization, the more likely it is to be laggardly in adapting to change demands. A case example of such reactive leadership follows.

> This case is based upon consultant experience with a large, long-established product organization. The organization was heavily centralized, vending its products trhough many statewide retail subsidiaries under its direct managerial control. The organization was founded under the placid-clustered environmental conditions described by Emery and Trist.[6] Its vending and factory locations ''fitted'' local centers of population and transport. The ''fit'' between organization and environment continued in steady equilibrium for many years. The organization's policy of heavy central control was consistent with the relative homogeneity, predictability—and pliability—of consumers of those days. As local communities began to change, however, the organization failed to sense the changing composition, demographic drift, and proliferating consumer wishes of the people in the communities where they operated. Operating on assumptions of consumer—and competitor—constancy, it made little change from one year to the next in its products, its advertising, or its marketing practices. Like most organizations in environments perceived as placid, strategies were based upon the steady-state assumption that loyal employees, suppliers, and consumers would behave in the future with precisely the same constancy they had displayed in the past. Little difference existed between strategies and tactics. These assumptions created perceptual blinkers limiting the organization's capacity to realize that many of its outlets were no longer located at centers of population or traffic. Oblivious to shifts in the market place, it also failed to detect early warning signs of competitive encroachment from retailing organizations that began to invade its traditional domains. The organizational blinders were only removed when the bottom line of successive years showed a waning of turnover and profit. At that point, there was belated realization of loss of market share to young, vigorous competitors. The organization thus eventually responded *reactively*. It did so by haphazard attempts to counter competition, repackage products and intensify sales. Impulsive decisions were made too little, too late, and too slowly. No overall appreciation existed for the organization's structural obsolescence and loss of competitive edge. Eventually, precipitous profit decline compelled the directors to appoint a new president, who was given the mandate to take charge and clean house. With the counsel of management consultants, many direct retail outlets were dismantled or sold. Emphasis was

placed upon the marketing of products through independent retailers. Unprofitable production plants were sold or closed.

Employees who had become redundant or obsolete were terminated. For the surviving managers, the cutback of employees generated poignant problems. The organization had always been benignly paternalistic, priding itself on taking care of its people. Its employees, in effect, had an implicit understanding that jobs were guaranteed from womb to tomb if they were loyal and conscientious. Managers who had to terminate such loyal, conscientious employees violated this psychological contract and suffered the pangs of consequent guilt, anger, and depression.*

The Turmoil of Transition

Given its assumption of system constancy, the organization had historically been structured for ease of control. Policies were developed at the apex of the organization and were uniformly applied. Little authority was delegated and independence was discouraged. The reorganization plan introduced by the new president ran counter to these long-established norms. The plan called for decentralization into locally responsive profit centers in which authority was delegated to local managers. However, no provision was made for the retreading of managers who for years had been inculcated with habits of regimented dependence. After years of subservience to established policy and procedure, they were now expected to make autonomous decisions on the basis of differentiated local conditions. Previously, decisions had been made at superordinate levels. Unable to respond to expectations of instant independence, employees were betwixt and between, confused and frustrated, poorly prepared for change, and overwhelmed by feelings associated with the loss of familiar moorings, habits, and relationships. They also bore the weight of emotions stemming from identification with employees who had been terminated or prematurely retired. Because they had been spared the same fate, they experienced survivor guilt. Everyone in the organization exhibited the psychological travail of transition. Demoralization, resistance, and increased absenteeism reflected this transitional turmoil.

Consultant Intervention

Some months after the reorganization, the president asked for consultation. The situation was rapidly assessed and diagnostic impressions conveyed to the leader and his management team. Some problems were so evident that an immediate remedial strategy was recommended—and accepted. Issue-focused workshops were held with all top echelon people, in which the

*Similar fat trimming and belt tightening (usually accompanied by a rhetoric of "biting the bullet") has occurred in countless organizations in the past few years. In the mid 1970s, we are witnessing managerial cutbacks in territory hitherto protected by patronage, such as civil service bureaucracies.

organization's transitional turmoil was explained, the stress of transition discussed, and employees' needs examined. Subsequent workshops helped their subordinates understand and express their grief and disappointment about the past, articulate anxiety about the future, and make sense out of the reorganization. As people became better able to understand what they were experiencing, employees could interact with their leaders and learn new ways of managing the business. They could commit themselves to the new ways when the president, in interaction with them, helped them realize that reorganization was crucial to their personal and organizational survival.

Management development programs were simultaneously installed. The effort has since expanded to include the development of substantial internal consultant resources. The indicators of transitional anomie are gradually declining and the organization's morale is significantly improved.

Too Much, Too Fast, Too Soon: A Cautionary Contrast

While older organizations tend to be slowly reactive in their responses to change demands, younger, aggressive growth organizations often commit an opposite error, exaggerated proactivity. They attempt to accomplish too much, too fast, and too soon.

This opposite situation is illustrated by a rapidly growing department store chain with conspicuous vitality and unique responsiveness to the tastes of multiple consumer groups. In its growth, the organization had been able to capture the burgeoning youth market without losing a secure foothold with older consumer groups. Consequently, it rapidly outdistanced longer established competitors. One chain of conservative competitors was eventually acquired by the younger organization.

As the stores of the established chain were incorporated, functional specialists from the parent organization began to impose their standards upon the newly acquired subsidiaries. The newly merged stores rapidly found themselves under pressure to accept the modus operandi and flamboyant style of the parent organization. This pressure was manifested in a decision to remodel the stores and change their image.

Consultant Intervention

Consultation was requested by the parent organization when it discovered that its change efforts were being vitiated in unexpected ways. Resistance was expressed in the passive–aggressive mode of the powerless. While saying "yes" verbally to parent demands, innumerable ways were found to say "no" behaviorally. Instructions from the parent would be followed to the letter, but their spirit would be systematically violated.

In consultation, systematic interviews were conducted with the managers of newly incorporated stores. Meetings were also held with the corporate staff officers with whom the local managers interfaced. The local managers were helped to articulate resentment of the "defacing" of their stores. The new style violated the conservative image with which they had long identified—and which they had incorporated into their personal identities. They had lost face in their own eyes as well as those of family, friends, and neighbors. They experienced impotent rage at being compelled to accept their new image and perceived the distant leaders of the parent organization as conquering Khans who had no care or concern for them.

In continuing discussion, they began to realize that they also harbored underlying resentment toward the departed chief executives who had founded the company and molded its previous image. They became aware of feelings of outrage about those leaders who had abandoned them by selling out. When the incorporating parent so hastily attempted to impose its preferred patterns upon them, all the force of their double outrage had bene mobilized to fight back at the only enemy that was visibly available to them. Pining for the past, they had been holding onto an idealized vision of their past leaders—and fighting their new leaders, whom they were portraying as entirely malevolent.

The diagnosis of the local people's unresolved mourning and transitional turmoil was shared with the officers of both local and parent companies. While doing so, opportunities were seized to offer "minitraining" about the impact of change upon people's feelings and self-esteem. A day-long meeting was then structured in which both groups were present. Over the day, they clarified their hopes, fears, and values. The meaning of each other's behavior was unraveled and both groups became better able to understand each other's respective positions. In a climate of enhanced trust and respect, appreciation for their shared interests grew and acceptable policy compromises were struck. A conjoint planning committee emerged in which crossfertilizing dialogue was sustained. "We–they" schism diminished, with the spirit of one family growing as some local managers were transferred to the parent—and some local officers recruited from it. Local managers were encouraged to visit their counterparts in other stores and participated in joint training programs.

Consultation thus provided an enabling structure, with the consultant monitoring psychological safety while grievances were aired, conflicts worked through, and new psychological contracts negotiated.

The Tasks of Transition: Bereavement

In each of these cases, the adaptive demands of transition wrought emotional havoc that was neither anticipated nor understood. Leaders were in considerable need of help to unravel the meaning of the behavioral consequences of their reorganizational decisions. Lacking clear understanding, they could not master the situation and were uncertain of their leadership roles. Consultation in each case therefore required explanation of the emotional experience of transition and the nature of its underlying psychological tasks. In addition, leaders needed authoritative guidance for the initiation of effective processes to deal with the psychological tasks of transition.

In consultation to changing organizations, it is consequently essential that the consultant be an applied crisis theorist, clearly understanding the psychological experience of significant transition. Axiomatic to such understanding is the fact that all change involves some measure of loss. This loss is actualized in the inevitable bereavement that accompanies organizational transition. Reorganization often precipitates multiple loss experiences and can demand that people simultaneously relinquish attachments to familiar people, places, habits, routines, functions, and roles. This is often compounded by temporary loss of the security, potency, and self-esteem that accompany habitual accomplishment and effective role performance. Reorganization disrupts settled niches in relationships patterned over time and lubricated by familiar habit.

The Crisis Experience

When reorganization is massive, the grief process intensifies and becomes manifest in such forms as aggrievement, outrage, physiological disturbance, emotional distress, tension, and irritability. People's habitual patterns are disrupted; they become off balance, function erratically, and are not themselves. Subject to bouts of fatigue, they mourn the loss of familiar attachments while attempting to meet the immediate survival demands of a changed situation.

In reorganization, an employee confronted with many change demands is like a man whose house has collapsed. Pining for his familiar home and objects, he does not know where or how to build anew. Like the West Enders described by Fried[7] and Marris,[14] he cannot settle down because he is too unsettled by loss. While grief and worry sap his emotional energies, he has little residual energy or appetite for the tasks of daily organizational life.

The depth of grief and worry experienced is greatest when transition is of massive proportions and when it is a first-time experience for the people concerned. Distress, hurt, and outrage are intensified when change is sudden, unanticipated, and imposed. When change is introduced summarily, people have no opportunity to understand *what* is being done, *how* it is being done, or *why* it is done. Credibility is questioned, confidence reduced, and resistance mobilized.

Defense and Mastery

When reeling under the impact of change news, people defend against emergency affect by resorting to psychological defenses. As the news is assimilated, tentative attempts at problem mastery begin. As people do their grief work, reorganizing their lives to cope with their changed situation, defensive behavior diminishes. Early in transition, therefore, psychological defenses serve to sustain psychological balance—and are to be expected. As transition proceeds, the newly generated adaptive tasks become clearer. Energy then gradually moves from defense against these tasks to attack upon them. If this shift does not occur, defense becomes retreat; when it does, defense is a way station en route to mastery.

In consultation under conditions of transition, defenses therefore require careful monitoring. The early numbness and denial evident when people receive bad news meets immediate psychological needs; however, when excessively prolonged, denial, like projection, can become a defense of malignant rigidity. In organizations, it may be manifest in role clinging—when people behave *as if* they were still in relinquished roles. Mass denial is also apparent when people avoid exposure to sources of information about change and tune out or distort what they do hear.

Conspiracies of mutual denial occur when members of the organization aid and abet one another in such ostrichlike activity as holding on. People hold onto cherished habits, routines, and rituals even when these are rapidly succumbing to obsolescence. Holding on, actually or symbolically, is a maneuver to maintain attachment, delaying the work of mourning; emotional energy remains invested in the old and cannot be released for adapting to the new.

Malignant Denial

An example of the maladaptive consequences of denial follows.

In one organization, survival was imperiled by excessive denial on the part of its president and his closest ally, the marketing vice-president. They had both been highly successful salesmen with noteworthy capacities to sell their buyers—and themselves—on the potential of the electronic product that their organization had pioneered.

The organization's original president had been a technically innovative engineer dedicated to quality production and service. With its rapid growth, the organization had become dominated by its marketeers. In the transition to a new generation of product, the marketing strategy of the new leadership team proved on analysis to be impulsively conceived and poorly planned. The marketeers were tenaciously committed to a roseate vision of rapid growth. This vision was sustained by strong denial defenses that made them impervious to their engineers' warnings that the newly developed version of the product still had bugs in it—and they did not warn purchasers of these potential bugs. In their zeal for sales, their growth planning was haphazard; they overpromised and oversold. The resulting sales volume left the engineers with insufficient time to debug the product, while the demand for production caused the president simultaneously to relax quality control standards. Since purchasers had been highly satisfied with the technical excellence and service of past purchases, the first year of the changed product's introduction reflected dramatic profits for the company, which simultaneously grew dramatically in size and managerial complexity. In the second year, both the bugs and the errors stemming from relaxed quality control became increasingly visible. The third year became a full-blown crisis year punctuated by mounting dissatisfaction, with many customers canceling or failing to renew leases. Product return wreaked mounting havoc with inventory control. New sales diminished to a trickle as the organization's reputation for integrity declined. In consequence, dramatic retrenchment followed dramatic growth. In responding to this precipitous decline, the president oscillated between denying that any real problem existed and angry scapegoating of the engineering and production departments. Partial denial continued as the president and the marketing vice-president became able to rationalize many of their product returns as "because of the recession." Planning for the future was colored by such blue skying as, "When the economy turns around . . ." Attention was thus deflected from their own contributions to the crisis.

At this time, this organization has so alienated its customers and has so much internal dissension that it is unlikely that the more realistic leader recruited by irate directors can do much to develop credibility. The organization faces only two likely fates: acquisition by competitors or liquidation.

This case illustrates how survival was imperiled by the psychological defenses of its leaders; denial was of so high an order that the leader could not perceive or accept the realistic consequences of ill-conceived, poorly timed marketing strategy.

Mismanagement of the Tasks of Transition

In the ideal planning of reorganization, psychological cost accounting anticipates—and budgets—the time and resources needed to help people with their grief work. People need time to experience and express their grief while seeking substitutes for what has been lost. In transition, leaders are therefore wise to structure opportunities for the organization's people to share distress, meet their temporarily heightened dependency needs, mourn for the past,* and exchange information that can help them master the tasks of transition. As the earlier cases indicate, the necessary psychological cost accounting rarely occurs.

Consultation to many organizations in the throes of change suggests that the mismanagement of change stems as much from ignorance of the psychological tasks of transition as from outmoded assumptions about man, motivation, and leadership. Some leadership assumptions and styles that contribute to the mismanagement of the tasks of transition follow.

1. *"Carrot-and-stick" theories of man and motivation.* In spite of mounting evidence that people's needs for freedom and autonomy require support and interactive involvement from leaders, there is often vain reliance upon material inducements or controlling threats to coax or compel employees to follow their leaders.†

2. *Insensitivity to basic emotional needs.* In times of change, people's dependency and affectional needs increase. Organizations that cope poorly fail to meet these needs.

3. *Disregard for cherished values.* When change is designed or implemented in ways that violate the values of organizational participants, identification with the organization is compromised. When *what* is done or *how* it is done runs counter to their ideal values, employees feel trapped; they cannot identify with their employing organization or its leaders and experience impotent fury. They may go along with what is expected out of survival necessity but resolve their psychological conflicts by disengagement.

4. *Failure to appreciate complexity.* Our society, its organizations, and its institutions, are all becoming increasingly complex. Organizations, their environments, and their people are becoming more pluralist, more differentiated, and more interdependent. With realization of the complexity of human organizations and the multiplicity of human needs, the adaptive planner mounts strategies responsive to these multiple needs.

*In all situations of loss-loaded transition, the working through of grief requires repetitive review of the past. The decathexis of lost objects is achieved by active reminiscence. By the laying of the past to rest through remembrance, dismemberment becomes tolerable.

†This philosophy was nakedly asserted in a recent statement by the chief executive officer of a large corporation who spoke of "having" his corporate officers "by their Cadillacs."

5. *Failure to budget adequate lead and lag time.* In coping with change, energy is depleted by grief and worry; until reorganization evolves stable norms, human behavior is erratic. During the weeks preceding anticipated change and in the subsequent weeks of turmoil and adjustment, decline in available energy for productivity is therefore to be expected. The effective organization accepts that optimal productivity is not realized for some months after reorganization. When it does psychological cost accounting, it budgets the necessary lag time for psychological turnaround to occur.

6. *Reactivity versus proactivity.* In response to the uncertainty of their environments, most organizations have developed differentiated planning subsystems. These attempt to make forecasts on the basis of computer-simulated models. However, planners are often compartmented, underutilized, and depreciated by action-oriented executives. The effective integration of planners into strategic planning teams is unusual. Too often, planning becomes an arid exercise to provide "numbers" so that long-term plans are written for the record. *Strategic* planning directly influences corporate policy and procedure. When planning plays little part in leadership decisions, the style is reactive, not proactive; when actual decision-making in such organizations is analyzed, policy decisions are seen to occur after immediate crisis not in anticipation of them.*

7. *Attempts to control rather than interact with relevant constituencies.* Many organizations have enjoyed organization–environment stability because they have effectively established oligopolies with allied organizations. They have therefore exercised effective control over consumers and competitors. The health industry is a classic example in which consumer pressures have been met with paternalistic attempts at co-option or control. A recent study of citizen participation by Warren[17] has highlighted the conspicuous differences between providers and users in their respective translations of "participation."

The Management of Transition

When the consultant identifies leadership patterns that do *not* help, the consultant can curb these; simultaneously he promotes and strengthens

*Leaders of organizations in which reactive crisis management is rampant do little proactive planning because of a personality style characterized by high denial; leaders are sensitive to the winds of change only when they assume hurricane proportions.

processes that *do* help. These processes serve to ease the emotional travail of transition and promote mastery of its multiple tasks.

Since reorganizations are planned prospectively, early intervention by the consultant can ensure the preparatory involvement of people *prior* to reorganization. When anticipatory involvement occurs, many helpful consequences accrue: people *understand* the causes and goals of change; by participation in strategic planning, they can influence the organization's course and their roles within it. The process of interactive engagement in the planning of change permits energies to be enlisted in constructive assault upon the organization's changing reality. Denial and distortion—and the rumor mill—are thus neutralized and psychological acceptance promoted. When imminent change is realistically discussed, anticipatory grief and worry work begin. It is of considerable related interest that Toffler,[15] discussing effective ways to cope with change in communities, describes a similar interactive process that he calls "anticipatory democracy."

Analysis shows that processes that promote adaptive mastery in organizations include the following ingredients.

1. *Understanding*. When an organization's people can discuss the facts and criteria that guide planning strategies, understanding, realistic coping, and high confidence result. Strong evidence for this assertion is provided by a study of patients before and after surgery.[5] Patients who had precise understanding about what to expect prior to surgery coped better and subsequently reported a 98% level of confidence in their surgeons compared to 69% in a control group that had been given "standard" information. In the absence of realistic information, imagination invariably fills the gaps. Paranoid suspicion and contagious emergency emotions are then exacerbated in the rumor mill. Fears and fantasies run wild, with energies uselessly dissipated in their pursuit.

2. *Involvement*. When the *process* of information sharing provides opportunities for employees to influence the future course of events, they feel included as team members. Participatory involvement across, and between, echelon levels of the organization mobilizes constructive forces for problem solving; commitment to implementation increases when employees can influence the architecture of their new roles.

3. *Support and reassurance*. During change, people's dependency needs increase. They look to each other and to sources of respected authority for reassurance, comfort and counsel. They need assurance that superiors care, understand their needs, and are able and willing to meet them.

4. *Guidance*. In new situations, people require guides who can provide maps, translation, and interpretation. In exploring new territory, one needs help with reconnaissance, planning, and the learning of new patterns. *Anticipatory* guidance is particulary valuable for the practice of new patterns and the rehearsal of new roles. By taking time out to project themselves into an uncertain future, anticipating what it will be like, people acquire some preliminary orientation and build immunity to the grief and anxiety that will be experienced in the new situation.

5. *Proximity*. With the uncertainty, ambiguity, and heightened dependency of the transition state, the ready availability of leaders is helpful. Such availability meets needs for contact comfort and can be realized through increased frequency of supervision and ease of access. The leader structures team meetings so that co-workers can share the pain and grief of loss, while trading experiences that can help them consolidate their new roles.

6. *Interaction*. Increased frequency of interaction expedites the restitution process by which people bury the old and build the new. As co-workers interact, they talk about the good old days, reviewing the past as they move toward the future. The leader's discussion of his own feelings can stimulate shared reminiscence and give emotions legitimacy. When feelings are acknowledged and expressed, energy bound in psychological defenses is freed for daily tasks.

7. *Clarity*. While the organization's people struggle with the experience of loss and change, it is difficult for them to maintain the boundaries of newly ascribed tasks and roles. In the early turmoil of transition, comprehension and attention are strained. The phenomenon of role clinging, unconsciously manifested as continuance of previous role behavior, also impairs learning of the new roles. Role expectations consequently may have to be frequently clarified and reclarified. Role strain and task ambiguity are reduced by such repeated discussion.

8. *Self-respect*. In times of change, people experience loss of self-esteem. Deprived of opportunities to perform with accustomed competence, they struggle to preserve meaning, identity, and self-worth. They often feel that they are no longer valued or of value. The devaluation of self can be neutralized in meetings in which their views are respected, their values supported, and their personal dignity reaffirmed.

9. *Hope*. Meetings can generate confidence in work teams and their leaders, serving to neutralize the transient hopelessness and helplessness experienced in unfamiliar situations. The realization that everyone is struggling together to surmount transitional difficulties in an atmosphere of

support and concern sustains the hope of eventual mastery. The maintenance of hope is a *sine qua non* for the successful navigation of change. Harold G. Wolff,[18] a physician deeply sensitive to the influence of social contexts upon health, once wrote:

> prolonged circumstances which are perceived as dangerous, as lonely, as hopeless, may drain a man of hope and of his health; but he is capable of enduring incredible burdens and taking cruel punishment when he has self-esteem, hope, purpose and a belief in his fellows. (p. 1082)

Visible Management

Effective leadership processes under conditions of transition are exemplified by Carlson[1] of United Airlines. His intuitive appreciation for the involvement of his people is recorded in a recent interview:

> if my constituency—the employees—don't support the programs that management develops, there's no way these programs can succeed. . . .
>
> I started out to meet as many people as I could to explain to them what was happening to their company and to solicit questions from them as to what they thought should be done, and openly to establish some credibility. (p. 94)

This statement illustrates the composite helping ingredients of understanding, involvement, support and reassurance, guidance, proximity, and interaction.

Carlson acknowledged that his visible management style requires a capacity to tolerate and accept—and deflect—aggression: "You have to be willing to accept criticism that comes from face-to-face meetings with employees." He is sustained by his belief that "A manager's job is to try and get people committed to a program they believe in."

In summary, people in transition benefit from heightened interaction with one another. Frequent contact meets heightened needs for closeness, affection, and dependency and encourages the mobilization of mature defenses to deal with the pain of loss and change. With a determination to help people share what they really feel, think, and value, pluralistic ignorance is dissipated and people can do business with one another. When they move closer to one another during transition, solidarity sentiments increase. "Membership of one another" closes ranks, mobilizing concerted attack upon external threats. The organization becomes a company.

Transitional Supports

The psychological travail of transition is compounded by the sink-or-swim management style of some organizations. Few bridges are prepared or support vehicles constructed to ease adaptive distress during the work of transition. In consultation, we often identify the support supplies that are lacking—and help leaders design vehicles for their delivery. In doing so, we tread gently, realizing that the stage must be carefully set before some leaders can hear, let alone accept, concepts about psychological man that violate deeply held assumptions about themselves. Many leaders have been reared with counterdependent (overindependent) assumptions of manliness. In order to sustain a self-image based on these assumptions, they are psychologically compelled to deny their own dependency needs and defend against awareness of the heightened needs for dependency, contact comfort, and affection that surge in times of transition. It is often wise to reexamine these basic assumptions in in-service training programs. When leaders are exposed to sensitizing seminars, they can be helped to grasp the universality of emotional needs in transition—and to understand *why* counterdependent sink-or-swim assumptions are perilous to organizational adaptation. Without such sensitization, the consultant may be perceived as talking a soft-headed foreign language, irrelevant to the real world of business. In consequence, he may not survive the tests of entry.

When leaders understand and accept the nature of human need in transition, it becomes possible for the consultant to help them built support vehicles in which to deliver the requisite transitional supplies.

Through the vehicles of support systems, needs can be met at two interrelated levels. At the *socioemotional* level, supplies meet increased needs for closeness, affection, dependency, and reassurance—the comfort that derives from being in touch. Because pain is assuaged by contact comfort, proximity to supportive others makes it possible to confront the situation that is occasioning distress. Supportive contact thus has the effect of reducing otherwise overwhelming distress to a tolerable level. Once pain becomes tolerable, *problem solving* needs can be met. With emotional needs met, and tension reduced to a working level, defenses diminish and people can move from an emotional to a *task mastery* level. They can then sharpen their understanding of their changed situation and exchange tactical plans for coping with it. There is thus, in interaction, an alternation between the socioemotional, tension-reducing level of interaction and the task-related, instrumental level.

The Transition Sequence

The availability of support systems stabilizes people and speeds them through the predictable phases of the crisis sequence that unfolds during transition. I have summarized the transition sequence as follows[16]:

> The responsible—and sensible—organization seeks to adapt to change demands so that risks are minimized and opportunities for growth are maximized. In terms of its people assets, these goals can best be achieved when managers understand that the feelings engendered by loss call for understanding and expressing them, particularly when loss of familiar competencies, disrupted attachments, and fractured identity accompany the change process. In the navigation of change, it is helpful to realize that transition has a predictable sequence of phases: A period of impact, in which the newness is assimilated, is followed by phases of recoil–turmoil, adjustment, and reconstruction.
>
> Impact produces a state of daze–shock, especially if the change event is undesired and unexpected. This assimilation phase may last for a few hours or a few days. The recoil-turmoil phase that comes next continues for one to three weeks; subsequent adjustment takes two to four weeks, but the eventual reconstruction may require many months. Time periods are, of course, subject to considerable variation. The specific duration of these phases in individual cases is influenced by determinants that include forces within the personality, such as ego strengths and coping resources; the subjective meaning of the life-change event; and the availability of external assistance.
>
> During the impact phase, a person is numbed. He is in Time Present. But as he absorbs the news of change, he is preoccupied with what has been, a world now irretrievably modified. Here, he recalls Time Past. As detaching tasks are carried out, however, he begins to explore new relationships and tests solutions to the fresh problems that confront him. Thus, his perspective moves toward Time Future.
>
> These steps are accompanied by predictable emotions. In the impact phase, a person is impelled by emergency, fight–fright–flight responses, and, entangled in them, he may seem almost "frozen." The person is disoriented and distracted. The level of apparent consciousness fluctuates; disorientation, perplexity, and impaired perception are common. In severe situational crises, a state of acute confusion may be mimicked.
>
> In the phase of recoil–turmoil, emotions may be rage, anxiety, depression, guilt and shame, openly expressed, as in weeping, or concealed behind a facade of overcontrol.
>
> When the person moves toward adjustment and reconstruction, his painful feelings become muted and are gradually tempered with some hope about the future. (p. 13–14)

In developing transitional support systems—which can be reactivated as needed—leaders are influenced to change their patterns by *evidence* that support systems are necessary and by a *rationale* for their use. Such a rationale requires that leaders be aware that their unique vantage points in the organization give them ready access to information that is not equally available to others. The positions they occupy on the decks of their organizational ships often permit leaders to scan their environments farther out in space and further ahead in time than is possible from lower decks. Consequently, the reality of what leaders perceive in their global environments and the change demands generated by these perceptions are obscured from the view of others in the organization. As environments change, subordinate resistance often stems from this information lag.

The subordinates cannot follow their leader because they do not understand, do not follow, the rationale for his behavior. Resistance can readily become schism as mutual frustration diminishes interaction, reducing opportunities to correct the misreadings of each other's behavior by the exchange of relevant information. Pluralistic ignorance then compounds the schism.

The Problem of Pluralistic Ignorance

When unsettled by what they see, leaders often fail to transmit precise information about what is in view. However, they cannot avoid emitting unsettling cues. As these unsettling cues are sensed at contact points in the organization, the news of leaders' unsettled states is transmitted and amplified through the organization. Uncertainty and anxiety then spread by group psychological contagion to become manifest in impaired productivity and disrupted morale. When change is in the air, anxiety, churning emotions, and milling rumors then abound—to the immediate and ultimate detriment of organizational adaptation. The greater the level of pluralistic ignorance—ignorance of information, plans, and sentiments—between leaders and their subordinates, the greater the likelihood of the substitutive exchange of rumors, paranoid distortion, and insurrectional sentiments.

Nonetheless, irrelevant information exchange may not be countered by *relevant* information exchange. Strategic planning may remain confined to the people on the captain's deck, the chief executive, his line generals, and staff officers. These leaders often lack the time, the inclination, or the sanction to involve their subordinates in the planning of change.

Reorganization plans tend, therefore, to be introduced in *fait accompli* fashion. When the reasons for reorganization are unknown, they cannot be *understood*. When plans are announced, the guiding criteria, rationale, and value assumptions are obscure. No vehicle may be available with which to sharpen people's appreciation of the changing situation. When people lack access to information sources that can make sense of the changes, the plan may fail to *mean* anything. If it lacks meaning, people cannot *accept* it. When new assignments descend upon them, resistance occurs and psychological defenses are mobilized. People struggle to maintain personal autonomy and to counter feelings of impotent rage. Morale, cohesion, coherence—and mastery—consequently suffer.

A Rationale for the Mastery of Change

Given the scenario I have described, a rationale for the mastery of change must encompass dimensions that include, but transcend, people's needs for relevant facts. It should be firmly grounded in the realization that people organize perceptions into widely varied structures of meaning. When the organization is unsettled, there are often startling differences in the ways in which sense is made of environmental intelligence, in the *meaning* given to it. Differences in meaning attribution interrelate with profound differences in perceptive and cognitive style and the influence upon these of value anchors.

Profound differences in *Weltanschauung* stem from man's early acquisition, in culturebound socializing institutions, of distinctive ways of organizing sensory experiences into structures of meaning. He makes sense of initially meaningless information by the schematic organization of perception into conceptual structures that frame events and give them coherence. Once established, these structures function conservatively to regulate the selective perception of sensory data in a field; data that cannot be assimilated into an existing cognitive frame may be ignored or selectively filtered. Another set of orienting frames provides members of a community with internal coherence and intergenerational continuity. The ethos of a community bonds people, providing binding structures of shared meaning and purpose. The collective ethos is incorporated as an existential value anchor that amalgamates sensory experience, fact-organizing cognitive structures, and value-anchoring judgments.

What is perceived, how it is perceived, and meaning attribution thus occur at the intersection of socioculturally coded readinesses within people's perceptual, cognitive, and value structures. This intersecting organization of percepts, meanings, values, and judgments has been called by Vickers[16] an "appreciative system." The appreciative system codes out people's appreciation of a situation and contributes to the differences encountered in what situations *mean* to people.

The implications and applications of awareness of differences in human appreciative systems in leadership and consultation emerge in the ensuing discussion of a model for the modulation of change.

A Model for the Modulation of Change

For the guidance of executives, I have formulated an explicit model that describes a process of sequential steps involved in the process of flexible adaptation to changing task environments. Figure 1 attempts to depict one loop of a three-dimensional spiral in dynamic movement. The dynamic movement stems from the fact that no contemporary organization is ever completely settled; given the lability of its environment, differentiation, reconfiguration, and directional change evolve continuously or discontinuously, in response to environmental intelligence captured by the

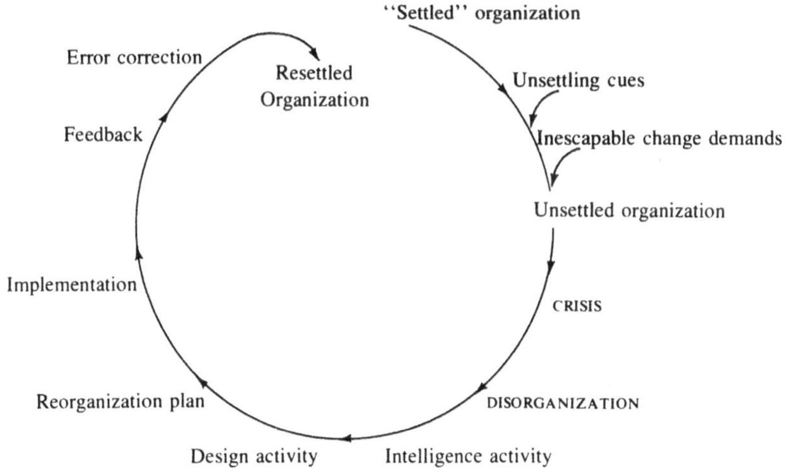

Figure 1. One loop of a three-dimensional spiral in dynamic movement in the model for modulation of changes.

organization's "sensors" located in such differentiated divisions as marketing or planning.

Figure 2, depicted, for convenience, as a linear process, also has ever-evolving organic qualities. Its steps flesh out the ideal process of interactive engagement by which the organization molds and modifies its adaptive strategies.

Figure 2 illustrates the process by which an organizational team can move from awareness of unsettling cues to the implementation of a corrective strategy. It advances through five steps: understanding, appreciation, acceptance, contracting, and commitment. The steps represent an inexorable sequence: when any step is omitted, adaptive distress will be accentuated and retracing of steps will be required.

Understanding refers to cognitive awareness of cues, clues, and facts about the unsettling environment. The unraveling and sifting of environmental information is governed by cognitive maps. When such information is profoundly unsettling, calling an organization's mission, integrity, or identity into serious question, personal value frames—ontological maps—will strongly influence the patterns of information seeking and processing. The use of different cognitive and ontological maps causes people to explore the same terrain in very different ways: much confusion is generated in the planning of change by the failure to appreciate the disagreement that stems from the use of these different maps.

Exchange of facts
↓
UNDERSTANDING
↓
Exchange of meanings
↓
APPRECIATION
↓
Exchange of planning perspectives
↓
ACCEPTANCE
↓
Negotiation of needs
↓
CONTRACTING
↓
COMMITMENT

Figure 2. Linear representation of the movement from awareness of unsettling cues to the implementation of a corrective strategy.

In introducing the principle of *acceptance*, we address a *psychological* process. The difference between understanding and acceptance is illustrated by a phrase commonly heard in times of change, "I can understand it—*but* I cannot accept it." Acceptance is a process that unfolds as people actively come to terms with loss and change. When acceptance occurs, its polar opposite, denial, diminishes. The goal of acceptance is reached by successful passage through a period of transitional crisis punctuated by turmoil and disruption. While *complete* acceptance, with detachment from past objects and reconstruction of new attachments, can occur only after total immersion in the new situation, a high level of prior acceptance can be achieved by anticipatory preparation; evocation of what lies ahead encourages prior detachment from the familiar objects to be relinquished.*

As future team members explore preliminary expectations, *contracting* is possible. *Contracting* is not used here in a mechanical or legal sense: it refers to Levinson's[12] "psychological contract." The psychological contract was a construct devised by Levinson and his associates to interpret "emotional health in the world of work." When people's legitimate needs for dependency, affection, and coping support (all of which are greatly magnified in transition) are contractually met, *commitment* occurs.

Discussion of the Model

The steps suggested here are often resisted because they are time-consuming. The process is also often ego-alien to the action-oriented executive whose image of self is that of a doer. (This orientation is reflected in the commonest question put to a consultant: What should be *done?*) The process of interactive engagement is emotionally exhausting and the action-oriented leader may readily lose patience with it. He often needs considerable support—and sometimes auxiliary help—to sustain the process.

While the process is most fatiguing for leaders when first embarked upon, its revitalizing efforts usually become so rapidly apparent that leaders are encouraged to continue. As a leader practices the process, he becomes more skilled and can lead his people through subsequent process steps with greater ease. Also, the leader comes to appreciate the psychic

*The analogous process of anticipatory mourning has been described prior to the death of loved ones known to be dying from fatal illness. See, for example, the work of Chodoff, Friedman, and Hamburg.[2]

economy of engaging his people in change processes *before* reorganization occurs rather than *after*.*

The model presented here is an ideal type. In times of survival emergency, its application is impractical. When a new leader inherits an organization significant components of which have succumbed to malignant obsolescence, the leader may have to make decisions about people that will never be appreciated or accepted. The model best fits situations of potential consensus. It is not a model for situations of irreconcilable dissensus; for these, mediative processes are required.

For many members of an organization, conservative impulses may be so tenacious that participation in radical change may be precluded. In such a situation, attempts are best made to mesh people with high psychological needs for stability to positions in subsystems where the prospects of continuity are highest.

Finally, the model is descriptive and heuristic rather than prescriptive. Its flexible application requires consideration of such factors as the organization's norms, its emotional climate, and the leader's stomach for interaction.

The model can also be used to illuminate the implicit processes operative in some classical contributions to the literature of organization psychology. For example, Coch and French's[3] study on "overcoming the resistance to change" described the value of "group meetings in which management effectively communicates the need for change and stimulates group participation in planning the changes."

Applications of this model to the practice of consultation are explored in the next chapter.

References

1. Carlson E. E. "Visible Management" at United Airlines, interview with Edward E. Carlson, *Harvard Business Review*, 1975, *53* (4), 90–97.
2. Chodoff, P., Friedman, S. and Hamburg, D. Stress, defenses and coping behavior: Observations in parents and children with malignant disease. *American Journal of Psychiatry*, 1964, *120*, 743–749.
3. Coch, L., and French, J. R. P. Overcoming resistance to change. *Human Relations*, 1948, *1*, 512–532.
4. Drucker, P. F. *Management*. New York: Harper and Row, 1973.
5. Egbert, L. D., Battit, G. E., Welch, C. E., and Bartlett, M. K. Reduction of post-operative pain by encouragement and instruction of patients. *New England Journal of Medicine*, 1964, *270*, 825–827.

*This process has long been practiced by Japanese leaders. See Drucker.[4]

6. Emery, F. E., and Trist, E. L. The causal texture of organizational environments. *Human Relations*, 1965, *18*, 21–31.
7. Fried, M. Grieving for a lost home. In L. Duhl (Ed.), *The urban condition*. New York: Basic Books, 1963. Pp. 151–171.
8. Hirschowitz, R. G. An attempt to delineate the field of community psychiatry. *Hospital and Community Psychiatry*, 1970, *21*(7), 209–212.
9. Hirschowitz, R. G. Community mental health and the community physician. *Current Medical Dialog*, 1972, *39*(7), 726–734.
10. Hirschowitz, R. G. Crisis theory: A formulation. *Psychiatric Annals*, 1973, *3*, 33–49.
11. Hirschowitz, R. G. The human aspects of managing transition. *Personnel*, 1974, *51*, 8–17.
12. Levinson, H., Price, C. R., Munden, K. J., Manell, H. J., and Solley, C. M. *Men, management and mental health*. Cambridge, Mass.: Harvard University Press, 1962.
13. Lodge, G. C. Business and the changing society. *Harvard Business Review*, 1974, *52* (2), 59–65.
14. Marris, P. *Loss and change*. New York: Pantheon, 1970.
15. Toffler, A. *The eco-spasm report*. New York: Bantam, 1975.
16. Vickers, G. *Value systems and social process*. London: Tavistock, 1968.
17. Warren, R. L. Citizen participation and community mental health centers. In R. G. Hirschowitz and B. Levy, (Eds.), *The Changing mental health scene*. New York: Spectrum, 1976.
18. Wolff, H. G. *Journal of the American Medical Association*, 1969, *209*, 1082–1083.
19. Yankelovich, D. *The new morality: A profile of American youth in the 70's*. New York: McGraw-Hill, 1974.

11

Consultation to Complex Organizations in Transition

The Practical Techniques of Consultation

RALPH G. HIRSCHOWITZ

The previous chapter described ways in which contemporary complex organizations manage—and mismanage—the tasks of transition. In these organizations, the leader struggles to reconcile role demands that are often inherently at odds. When aware that the organization is losing its competitive edge, the leader must unsteady the organization by confronting its people with the reality of inescapable change demands. He must also ensure that stabilizers are provided to steady the organization as it changes course. Principles have been established to guide the leader—and his consultant—in processes that can balance these unsteadying and steadying roles. I have argued that motivation during change is sustained when people *understand* the change imperatives facing the organization, *appreciate* their meaning, *accept* their implications, participate in response strategies, and have some freedom to *negotiate* aspects of their roles in the

RALPH G. HIRSCHOWITZ · Assistant Professor of Psychiatry, Harvard Medical School.

changing structure. Appropriate strategies for adaptive action are derived from careful psychological cost accounting.

A model for the modulation of change has been developed from the psychological experience of people coping with the tasks of organizational change, and a rationale has been provided for the adaptive planning of transition.

The principles and processes described in the previous chapter are applied in this chapter to the *practice* of consultation to complex organizations in transition. An orderly process of consultation to complex organizations in transition is delineated. The complexity of organizations, the differences in their evolution, the multiplicity of their environments, and the variance in their salient issues demand that this process be flexibly interpreted and applied. Consultation processes are tailored to the differentiated realities of organizations, their norms and values, and their readiness to engage in self-scrutiny.

The Phases of Consultation

While phases overlap and telescope, an orderly sequence can be discerned. The phases are preliminary contact, exploratory reconnaissance, and organic consultation.

Phase One: Preliminary Contact

Preliminary contacts vary. Someone may be seriously seeking consultation for himself and his team; he may be empowered to commit resources; he may be well informed about the consultant and his distinctive competencies. Someone else may be seeking help for some other person in his organization; he may have no mandate to represent the other or authority to purchase consultation; his knowledge of the consultant may be limited and his expectations magical.

After preliminary contact, therefore, the consultant needs precise information about the help being sought—and the seeker. He might need answers to such questions as: What previous help has been sought or given? What help is being sought now, why now, and why from him? He screens the information received to decide whether interest is serious and whether it merges with his capacities and interests. If mutual interest is high and consultation is likely to be feasible, preliminary contacts made by telephone or letter are followed by face-to-face meetings with the organization's sanctioning authorities. In continuing exploration, any declaration of consultant interest is accompanied by information about his available commitment, fees, consultant approach, and suggested next steps.

In his exploration, the consultant pursues the issue of fit. From his point of view, will he fit the organization, its style and values sufficiently to do the work required—and sustain his integrity? Does he have the competencies and motivation to respond to its needs? From the organization's point of view, he helps prospective consultees understand what he has—and does not have—to offer, what rules he operates by, and what his conception of consultation is. Often, organizations have a "doctor, tell me" expectation that the consultant will diagnose all their problems and prescribe quick-fix solutions. If the complexity of any particular consultation situation precludes this prescriptive approach, the consultant does not offer promissory notes that he will not be able to meet.

The consultant indicates the limitations of what he may be able to offer, advising that he may be identifying problems for which elegant or quick solutions may not be available. His stance is that he enters to diagnose; he cannot enter with prior knowledge of what he can offer the consultee organization. In a complex organization, his stance is often that of asking an organization to invest time and money so that he can enter the organization to gather enough additional information to assess where and how—and if—he can be helpful.

The effective consultant develops a repertoire of testing and screening interventions that guide him in deciding when to pursue preliminary contacts—and for how long. Without screening principles, considerable time may be wasted in random exploration. An example of such wasted exploration follows.

> The director of a state hospital met the consultant in a training program in which the consultant lectured. After the lecture, the director explored the possibility of consultation. Since this was a coffee break, the consultant had little time to do much more than indicate interest. Subsequently, the director wrote to the consultant. The consultant called the director to find out what the consultant issues were. The director had difficulty defining the problems for which help was being sought. The consultant then suggested that he visit the hospital, interview key people, and report his diagnostic impressions. However, he neglected at this stage to explore fees. In discussing his reasons for not talking business, he said that he took it for granted that the director would pay an appropriate consultant fee. In a later discussion, he discovered that no payment for services was contemplated. When this was finally broached, he learned that the medical director required superordinate authority to hire him as a consultant; were such authority granted, the con-

sultant fees that could be authorized were lower than his going rates. Had he explored this question earlier, much time could have been saved.

The fledgling consultant, like some human services professionals who seek consultation, often suffers from the "myth of dirty hands." Growth—and reality testing—is fostered when business is talked early, clearly, and crisply.

Preliminary contact, in summary, is pursued until the consultant has determined whether or not the consultation is of interest to him—and whether a service contract is feasible; in the above case, the consultant should also have given the organization's representatives enough information for them to make a similar determination.

Phase Two: Exploratory Reconnaissance

When the phase of preliminary contact encourages the consultant to predict that a mutually productive relationship is likely, he establishes a reconnaissance contract to explore the organization's needs. He asks for orienting materials such as annual reports, company newsletters, and the minutes of recent meetings. He specifies how much time he will need for exploratory assessment and undertakes to report his preliminary diagnostic impressions by a defined date. As the consultant moves from preliminary contact behind the scenes to formal on stage meetings with organizational informants (and with prospective consultees), exploratory reconnaissance begins.

In negotiating his formal entry, the consultant is wise to be formally introduced to members of the organization. This is often best done in formal meetings so that his credentials and intent—and the intent of the consultation brokers—can be clarified. In the absence of such clear communication about the reasons for his presence, exaggerated distrust and suspicion is likely.

Entry. The mental health consultant entering a complex organization is like an anthropologist entering a strange territory. If he is to be effective in his ultimate consultation objectives, the consultant must prepare and present himself so that he gains acceptance. While acceptance is his ultimate goal, his immediate task, like that of the anthropologist, is to avoid exclusion. Each therefore arms himself with information about local language and folkways. He also buttresses himself by building relationships with people who are potential introducers and translators to interpret local nuances of custom and language. The organizational consultant is wise to establish a prior relationship with at least one person who is strategically placed to play this interpretative role. Often, the personnel director plays the role and is easily sanctioned in it. It is usually wise for the consultant to develop an informal ad hoc committee of representative key people who can help him interpret his data and with whom he can test his diagnostic formulations.

With consultees, the consultant clarifies that *sources* of information will not be identified in the formulation of organizational diagnoses. He unambiguously declines such proferred roles as company spy, message broker, or advocate. He should anticipate a variety of tests by the consultees.

The Tasks of Exploratory Reconnaissance. In exploratory reconnaissance, the consultant has formal *diagnostic* tasks and informal *process* tasks. His diagnostic tasks are often contractually defined as assessment of the organization's salient problems with recommendations for their solution.

His process tasks are less visible: in order to discharge his formal task, he must build relationships and establish sanctioned beachheads for continuing involvement. He negotiates sanctions for continuing involvement by anticipating—and passing—repeated tests. These are intensified whenever he presents his credentials at some new organizational gateway.

In his first encounters, the consultant explores who in the organization is distressed, in what way, and why. He gathers information about the organization's history, style, present adaptive struggles, and orientation to the future.

In searching for symptoms and signs of adaptive distress, the consultant guards against glib agreement with informants' diagnostic statements. The organization is viewed internally from the positions people occupy. Their perceptions are thus colored by both *positional* and *psychological* screens. Psychological screens are often colored by emotions that surge during transition. In defending themselves against such emotions as rage and depression, people often reduce complex situations to preparanoid formulations about the malign motives of influentials in the organization. In attempting to maintain a spurious sense of cognitive mastery, they reduce multifactorial behavioral problems to simple "bad guys and good guys" formulations. Symptoms defined by consultees at one interface may therefore signify strain at any or many of the organization's other interfaces: between organization and external environment, between divisions, between people, between hierarchical generations, and so on. The entire organization may be fighting a rearguard action, holding on to familiar but obsolete ways of doing business; the system may be aware of change imperatives, but it may be paralyzed or sluggish in its response. Symptoms may be consequent upon impulsive, haphazard attempts to adapt. Stated problems may conceal a whirring, blurring, running, jumping, and standing still mode of frenzied crisis management. Such social and psychological defenses against anxiety as massive denial, rationalization, projection, or displacement must all be taken into account in the interpretation of informants' testimony.

Assessing Consultee Commitment. During the phase of reconnaissance, the consultant monitors—and strives to sustain—the leaders' commitment to consultation. Most leaders are oriented to action, not reflection; when an attack upon their problems is not foreshadowed by the consultant, they become impatient for action. Also, recruitment of a consultant is often in response to the heightened suggestibility and dependency of crisis. Unless the consultant capitalizes upon this temporary leverage by meeting frequently with the leader, the leader's impulsive need to act may cause him to apply some symptomatic bandaid to areas where distress has surfaced. While symptom removal reflects crisis management (removing the symptom, but not the underlying problem), the leader, who thinks he has solved his problem by extinguishing a brushfire, may have no awareness that he moves from brushfire to brushfire; his immediate crisis abated, he may have little motivation to explore the ashes of abating fires or learn how to prevent future ones. As the heat of his own crisis emotions diminishes, his enthusiasm for consultation cools.

It behooves the consultant who is aware of a leader's action-oriented propensities to maintain the closest possible proximity to a leader in crisis; he should seize frequent opportunities to drop in. In talking, he provides crisis consultation without the leader's asking for it (or sometimes without knowing that he has received it). By providing presence, reassurance, and support, the consultant can curb the exuberances of crisis management and model reflective planning. He can maintain a fluid situation "open" by focusing the leader's attention on relevant areas of the social field missing from his immediate vision. He helps the leader to *plan* action. Against a confident diagnosis of reality, strains toward anxiety reduction by premature closure are reduced when an ego-sustaining alliance is rapidly forged. In crisis situations, the consultant, like the clinical crisis counselor, infuses calm, cool, and auxiliary ego support.

Exploratory Reconnaissance: Reporting Back. When he reports on the organization's most salient problems, the consultant may have to recommend that more precise diagnostic exploration be continued in concert with the organization's leaders. When leaders are patently out of touch with influential constituents, a combination of survey research and structured meetings for upward feedback may be a required next step. This is illustrated by a case vignette.

> Consultation was requested by the administrator of a psychiatric hospital to explore problems of declining referral. Consultation disclosed that the declining referrals substantially stemmed from failure to maintain interactive dialogue with referring physicians. These physicians reported that they were treated in summary fashion by the hospital gatekeepers and that continuity was poorly sustained. Further exploration revealed that the social workers who were responsible for external communication were demoralized by recent policy and personnel decisions. A new medical director was perceived as depreciating them by reducing previously entrenched positions of influence in the hospital hierarchy. They had lost out in salary negotiations and felt unable to influence recent administration decisions that increased the status of hospital physicians—but diminished theirs. Because they were impotent to negotiate upward in the organization, their frustration had been unconsciously directed to available displacement targets, the referring physicians.
>
> The consultant recommended focused questionnaire surveys of the referring physicians and hospital staff, following by his help with interpretation and discussion of the issues that emerged. Corrective action required the repair of communication bridges and the restoration of eroded equity. Eventually, some of the social workers' grievances were resolved and new understandings established. Simultaneously, representative referring physicians were included with representatives of the hospital staff on a policy advisory board.

When the consultant reports back to the organization's leaders, he formulates his diagnostic assessment, presents evidence of adaptive problems, and recommends possible courses of action. For example, when problems stem from substantial gaps in knowledge of the psychological dimensions of leadership and motivation, the consultant may recommend training programs as well as consultation.

The exploratory phase of consultation may end with a consultant's report or be followed by a new contract for continuing services. When this occurs, the contractual intent, content, and implications should be clearly understood by the contracting parties and the people in the organization. The consultant should know what will be communicated about his continuing presence and should anticipate with the leaders the questions that are likely to ensue. The consultant's continuing presence often needs to be discussed in meetings with managers in, and across, all divisions likely to be affected by consultation. In the absence of meetings at all relevant levels, misreadings and paranoid interpretations are likely.

Phase Three: Organic Consultation

The stage is now set for the third phase: organic consultation. Where the primary goal of reconnaissance has been the *diagnosis* of problems, organic consultation's goals are their *resolution*. The organic consultant assists the organization's leaders to refine diagnostic issues and develop corrective strategies. The essence of organic consultation is the catalytic involvement of the organization's people in the *ownership* of their internal problem-solving process.

With movement into the organic consultation phase, tests of the consultant's motivation, values, and objectives will be renewed. People who had tolerated him as yet another consultant passing through may now display behavior that ranges from reverence to suspicion. The consultant will be tested by what he does as much as by what he says. Tested anew, he is wise to answer questions about his presence with candor. He freely discusses the ends he pursues and the sanctions he has established, clarifying what he intends to do—and *not* to do. By his words and behavior, he indicates that he will not play such roles as judge, policeman, rescuer, or therapist.

A consultant who is by profession a psychiatrist or a clinical psychologist may need to emphasize that his purpose is to improve the *organization's* adaptive performance; he is not there to diagnose or recommend treatment for individual psychiatric problems.

Sanctions and Sanction Maintenance. Organic consultation may require intensive delving by the consultant into the organization's operations. His role boundaries and constraints should therefore be unambiguously negotiated—and clearly communicated. Consultees will be uneasy unless they know where the consultant is sanctioned to probe and what he is sanctioned to do—and what they are sanctioned to share with him. Sanction and sanction maintenance is intrinsic to the professional consultation process and should be rigorously addressed. The consultant establishes contractual sanctions with the organization's chief executives, ensures that the sanction is passed to other levels, and negotiates extension of sanctions when they are needed.

What Does the Organic Consultant Do? In organic consultation, the instrumental and socioemotional demands upon the consultant intensify. In his instrumental role, he focuses upon people's performance of their tasks and their relationships with one another. He scans for strains at the interfaces between people and groups and identifies the characteristic patterns of coping with conflict and anxiety. Examination of their behavior is threatening to consultees. In the course of organic consultation, feedback is promoted and suppressed conflicts surface. These acts generate tension that is exacerbated by the fact that problem awareness places demands for new behavior upon the consultees. As consultees are compelled to relinquish sustaining illusions about themselves, the consultant will experience the emotional backwash of the loss experience to which his intervention contributes. The consultant's relationship with consultees is thus imperiled whenever the consultant's acts influence—or are likely to influence—changes in structure, policy, or practice. Task-directed acts that threaten change must therefore be counterbalanced by socioemotional acts that clarify intent, reduce tension, restore confidence, and replenish reserves of eroded equity.

The process of consultation is dialectical, oscillating between acts that promote change and acts that stabilize, restore cohesion, and renew sanctions for continuance.

The consultant's behavior is perforce delicately responsive to perceived differences in consultees' flexibility, motivation, and personal styles as he harmonizes the balance between interventions that spur change and those that promote coherence and sustain continuity.

When significant changes are under consideration, the consultant stimulates a process of *planning* followed by *action*, followed—and therefore logically preceded—by *reflection* and *analysis*. He enters this process at any needed point in the cycle. Given the orientation toward *action* of most executives, his behavior is often weighted to strengthen the practice of reflection, analysis, and planning.

Techniques. A *technique* is defined by the Oxford English Dictionary as "an artistic manner of execution or performance." However, too exquisite a focus upon technical artistry may obscure the pragmatic reality that techniques are tested—and best evaluated—by their adaptive outcomes, not their elegance. An adequate repertoire of technical interventions to draw upon is, simply, a necessary but insufficient condition for consultant effectiveness. Techniques, like surgical procedures, may be applied with random impulsivity; brilliance of technique must be adequately complemented by overall competence in organizational diagnosis. The consultant, like the executive, may be propelled by a need to sustain the illusion of role competency and potency by premature resort to technical action. The effective technical intervention follows a firm diagnostic grasp of the multiple, intersecting processes operative in a consultant's situation. Until these are adequately assessed, the consultant endures the psychological burden of ambiguity and anxiety inherent in every consultation.

Evaluation. Discussion of *what* the consultant does and *how* becomes a hollow exercise unless it is cast within a frame encompassing such questions as: In response to what? With what ends in mind? Evaluation of acts isolated and analyzed bereft of goals and context, space and time, is unproductive. Analysis of acts requires a temporal context because evaluation is confounded by difficulty in comprehending why some interventions work when they do and fail to work when they do not. A technique that flops or plops at one point in the evolution of a consultant relationship in one organization may prove effective at the same evolutionary point in another organization—or at a later point in the same organization.

For evaluation, learning, and teaching, my preference is to cast the question "What does the consultant do?" in an open systems framework that interrelates the consultant's technical acts with *primary targets,* target *fields of concern,* intervention *vehicles,* and *salient issues.* These interrelationships are illustrated in the next case study.

> In consultation to an organizational team, the consultant decided that the initial problem presented to him was the reductionist simplification of a much more complex package of problems. As presented, the problem was declared to be the personality pathology of an organizational team member who was described as an abrasive troublemaker. As evidence accumulated, it became apparent that this team member was expressing feelings that other members of the team were repressing—and surfacing questions that others preferred to avoid. His questions consequently detonated repressed emotions, especially fury toward the team's leader. During months of prior organizational turbulence, the leader had often been physically absent from the organization and, when present, was psychologically unavailable. While struggling to maintain psychological equilibrium under conditions of considerable uncertainty, team members' legitimate needs for information, support, and guidance had been inadequately met. The leader's absence had been experienced as abandonment and had triggered emotions of aggrievement. When the "abrasive" team member came on strong, the intensity of his feelings rasped upon their own, disrupting their psychological defenses and bringing their own emotions close to dangerous awareness. The feelings of anger that did surface were displaced on to the "troublemaker."
>
> The salient issue here was not therefore the personality of the "troublemaker" but family pain. In an eventual climate of psychological safety, emotions were interpreted and given legitimacy. Team members were then able to articulate feelings about past deprivation. As the diagnostic scenario unfolded, it became clear that the *primary target* for corrective action was the

leader; the immediate *field of concern* was his executive team, the organizational family. The consultant interviewed the leader and each team member, rehearsing them for eventual family meetings in which shared issues were addressed. The primary *vehicles* were structured meetings with the leader and the team. The *salient issues* crystallized around abandonment and deprivation. The consultant rehearsed with the leader so that he could accept their aggrieved feelings nondefensively. In the meetings, he interpreted relevant psychological and group processes. The consultant's *acts* included *socio-emotional acts* of acceptance, support, and legitimation; *educational acts* to make sense of recent behavior; *administrative acts,* building and maintaining retreat structures for interaction; and *analytic, interpretive* acts during team confrontation of salient issues. His behavioral acts thus aggregated to reduce pluralistic ignorance on the team, enhance psychological understanding, stimulate mastery of interpersonal problems, and establish new psychological contracts.

This case vignette illustrates how the organic consultant's diagnostic scanning requires spanning of the boundaries of interdependent fields. His scanning gradually sharpens to focus upon primary targets, relevant fields of concern, and salient issues. In a field of any complexity, there is usually no dearth of targets and issues. In determining target feasibility and issue saliency, he *acts* as, and when, transitional disequilibrium creates leverage opportunities.

With this perspective upon acts as integrally related to targets, fields, vehicles, and issues, some illustrative acts in the consultant's repertoire of interventions can be discussed. They are classified as:

1. *Tension-reducing acts.* Consultee and consultant encounter one another as strangers, unfamiliar with each other's language and values. In discussing problems, consultees are often defensive, fearing the consultant's criticism or judgment. Defenses and defensive communication are often magnified during the disequilibrium of critical transition. The consultant acts, therefore, to reduce defensive communication with messages, verbal and nonverbal, that are supportive, acceptant, and revealing. He may inject humor and legitimate respites of rest and recreation.

2. *Information-seeking acts.* The consultant's probing questions are designed to help consultees approach their problems from new vantage points. The consultant's questions serve to clarify for the consultee to what extent his difficulties stem from *logical* deficits such as information lack or overload, difficulty in conceptualizing, or poverty of solutions. More often, *psychological* obstacles to objective evaluation have to be weighed. Psychological difficulties may be associated with disrupted self-confidence or emotionally charged themes that obscure the consultee's perceptual or

cognitive operations. Once the source of the consultee's problem-solving difficulties is located, the consultant designs his interventions to help the consultee improve his logical operations or repair his psychological operations. Psychological needs are addressed by such techniques as nonspecific ego support or theme interference reduction.

3. *Analysis-promoting acts*. When the consultee is immersed in an overabundance of data, the consultant's presence and questions serve to help the consultee step back to a point of objective vantage from which he can abstract sense and meaning from his data. The consultant helps to establish connections, generate exploratory hunches, or loosen rigidities in the consultee's cognitive frame. When the consultee is jumping to premature conclusions, the consultant maintains exploratory openness by posing relevant analytic or evaluative questions. More rarely, with obsessive consultees whose analysis has been adequate but whose decision dither contributes to postmature nonclosure, the consultant acts to confirm ripeness for decision. (Both postmature nonclosure and premature closure are common in crisis, since psychological disequilibrium intensifies decision avoidance in consultees who are obsessive or lack self-confidence, and spurs impulsive decisions in action-oriented "busy" consultees.)

4. *Solution-seeking acts*. When a consultee is exploring alternatives for action upon a complex problem, the consultant frames questions to ensure that the consultee has a model and criteria for decision. He helps the consultee explore the likely consequence of alternative solutions. His questions and comments are designed to help the consultee predict and weight the likely human costs of alternative solutions in all the areas likely to be affected by them. By the facilitation of psychological cost accounting, solutions are then cast in a risk-choice decision frame.

5. *Value-crystallizing acts*. In reorganization, when fundamental questions of motivation arise, the consultant's exploratory questions focus on issues of value and ideology. By ensuring that employees' values are surveyed, he refines the calculus by which consultees predict the impact of possible decisions upon morale and commitment.

6. *Educative acts*. As the tasks of complex organizations in transition grow, the consultant may discover that difficulties in problem resolution stem from consultees' lack of the requisite knowledge or skills. The consultant may provide relevant information, offer ad hoc instruction, link the consultee to learning resources, or stimulate the development of in-service training programs.

7. *Conflict-resolving acts*. When fight–flight emotions escalate during transition, the consultant may help leaders analyze the sources of conflict and explore tactics for conflict resolution.

8. *Encouraging acts*. When the consultee seeks to change such common patterned behavior as habitual conflict avoidance, the consultant can encourage the consultee to break set by anticipatory rehearsal. Preparatory evocations of potentially tense situations provide emotional prophylaxis against the feared consequences of confrontation.

9. *Prescriptive acts*. A common posture of the consultee is "What should I do?" At times, the consultant may be compelled to respond with a behavioral prescription. He does so when the consultee is overwhelmed or paralyzed or has no action possibilities in his own repertoire. Where he is legitimately in the role of expert who has technical expertise that his consultees are entitled to draw upon, he makes specific suggestions. The consultant may also choose to prescribe—or proscribe—action in an emergency crisis conflict when the consultee is hell-bent upon a course of action fraught with unseen danger for him and his people. Red-light signaling by the consultant is then appropriate. He warns against action and gives clear reasons. While cautionary intervention of this kind can place a consultation relationship in some jeopardy, eventual appreciation for the consultant's stance may nonetheless ensue. The consultant is strategically placed to take risks that salaried employees may fear to take in the prevention of decision disasters.

This list has been introduced to suggest some examples and tentative categories of consultant intervention acts. No claim to inclusivity or exclusivity is made and categories overlap with some arbitrariness. In the process of consultation, acts are purposively sequenced to carry the consultee through the successive problem-solving steps of information gathering, systhesis, problem definition, solution seeking, risk analysis, and solution choice.

This description of intervention acts has emphasized the instrumental, task-related acts of consultation. These are complemented by socioemotional acts that maintain the consultant relationship, relieve distress, reflect concern, provide support, and sustain self-esteem.

In the field, acts of consultant intervention merge and blend in flexible strategic response to the demands of present and future, issues of immediate and ultimate saliency, and situational feasibility.

The Prescriptive Consultation Dilemma

Organic consultation includes, but transcends, prescriptive consultation. Prescriptive consultation follows a clinical paradigm: the doctor diagnoses and prescribes for a patient who is rewarded for his patience by being told what to do. Organic consultation's paradigm is one of interactive education. It pursues the goals of consultee development by catalyzing processes of active consultee involvement in self-scrutiny and diagnosis. Its ultimate goal is that consultees generate and eventually *own* their solutions. Pure prescriptive consultation accepts the dependence of consultee upon consultant; organic consultation's ultimate objective is the consultee's growth and independence of his consultant.

Since organic consultation is a development process realized through growth in consultees' generic capacity to solve adaptive problems, the consultant ensures that adequate time is allocated for the consultee to sharpen his understanding of the problems he presents. By raising questions that clarify problem boundaries and dimensions, the consultant promotes consultee ownership of problem analyses. The process helps consultees weigh and choose solutions, translate them into action plans, and follow action with subsequent outcome analysis. In the evolving, unfolding course of consultation, the norms of the process and the roles within it are gradually stabilized. Once the consultee plays a coordinate role in problem solving, he is as likely to resent the consultant's taking over of a problem as he is to expect it in his initial encounters. A dilemma thus emerges *early* in consultation. Unless *some* prescribing is done early in consultation, the consultant may lose his consultee. As the consultation relationship matures and prescriptive expectations diminish, the relationship may be threatened by another horn of the dilemma, overprescribing.

The consultant's early failure to respond to a prescriptive request is likely to be received by consultees as capricious, depriving behavior. When a consultee has problems of pressing immediacy, the consultant is therefore wise to defer to a consultee's preference for prescriptive consultation. By meeting a consultee on the consultee's terms, the consultant builds a base from which organic consultation can later evolve.

Failure to prescribe may be particularly prejudicial to consultant relationships where consultees are embattled in acute or recurrent transitional crises. Heightened dependency needs, turbulent emotions, and battle fatigue may occasion a legitimate need for the consultant to offer authoritative guidance for action.

A particularly vexing problem may demand prescriptive attention when leaders defend against awareness of their people's distress by moving out of reach. Some leaders insulate themselves against bad news by avoiding subordinates during transitional turbulence. Leaders may respond to emotional early-warning signs with subjective dyscontrol, which is compensated for by hypercontrol of their environment. This control effectively gags their subordinates. In the first case, the leader insulates himself from relevant psychological input; in the second, the leader's control suppresses corrective upward feedback. In such situations, the consultant may be compelled to call plans into question, present essential data, or promote upward feedback by techniques of survey research or structured interaction. When decisions have disaster potential, he may risk invasion of the leader's domain by warning against the decisions.

Authoritative assurance is a technical intervention that overlaps the boundaries of organic and prescriptive consultation. A consultee poised on the brink of an important decision may need the consultant's sapiential authority for assurance that his perceptions, cognition, and planning are realistic. This is commonly the case when decisions are risky, when consultees are obsessive, or when self-confidence is shaky. The consultant's authoritative assurance can appropriately speed a decision in such circumstances.

The Effective and the Popular

Because prescriptive consultation, while popular, has limited effectiveness, consumer satisfaction does not suffice to evaluate a consultant's effectiveness. Despite its popularity, prescriptive consultation lacks the long-term developmental thrust of organic consultation. The slow, deliberate sharpening of issues in organic consultation refines consultees' problem-solving skills, increases their knowledge, sharpens their understanding of process, and strengthens confidence. Forces that cloud perception, impair cognition, or paralyze action diminsh as coping strengths increase. The goal of effective consultation is growth in the consultee's knowledge, objectivity, and adaptive mastery. The solution of a specific problem is a means toward the larger end. Evaluation should therefore assess the extent of growth in consultee competencies.

Organic consultation is uniquely useful for correction of problems of consultee objectivity, the understanding and mastery of affects, the working through of conflicts, and the mobilization of corporate and personal confidence. It is also an exceptional vehicle for the identification and unraveling of emotion-laden themes that impair understanding or paralyze volition.

When the consultant relies exclusively upon techniques of prescriptive consultation, he increases the likelihood of undue dependency upon him. If the consultee is unable to generalize from one problem situation to another, eventual disappointment, impotence, and ambivalence may dilute the consultee's dependency gratification. Prescriptive techniques are thus to be regarded as useful relationship-building tools but limited growth-promoting tools in the organic consultant's armamentarium.

In the early negotiation of his contract, it may be wise for the consultant to stress his commitment to helping consultees work at their problems and own their decisions. This safeguards against later perceived contractual violation by consultees whose expectations of the consultant were prescriptive. Without preliminary sensitization, they may become deeply resentful of the Socratic style of a consultant who appears to be declining *his* task responsibility while expecting *them* to do the work for which they assumed the consultant to be hired. Their outrage at perceived violation of contract intensifies if the consultant is thought to be playing psychiatrist by countering questions with questions. The consultee's resentment of a role for which he has not contracted is best countered by clarification and renegotiation of the consultant contract.

Despite his commitment to organic consultation, the consultant may find himself repetitively prescribing for consultees because they lack the analytic competencies to prescribe on their own behalf. When this occurs because many consultees' conceptual grasp of psychological and adaptive processes is limited, the consultant alerts the organization to the need for crash training programs.

While pure prescriptive consultation lacks long-range developmental payoff, it is popular and eases the entry of the consultant. Consultees rarely share the organic consultant's concern that direct advice can lead to the mastery of only a specific problem. Advice gratifies the immediate felt needs of a consultee for whom development of *generic* problem-solving skills is, at best, a remote goal. Prescriptive consultation provides immediate relief.

The consultees' expectation of immediate relief is not the only reason to practice prescriptive consultation. Prescriptive consultation *is* always appropriate when knowledge of the psychological experience of transition is scanty and skills in easing transitional distress unknown or untried. Where consultees lack lexicons, concepts, or skills, the consultant's thoughtful evaluation of a situation can help to repair these deficits. When consultees have a limited action repertoire upon which to draw, the consultant can multiply the range of possibilities by listing tactics known to have been effectively used in other organizations.

The consultant thus alternates between playing the role of the expert by prescriptive consultation and transferring his expertise by organic consultation's interactive problem-solving with his consultees. The evolution of consultation is from early, heavy reliance upon prescriptive consultation to more organic consultation.

The Modulation of Change: Accents and Emphases

When the consultant encounters crisis disruption associated with actual or anticipated transition, his consultation ideally guides leaders to an appreciation of:

1. What are the organization's adaptive tasks and the associated hazards or opportunites for its people.
2. How to design the human environment in which transition is imminent so that dangers are reduced and adaptive opportunities maximized.
3. How to enhance people's coping capacities by involvement, preparation, or training before and during the transition.

In the introduction of this guiding frame of reference, the consultant is in the role of expert. Given the pragmatic orientation of business leaders, he is wise to buttress his position with evidence that the adequate preplanning of change strategies, meeting needs for involvement, support, and guidance, is in the organization's self-interest.

The Leader as Modulator of Change: The Consultant's Role

As organizational environments become volatile, leaders are pulled into two directions; the external environment demands proaction while, simultaneously, internal environmental turmoil demands interaction. When survival needs compel the leader to direct his energy and attention to external adaptive tasks, he cannot simultaneously sustain adequate internal interactivity. In such a situation, the consultant can help the leader and his people by ensuring that unmet internal needs are recognized. When the leader is unable to sustain his people's interactive needs, he may choose to delegate some interactive tasks to a trusted in-house deputy. A division of leadership labor is adaptively struck by a complementary alliance between an externally oriented Number One leader and a Number Two who acts as an internal communications center, interacting freely and frequently with members of the organization.

The consultant whose relationship with leaders has been confidently consolidated plays a particularly vital role as the leaders' support system through times of escalating change. This places a responsibility upon the consultant to increase his availability to leaders at times of adaptive pressure. The consultant provides an oasis of time out for the harried leader to take stock, assess needs, and plan responses. In frequent meetings with the leader, the consultant ensures that the leader is clarifying for his people the rationale for corporate decisions about change. In the course of such unfolding discussion, the consultant helps the leader identify what aspects of a proposed reorganization are open to negotiation—and what are not. He thus provides the leader with an opportunity to rehearse what he will be *telling* his people and what it is that he will be *asking* of them. In rehearsal, they anticipate what the likely responses of his people are going to be to the unsettling news of change—and what his responses will be. This process of contingency rehearsal increases the likelihood that the leader will be able to regulate the emotional climate of potentially tense meetings and behave nondefensively. It is sometimes helpful for the consultant to share the process leadership in such meetings; when he does so, the division of labor between leaders and consultant should be scrupulously negotiated so that the consultant does not invade the leaders' domain.

Application of the Model for the Modulation of Change

As an organization embarks upon the tasks of transition, the model for modulating change* can provide leaders with authoritative guidance on the *process* steps to be taken. The model is initially applied by an exploration of the flow of unsettling information to relevant sectors of the organization. When relevant information flow is restricted or distorted, the consultant encourages interactive engagement so that people can make sense of the change and exercise some control over their changing lives.

During the stress of imminent or actual transition, the consultant increases proximity by dropping in, heightening his visibility and availability. He grasps and generates opportunities to interpret people's experiences and their expression in behavior. He advises leaders about evident needs for such adaptive supplies as information and interaction. He operates from multiple vantage points to sharpen awareness of the tasks and processes of transition—and to ensure that people's augmented aggressive energies are harnessed for attack upon the organization's adaptive tasks, not each other.

*See previous chapter.

While seizing every opportunity to influence policy and practice, the consultant pays due heed to the limits of his sanctions. In unsanctioned territory, he seeks out the formal gatekeepers and negotiates his sanctions.

By maintaining objectivity in situations that are emotionally overheated, he provides a role model for keeping cool. When planning decisions are about to be made under impulsive pressure toward premature closure, he raises questions that assure that problem solving will remain appropriately complicated. He is alert to maladaptive expressions of resistant anger in the form of scapegoating, pot stirring, or sabotage and helps leaders understand and curb these.

Where change has been introduced so that organizational continuity has been severed or coherence paralyzed, the consultant helps leaders stimulate interactive discussion to ensure that buried psychological meanings are explored, emotional expression legitimated, grief expressed, and continuity between past, present, and future restored. When grief is overwhelming and conservative needs profound, the consultant may influence the design of specialized support structures to meet people's adaptive needs.

In the not uncommon situation in which reorganization is introduced without adequate prior preparation, the consultant helps leaders back up and design strategic retreats. In these retreat structures, the steps that the organization's decision makers have been through are retraced: information is given about the reasons for reorganization and understanding promoted. Negotiations of need are encouraged so that people are assured of specific help to ease their transitional distress.

The consultant thus applies the model for the modulation of change both diagnostically and reparatively. He diagnoses the process steps that have been neglected in reorganization, encourages leaders to retrace these steps, and guides the repair of errors of omission or commission. When change is prospective, he is strategically placed to help leaders anticipate and rehearse the necessary modulating steps.

In modulating change, the consultant deploys himself flexibly. He builds new relationships and strengthens existing ones; he provides specific and nonspecific support wherever he can. His increased availability provides contact comfort and an objective sounding board. While mutual convenience often requires that he meet at prestructured times, he leaves time available to respond to ad hoc emergencies. As he becomes dynamically involved in a changing enterprise, he often extends his availability by providing readily available telephone consultation. This communication of concerned availability is a powerful spur to confidence in him. It is important, too, that the consultant appreciate that counterdependent leaders may not avail themselves of proffered consultation; when he encounters leaders for whom seeking help is painful, the consultant should exercise considerable initiative. He seizes opportunities to telephone or visit about "what's cooking?"

The Evolution of Consultation: Becoming the Internal Consultant's Consultant

As consultation evolves, leaders vary in the use made of the consultant. While heavily action-oriented executives may blow hot and cool in their utilization, more reflective, psychologically minded consultees are likely to avail themselves of the consultant frequently and appropriately. As these consultees grow in conceptual sophistication and the mastery of process skills, they play enhanced roles as supports, guides, and mentors within the organization. Such avuncular organizational leaders are often concentrated in personnel departments, where the demands upon them intermesh naturally with their personal styles and proclivities. In consultation's evolution, impact upon the organization can be considerably extended, by the teaching of consultation skills to these informal, internal consultants—and by advocacy of formal internal consultant roles for some of them. The external consultant supports the efforts of internal consultants and can strengthen their roles by becoming the "consultant's consultant."

The internal consultants' efforts can formally be expanded by educational seminars and case-focused support groups for them. The certainty of continuing transition in organizations increases the need for substantial consultant resources within the organization; since external consultants cannot meet day-to-day needs at all levels, the consultant can imaginatively multiply his impact by this development of an internal consultant cadre. As organic components of an organizational network, internal consultants are uniquely placed to maintain the velocity of an external consultant's support efforts. In his strengthening of organizational support systems, a natural evolving role for the external consultant is to develop, support, and supply these indigenous suppliers of support.

The Support of Supporters

The leader of an organization is in a lonely and vulnerable position. The many change demands upon him, intensified by Daniel Bell's "revolution of rising entitlements,"[1] strain his adaptive resources and drain his emotional reserves. Without opportunities to replenish these reserves, he will find it difficult to infuse his constituency of internal supporters with the support they need. For the leader to sustain others, the leader, like internal consultants, needs the external support that the consultant is uniquely equipped to provide.

During some phases of transition, the leader must anticipate that some of his habitual organizational supporters will withdraw their support of him. In confronting his supporters with tidings that threaten loss, he inevitably triggers aggressive and regressive responses. Before and after such meetings, the consultant plays a crucial role in meeting the leader's needs for guidance, reassurance, and support.

Conclusion: Support Systems

In transition, support supplies are strengthened by fine tuning of the strands that connect people to one another. A support system emerges by the transformation of a static, formal organization into a dynamic network for the reciprocation of psychological needs.

Organic consultation affirms the universality of psychological needs for ministration, maturation, and mastery—and stimulates transactions that legitimate and nourish these needs. (For elaboration of these clusters of needs, see Levinson.[2]) Organic consultation emphasizes the heightening of these needs when people are confronted with change demands.

The organic consultation process provides the comfort of human support while promoting cognitive and strategic mastery. It is a process that supports leaders in supporting their people as they struggle to master the complexity of tasks generated by the adaptive imperatives of transition.

References

1. Bell, D. The revolution of rising entitlements. *Fortune,* 1975, *41,* 98.
2. Levinson, H. *The exceptional executive.* Cambridge, Mass.: Harvard University Press, 1968.

12

Some Considerations in Evaluating School Consultation Programs

PAUL I. AHMED AND FRANK M. TIMS

Introduction

Evaluation of social service programs is difficult under the best of circumstances. Problems of program variation, lack of control over the context in which evaluation is conducted, and difficulty in defining a single set of objectives and criteria applicable across programs all pose special challenges. An input-process-output model often proves inadequate because of difficulty in standardizing its components. In an effort to get beyond reliance on case studies, evaluators are urged to employ experimental and quasi-experimental designs.[1] Of course, the values which govern service delivery have generally mitigated against the random assignment of clients to groups from which services are withheld, thus making true experimental designs virtually out of the question. The use of quasi-experimental designs, using "comparison groups" rather than true control groups, provides a partial answer to this dilemma, but one far from satisfactory.

A starting point for any evaluation is defining the objectives of a

PAUL I. AHMED · Southeastern University, Washington, D.C. FRANK M. TIMS · National Institute of Drug Abuse, Rockville, Md.

program. Objectives are usually formulated as a level of generality such that the link between program activities and objectives remains vague. It becomes necessary to develop a model which specifies the process, the goals, and the objectives, and the linkages between these. Goals are, of course, somewhat more specific than objectives. We may set goals in terms of those persons or programs receiving direct services and objectives in terms of changes that follow from goal attainment. For example, a goal of consultation might be to increase a consultee's skills in dealing with intergroup conflict, and the objective might be defined as a reduction of such conflict through the consultee's intervention in the context of a program.

These are two of the major areas which will be addressed in this chapter—definition of goals and objectives, and problems of design. The purpose of the chapter is not and cannot be to solve the problems; it is rather to suggest to the reader an agenda of problems to be confronted in approaching such evaluations, and to provide some clarification of these key issues. There are, of course, other aspects of evaluation that might be addressed, but space considerations will necessarily limit our discussion.

Consideration of Goals and Objectives

Abrams, Vanecko, and Abrams[2] have correctly suggested that the need for school mental health services has grown so fast that existing programs have only begun to scratch the surface. Thus, any attempt to define objectives for consultation must seem ambitious. Nevertheless, objectives must be defined as a first step in a coherent evaluation strategy. This is complicated by the fact that there are different kinds of school consultation programs. Recent studies have identified types of consultation in terms of its focus and orientation. Haylett and Rapport[3] have defined three types of consultation: client-centered consultation, consultee-centered consultation, and program-centered consultation. A further source of difficulty is that few have been able to agree on the priorities among objectives of consultation programs. NIMH attempted to develop such a set of objectives several years ago, and the resulting list is partially presented here:

A. *Benefits to society,* which include:

1. Improvement in race relations in the school system. Improved attitudes and behavior toward members of other races.

2. A lower incidence of juvenile delinquency and anti-social acts by students in the community at large.

3. Improvement of health status of children in the school system.

4. Greater productivity of pupils in the school system (in terms of improved grades, greater participation of parents, students, and teachers in school affairs, and greater satisfaction with the system).

B. *Benefits to schools:*

1. Improved race relations in the school system.
2. Improved teacher performance.
3. Lower rate of absenteeism.

C. *Benefits to pupils:*

1. Reduced absenteeism and thus greater access to education.
2. Reduced dependence on teacher's instruction for routine tasks.
3. Reduced juvenile delinquency and anti-social behavior, which improves the climate for learning in the school.
4. Fewer brushes with the law for the individual pupil.
5. Improved productivity of school children.
6. Improved family life for pupils.

D. *Benefits to Community Mental Health Centers:*

1. Improved staff skills.
2. Enhanced communication with the community.
3. Improved therapy provided for children.

Aside from the redundancy of some of these, it is clear that they may be defined at various levels, varying degrees of specificity, and in terms of short-range or long-range objectives. To take one of these goals, improved race relations in the school system, and link it to the consultation process implies an almost blind faith in our ability to control events. If we observe that race relations improve in schools receiving consultation services, and they deteriorate in those schools not seeking them, it tells us more about the schools than it does about the effects of consultation. It becomes necessary to focus at a more specific level, and to identify goals, attainment of which will contribute to the objective. Rather than dwelling on the general objective, it is more appropriate to look at specific problems.

These goals might be stated in terms of increases in a consultee's ability to deal with different kinds of cases, or development of better understanding of the dynamics of intergroup conflict. Goal setting must reflect a realistic, problem-specific orientation. It should also be linked to verifiable indicators so that progress toward goals may be assessed.

Given the foregoing, one might be skeptical of any attempt to attribute improvement in such conditions as race relations in a school as an outcome of school consultation. Tenuous as this might be, our confidence in such an observation can be enhanced by establishing consultation goals at a level below that of objectives. The goals should be linked to the consultation process and objectives by means of a theoretically sound model. The consultation goals should be linked to verifiable indicators, as should objectives. Taking the race relations objective as an example, goals may be set in terms of improving intergroup attitudes and behavior of pupils, and assessing such improvement by means of self-reports, rating scales administered to teachers and other staff, and sociometric choices of pupils in task and expressive contexts. Can improvement in specific pupil attitudes and behavior be related to such indicators of improved race relations as a decrease in the number of hostile interracial confrontations? For example, are pupils who were previously involved in such events now less often involved? Do these pupils now assume more constructive roles, such as providing positive leadership and open advocacy of peaceful resolution of such disputes?

Once goals are established, it is desirable to link them to objectives in a larger context. As previously stated, objectives may be short-term or long term. Using the race relations example, the immediate goal may be the resolution of a particular crisis with a pupil. A short-term objective could be to develop staff capability to deal with such problems without immediate reliance on the CMHC. The longer-term objective may be to bring about behavior changes among pupils and staff which will result in a reduction of tensions in the school.

For any evaluation, it is important to define the goals and objectives of consultation, obtain agreement on objectives, measure progress toward objectives, and solicit consultee participation in the final evaluation. There should also be agreed-upon criteria to determine whether the objectives are reasonably being met. If, for example, reduced absenteeism is an objective, the expected change as a result of consultation should be stated in advance so we might know how close to the objective we are coming, as well as have a basis for comparisons with other agencies or systems of mental health intervention.

Problems of Evaluation

Problems Related to the Evaluation Context

Ideally, upon receiving an initial agency evaluation contract, the consultant must perform an effective survey of organizational needs. The extent of the problem(s), the severity, the priority of corrective actions required, the adequacy of existing remedial efforts, and the constraints influencing possible outcomes need to be laid out. While this is ideally a good thing to do, few consultants find the time to do the effective analysis, and naturally no evaluation is done in advance.

There is also a reluctance to proceed with evaluation during consultation. A partial explanation of this is found in the following observations:

1. There is often a lack of clarity and consensus regarding objectives.
2. Records at CMHCs are often inadequate to provide all data needed for evaluation.
3. CMHCs often lack follow-up procedures for assessing long-range results.
4. CMHCs and schools lack orientation to develop short-range and long-range objectives, and to specify in advance measures and criteria.
5. Like most social service professionals, there tends to be a view that time is better spent in consultation than evaluation.
6. Efforts in CMHCs tend to be diffuse, and commitment to evaluation is only partial.
7. For a number of reasons, there is a tendency to regard evaluation as an intrusion on the consultation process, and possibly as detrimental to consultation.

Problems Related to Design

Evaluation is also complicated by the fact that benefits from the school consultation programs may be received by society, by pupils, by schools, and by CMHCs. Because each has somewhat different goals and criteria of success, separate calculations of program benefits are required for each of these groups on the basis of the benefits as defined for the groups. The methodology of each calculation must be the same for all the groups. Each group seeks to determine the differences which exist in a set of measures with or without the school consultation program. Cost-benefit analysis for each group of benefits requires comparison between the experience, behavior, and attitudes of parties participating in the program and those expected if they had not participated. Thus, a control group is necessary in order to measure the absolute effects of a particular method of consultation.

At this point, the reader will no doubt recognize the problem of control groups as being the nemesis of evaluation. True experimental designs in social service or health service delivery are virtually nonexistent. Mental health professionals resist the systematic withholding of services necessary to establish experimental conditions, and it is understandably difficult to persuade them to change their views, although Wholey and others argue that there are good reasons for trying to allocate services in an experimental framework—including the fact that resources are usually inadequate to provide services to all who need them.[1] A compromise that has come into vogue is the use of "comparison groups" in what has been termed "quasi-experimental designs."[4] Comparison groups, like control groups, presumably have not been exposed to the treatment which is being evaluated, and is similar in most respects to the group(s) which do receive the treatment(s). This is accomplished by matching and trying to eliminate as much as possible of the bias due to selection. In addition, the groups should be physically separated from one another in order to minimize contamination between groups. This means that the control group must be in another school. If effects are to be observed at the level of objectives, this implies that the comparison will in fact be between schools. Particular problems with this approach are:

1. The range of variability between schools, in terms of school milieu, staff, pupil characteristics, and administration is potentially large, thus making it extremely difficult to make a case for a school being a valid "comparison group."

2. CMHCs tend to consult with the schools which have reached a maturity level such that the need for consultation is recognized. In addition, consultation is often provided on a particularistic basis such as the influence or political contacts of school administrators.

3. Another major problem is that no two schools receive the same type of consultation; the necessities of program and client-centered consultation differ from time to time and place. Hence, it is hard to compare one school's success in relation to the success of other schools.

4. But the final and perhaps the most difficult problem in determining the success of a school program is that the multitude of intervening and exogenous circumstances can create an effect which may not necessarily be due to school consultation. For example, the race relations in a given school may improve because of changes in the community, changes in the staff of the school, or because of other programs such as compensatory education, human relations courses, and staff development activities. Thus, it will be hard to distinguish what benefits in improving race relations were received specifically from the school consultation program. In the absence of a control group, there is clearly merit in comparing consultation benefits in several similar circumstances for the purpose of relative comparisons of effectiveness, even though we recognize that an absolute standard would not be possible.

Cost Benefit Analysis

The cost part of the cost-benefit analysis of a school consultation program is the easiest to handle. The direct labor cost of a school staff could be determined by multiplying the house devoted by each staff member to school consultation by the appropriate per hour labor cost (wages, taxes, fringe benefits, etc.). The transportation costs to and from schools are also easy to obtain. Materials and supplies,equipment and communications costs can also be obtained readily. A reasonable estimate of overhead costs and an analysis of other costs associated with school consultation are also possible.

It is the benefit side that presents the greatest problems. There is no consensus, for example, on what the benefits are and how to measure them. In an experimental study carried out by Behavior Science Corporation (BASICO) several new approaches were tried. In this cost-benefit study, an attempt was made to develop indicators of the relative magnitude of various benefit categories and the relationship of benefits associated with the sample projects. For example, teachers were asked the direct question, "How many children from your classes were helped in each of the relative benefit areas, and to what extent were these helped due to mental health consultation?" By combining their responses estimates could be made, for sample teachers, of benefits received by children in their classrooms in each benefit area.

The next step for a cost-benefit evaluation is to extrapolate from the sample-teacher-benefit estimates to the entire population. This is done by estimating the average classroom benefit level for each benefit category. By multiplying the number of classes receiving consultation times an estimate of average class benefit, an estimate for total benefits for each benefit category is obtained. Another approach BASICO tried was to ask school administrators whether they would pay for school consultation if some extra money were available. This question was asked on the assumption that if the service was viewed as important and of high priority, the administrators would allocate funds for it.

Conclusion

On the basis of what we know from existing studies, it would be reasonable to say that the definitive technology for evaluating the absolute impact of benefits from program consultation is not yet here. What we can expect from the present technology, however, is the following:

A. Some notion of ranking of benefits within the projects.

B. Some notion of ranking of benefits *across* the projects.

C. Some notion of the relative effectiveness of one project with respect to another project.

With the above measures we should be able to determine which projects are operating most effectively with respect to the economic benefit category we are investigating. We also believe that considerable benefit accrues to a program which attempts to analyze its procedures systematically—even though the outcomes may leave something to be desired.

NIMH funded a study in 1970 to discern some of the objectives of school consultation and to develop the methodology to measure them.[5] The products of this research included various forms of assessment of client-centered, staff development models. These forms include a record of administrative notices which define the problem, the goals of consultation, plans and strategy, consultee expectations, documentation of consultee participation, comparisons of actual with expected outcome, and estimates of the long-range benefits accruing to schools.

The standard form tends to be necessarily general, often missing the particular problem or point relative to a specific consultation case. Perhaps given the difference in school systems, it may be more appropriate for consultants to construct measures specific to each consulting situation.

Encouraging as these studies are, an array of techniques and methodology is clearly needed to establish the empirical linkages with consultation, consultation goals, and the achievement of objectives within schools, as well as for making meaningful comparisons between schools and programs. Such a methodology would require data with respect to the school environment, the family, and the community. In this connection, there is a clear need for a long-term study which would involve the best available approximation of experimental design conditions and longitudinal follow-up of pupils, and analysis of changes in pupils' attitudes, behavior, and adjustment in school, family, and community. Without such follow-up, it is impossible to assess fully the benefits of consultation.

The challenges of the evaluation task are considerable, and many questions remain which, due to limitations of space, could not be discussed in any depth here. The increasing demand for evaluation and for cost-benefit appraisals of mental health services assures that a great deal more thought will be given to the problem. We hope that the foregoing discussion will have stimulated forward movement in this important area.

References

1. Wholey, Joseph S., John W. Scanlon, Hugh G. Duffy, James S. Fukumoto, and Leona M. Vogt. *Federal evaluation policy*. Washington, D.C.: Urban Institute, 1970.
2. Abrams, Richard S., Michael Vanecko, and Irving Abrams. "A suggested school mental health program," *Journal of School Health, 42*,(3): 137–141, 1972.
3. Haylett, Clarice H. and L. Rapport, "Mental health consultation," *Handbook of community psychiatry and community mental health*. New York: Grune and Stratton, 1964.
4. Readers are referred to Donald T. Campbell and Julian C. Stanley, *Experimental and quasi-experimental designs for research and teaching*. Chicago: Rand McNally, 1963, for a systematic discussion of such designs.
5. Montague, Ernest K., and Elaine N. Taylor, *Preliminary handbook on evaluating mental health indirect service programs in schools*. Alexandria, Va.: Human Resources Research Office (HumRRO), 1971, (HumRRO Technical Report 71–18).

Index

GPSR Compliance

The European Union's (EU) General Product Safety Regulation (GPSR) is a set of rules that requires consumer products to be safe and our obligations to ensure this.

If you have any concerns about our products, you can contact us on ProductSafety@springernature.com

In case Publisher is established outside the EU, the EU authorized representative is:

Springer Nature Customer Service Center GmbH
Europaplatz 3
69115 Heidelberg, Germany

Batch number: 10854084

Printed by Printforce, the Netherlands